Apple Training Series

Mac OS X
Support Essentials

Edited by Owen Linzmayer

Apple
Certified

Apple Training Series: Mac OS X Support Essentials
Edited by Owen W. Linzmayer
Copyright © 2006 by Apple Computer Inc.

Published by Peachpit Press. For information on Peachpit Press books, contact:

Peachpit Press
1249 Eighth Street
Berkeley, CA 94710
(510) 524-2178
Fax: (510) 524-2221
http://www.peachpit.com
To report errors, please send a note to errata@peachpit.com
Peachpit Press is a division of Pearson Education

Editor: Owen W. Linzmayer
Project Editor: Bob Lindstrom
Managing Editor: Kristin Kalning
Apple Series Editor: Serena Herr
Production Editor: Pat Christenson
Technical Editors: John Parenica, Max Pruden
Copy Editor: Joanne Gosnell
Compositors: Tina O'Shea, Owen Wolfson
Indexer: Rebecca Plunkett
Interior Design: Frances Baca
Cover Design: Tolleson Design
Cover Illustration: Alicia Buelow, image © Alicia Buelow
Cover Production: George Mattingly/GMD

ISBN 0-321-33547-3
9 8 7 6 5 4 3
Printed and bound in the United States of America

Acknowledgments Thanks to Donald Pitschel, John Parenica, Max Pruden, Jeffery Parks, and the rest of the Apple training team responsible for the development of the Mac OS X Support Essentials course on which this book is based.

Contents at a Glance

Table of Contents

1

Time   This lesson takes approximately 15 minutes to complete.

Goals   Describe the topics covered in this book

Describe the Apple certification options

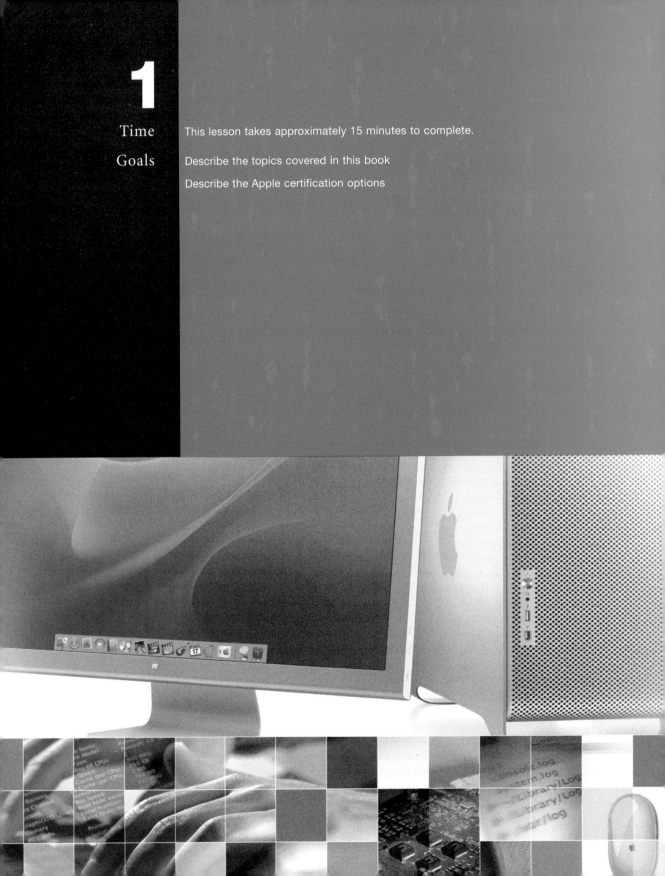

Getting Started

This book is based on Apple's official training course for Mac OS X Support Essentials, an in-depth exploration of the Macintosh operating system. It serves as a self-paced introduction to supporting and troubleshooting Macintosh computers running Mac OS X.

The primary goal is to prepare help desk personnel, technical coordinators, and system administrators to knowledgeably address customer concerns and questions. This includes the ability to return a Macintosh computer to normal operation, using the proper utilities, resources, and troubleshooting methodology.

Whether you are an experienced system administrator or just want to dig deeper into a Macintosh, you'll learn in-depth technical information and procedures used by Apple-certified technicians to install, configure, maintain, and diagnose Macintosh computers running Mac OS X.

This book assumes a basic level of familiarity with the Macintosh operating systems. Unless otherwise specified, all references to Mac OS X refer to Mac OS X 10.4.1, which was the most current version available at the time this book was written. Due to subsequent upgrades, some screen shots, features, and procedures may be slightly different from those presented on these pages.

The Methodology

This book is based on material provided to students attending Mac OS X Support Essentials v10.4, a three-day, hands-on course that provides an intense and in-depth exploration of how to troubleshoot Mac OS X. For purposes of consistency, we have maintained the basic structure of the course material, though you may complete it at your own pace.

This course is designed to help experienced users become experts who are able to support other Mac OS X users by:

▶ Providing *knowledge* of how Mac OS X works

▶ Showing how to use diagnostic and repair *tools*

▶ Explaining troubleshooting and repair *procedures*

For example, in Lesson 8, "Network Configuration and Troubleshooting," you'll learn basic networking concepts (knowledge). You'll acquire network configuration and troubleshooting techniques using Network preferences and Network Utility (tools). And you'll explore methods for troubleshooting networking issues (procedures). In addition, each lesson includes troubleshooting tips for dealing with common problems.

You'll also apply what you've learned by performing hands-on exercises.

Finally, you'll learn how to integrate your knowledge, procedures, and tools using the Apple troubleshooting process. The troubleshooting process is a method for systematically solving problems.

Lessons 1 through 7 focus on the elements involved in setting up, configuring, and troubleshooting a standalone Mac OS X computer:

- ► Mac OS X installation
- ► Users accounts
- ► File systems
- ► Permissions
- ► Application environments
- ► Command-line interface

Lessons 8 through 10 deal with configuring Mac OS X to work in a networked environment. You will troubleshoot issues involving network services, such as file and Web servers, and configure Mac OS X to provide network services:

- ► Network configuration and troubleshooting
- ► Accessing network services
- ► Providing network services

Lessons 11 and 12 introduce you to the support in Mac OS X for attaching hardware devices and printing:

- ► Peripherals
- ► Printing

Lesson 13 reveals the technical details of how Mac OS X starts up, and Lesson 14 explains how to implement Apple's General Troubleshooting Flowchart to correctly identify and fix machines that have unknown software issues:

- ► Startup sequence
- ► Troubleshooting

In an effort to be informative but not overwhelming, we have included several supplementary appendices. They may be valuable to you, though they are not considered essential.

Lesson Structure

Each lesson in this book begins with an opening page that lists the goals for the lesson and an estimate of the time needed to complete the lesson.

The explanatory material is augmented with hands-on exercises essential to developing your skills. For the most part, all you need to complete the exercises is a Macintosh computer running Mac OS X 10.4.1 or later. If you lack the equipment necessary to complete a given exercise, you are still encouraged to read the step-by-step instructions and examine the screen shots to understand the procedures demonstrated.

> **NOTE ▶** The exercises in this book are designed to be nondestructive if followed correctly. However, some of the exercises can be disruptive—for example, they may turn off network services temporarily—and some exercises, if performed incorrectly, could result in data loss or damage to System files.
>
> As such, it's recommended that you perform these exercises on a Macintosh that is not critical to your daily productivity. Instructions are given for restoring your Macintosh to its functional state whenever necessary, but reasonable caution is highly recommended. Apple Computer, Inc. and Peachpit Press are not responsible for any data loss or any damage to any equipment that occurs as a direct or indirect result of following the procedures described in this book.

We refer to many Knowledge Base documents throughout this book, and close each lesson with a list of recommended documents related to the topic of the lesson. The Knowledge Base is a free online resource (www.apple.com/support) containing the very latest technical information on all of Apple's hardware and software products. You are strongly encouraged to read the suggested documents, as well as learn how to search the Knowledge Base for answers to your particular questions.

At the end of each lesson is a short "Lesson Review" that recaps the material you've learned. You can refer to various Apple resources, such as the Knowledge Base, as well as the lessons themselves, to help you answer these questions.

Certification

After reading this book, you may wish to take the Apple Mac OS X Support Essentials v10.4 Exam (9L0-401) to earn the Apple Certified Help Desk Specialist certification. This is the first level of Apple's certification programs for Mac OS X professionals:

▶ Apple Certified Help Desk Specialist (ACHDS) — Ideal for help desk personnel, service technicians, technical coordinators, and others who support Mac OS X customers over the phone or who perform Mac OS X troubleshooting and support in schools and businesses. This certification does not include support of the Mac OS X Server platform. To receive this certification, you must pass the Mac OS X Support Essentials certification exam. This book is intended to provide you with the knowledge and skills to pass that exam.

> **NOTE** ▶ Although all of the questions in the Mac OS X Support Essentials exam are based on material in this book, simply reading this book will not adequately prepare you for all the specific issues addressed by the exam. We recommend that before taking the exam, you spend time actually setting up, configuring, and troubleshooting Mac OS X. You should also download and review the Skills Assessment Guide for the exam, which lists the exam objectives, the total number of items, the number of items per section, the required score to pass, and how to register. To download the Skills Assessment Guide, visit http://train.apple.com/certification/macosx.

▶ Apple Certified Technical Coordinator (ACTC) — This certification is ideal for Mac OS X technical coordinators and entry-level system administrators who provide technical support to Mac OS X users. In addition to user support, these professionals maintain the Mac OS X Server platform. This certification requires passing both the Mac OS X Support Essentials and Mac OS X Server Essentials exams.

▶ Apple Certified System Administrator (ACSA) — This certification is designed for full-time professional system administrators and engineers managing medium-to-large networks utilizing Mac OS X Server in demanding and relatively complex multiplatform deployments. The ACSA program is focused on individual job functions. Each passed exam earns a specialization certificate and a specific number of credits toward ACSA certification, which requires a total of seven valid (unexpired) credits.

The Apple Certified Help Desk Specialist certification can also be a step toward the Apple hardware service technician certifications. These certifications are ideal for people interested in becoming Macintosh repair technicians, but also worthwhile for help desk personnel at schools and businesses, and for Macintosh consultants and others needing an in-depth understanding of how Apple systems operate:

▶ Apple Certified Desktop Technician (ACDT) — This certification requires passing the Apple Desktop Service exam and a qualifying Mac OS X exam such as the Mac OS X Support Essentials exam.

▶ Apple Certified Portable Technician (ACPT) — This certification requires passing the Apple Portable Service exam and a qualifying Mac OS X exam such as the Mac OS X Support Essentials exam.

About the Apple Training Series

Mac OS X Support Essentials is part of the official training series for Apple products developed by experts in the field and certified by Apple. The lessons are designed to let you learn at your own pace. You can progress through the book from beginning to end, or dive right into the lessons that interest you most.

For those who prefer to learn in an instructor-led setting, Apple also offers training courses at Apple Authorized Training Centers worldwide. These courses are taught by Apple certified trainers, and they balance concepts and lectures with hands-on labs and exercises. Apple Authorized Training Centers have been carefully selected and have met Apple's highest standards in all areas, including facilities, instructors, course delivery, and infrastructure. The goal of the program is to offer Apple customers, from beginners to the most seasoned professionals, the highest quality training experience.

To find an Authorized Training Center near you, go to www.apple.com/training.

2

Time

This lesson takes approximately 2 hours to complete.

Goals

Ensure that a specific computer meets the minimum requirements to run Mac OS X 10.4

Perform an erase, upgrade, or archive installation of Mac OS X on either a single- or multiple-partition hard drive

Use Setup Assistant to create a new user account

Use Software Update to locate and install any software updates available from Apple

Perform quick fixes to troubleshoot installation problems

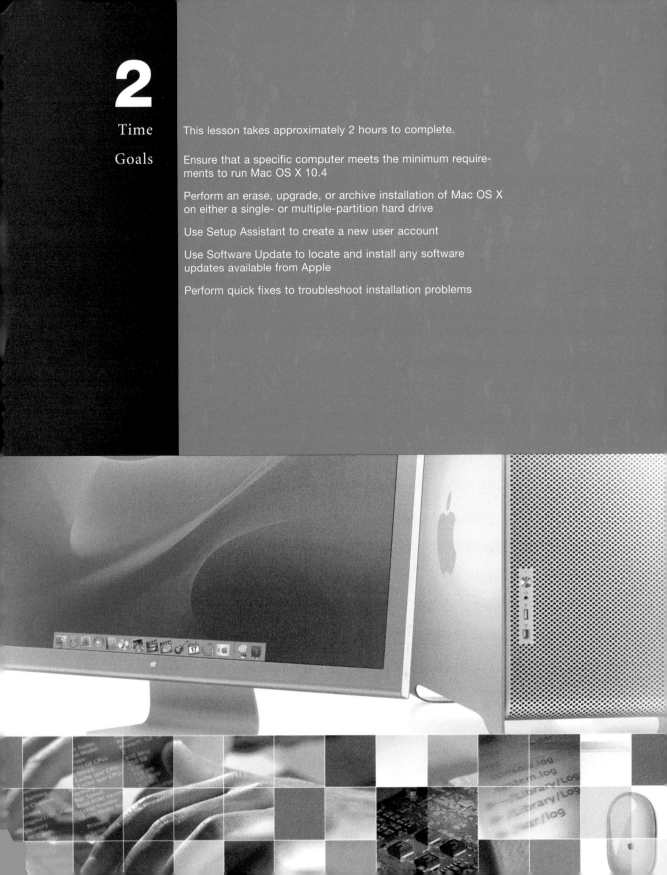

Lesson **2**

Installation

All Macintosh computers ship from the factory with Mac OS X already installed so that you only need to plug in the computer and turn it on to begin taking advantage of the world's most advanced operating system running on the most elegant hardware. However, not every Macintosh in use today is running the latest version of Mac OS X. (As of this writing, that's Mac OS X 10.4, also known as "Tiger.")

This lesson provides a brief technological overview of Mac OS X, followed by detailed instructions for installing, updating, and troubleshooting the installation. Although you do not need to perform an installation of Mac OS X as you read this lesson, doing so will give you a better understanding of the available options. If you do decide to install Mac OS X, it is suggested you do so on an extra computer or external hard drive so that you don't lose any productivity should you encounter difficulties working with a new, unfamiliar operating system.

Understanding Mac OS X

Since its release in March 2001, Mac OS X has been praised for its simplicity, elegance, and powerful UNIX-based core. Mac OS X combines three graphics technologies—OpenGL, Quartz Extreme, and QuickTime—that take Macintosh graphics capabilities beyond anything previously seen in a desktop operating system. The Aqua user interface provides a fluid look and feel for Mac OS X and showcases the graphics capabilities of the Quartz 2D graphics engine.

The power of UNIX in Mac OS X is provided by Darwin—the open-source foundation of Mac OS X. Modern operating system features, such as pre-emptive multitasking, protected memory, and symmetric multiprocessing, give Mac OS X greater stability and performance than previous versions of the Mac OS.

Finally, because most of today's major Internet technologies were developed on UNIX, the UNIX core of Mac OS X makes it a very Internet-savvy operating system. For example, Mac OS X uses the Berkeley Software Distribution (BSD) TCP/IP networking stack, which serves as the backbone of most TCP/IP implementations on the Internet today.

Mac OS X 10.4 includes revolutionary new features, and powerful upgrades to existing technologies. New technologies such as Spotlight and Dashboard improve the user experience over previous versions of Mac OS X. As a technical professional, you will find new programs in Mac OS X 10.4, such as Network Diagnostics, and upgrades to familiar tools that improve your ability to support Mac OS X in any environment.

Integration Through Standards

One of the strengths of Mac OS X is that it uses a rich set of standards, which enables Mac OS X computers to integrate with other platforms. At every level of the operating system, standards play a key role.

At the hardware level, Mac OS X supports key hardware buses such as Universal Serial Bus (USB) and IEEE 1394 (also known as FireWire) that allow Mac OS X computers to use devices that also work on other platforms. Mac OS X can read and write files on a wide variety of formats such as 32-bit File Allocation Table (FAT32), UNIX File System (UFS), and ISO-9660, providing access to storage devices formatted by other operating systems. For networking, Mac OS X relies on TCP/IP, allowing the computer to communicate with systems around the world. Mac OS X has extensive support for industry-standard formats such as Portable Network Graphics (PNG) and Portable Document Format (PDF), and creates archives in the PKZip (.zip) format, which allows documents and compressed files to be shared with non–Macintosh systems.

Layers of Mac OS X

From an architectural standpoint, Mac OS X consists of four distinct layers. From bottom to top, they are:

▶ Core OS — The foundation of Mac OS X. This layer is responsible for handling all I/O (input/output) and for managing memory and processor usage. It is commonly referred to as Darwin.

▶ Core Services — System components that implement the operating system services used by applications, such as QuickTime for playing movies, Quartz for 2D drawing, directory services, and so forth. New to Mac OS X 10.4 are the core services Core Audio and Core Video.

▶ Developer Frameworks — Application environments that allow you to run various applications on Mac OS X. Running applications in these environments is covered in Lesson 6, "Application Environments."

▶ Applications — The programs you run, using the appropriate environment provided by the applicable Developer Frameworks layer. The applications layer is where users interact with the Macintosh. In addition to running traditional Mac OS–specific applications, Mac OS X includes support for running Java and UNIX-style applications, including X11 applications, all of which are discussed in Lesson 6, "Application Environments."

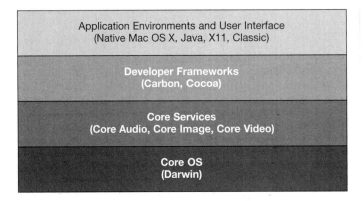

Installing Mac OS X

All new Macintosh computers come with Mac OS X preinstalled and most also come with Mac OS X on CD or DVD, in case the operating system needs to be reinstalled. This book assumes you are using Apple's Mac OS X 10.4 retail package that contains a single DVD with a simple Installer to guide you through the installation. If you are using the model-specific discs that came with your Macintosh, you may notice minor differences in the screens and examples used here.

Verifying Requirements

The first step to take before attempting to install Mac OS X is to verify that the intended computer meets the minimum system requirements. If you don't know your computer's specifications, use System Profiler (/Applications/Utilities) to determine its specifications.

Mac OS X 10.4 requires the following:

▶ Macintosh computer with a PowerPC G3, G4, or G5 processor

▶ Built-in FireWire

▶ At least 256 MB of RAM

▶ DVD drive

▶ Built-in display or a display connected to an Apple-supplied video card supported by your computer

▶ At least 3 GB of available disk space, or 4 GB if you install the Xcode 2 developer tools

NOTE ▶ For more information about installation requirements, see the complete list of supported computers at www.apple.com/macosx/upgrade/requirements.html.

Preparing for Installation

Although you can certainly dive right in and install Mac OS X without any forethought, you'll be better served in the long run if you prepare for installation by taking some precautionary steps.

▶ Back Up Important Information

Before upgrading any operating system, you should back up all important data for protection in case an error occurs during installation.

▶ Read the "Read Before You Install" Document

Before beginning the installation of Mac OS X, review the PDF document "Read Before You Install" on the Mac OS X Install DVD. This document contains important information about the disc and the Installer program.

▶ Collect Information

If you are upgrading a computer from Mac OS 9 to Mac OS X, collect your current network settings from the TCP/IP, Internet, Remote Access, and Modem control panels. You can run Apple System Profiler to generate a report with information that may prove useful during the upgrade process. Also, if you have a .Mac account, have your member name and password available.

▶ Update Firmware

If your computer's firmware is out-of-date, the Mac OS X Installer will alert you when you attempt to install the new OS. You can use System Profiler to find the current version number of the firmware. (It's listed as the Boot ROM Version in the Hardware Overview.) You can also get the version number by restarting the computer and pressing Command-Option-O-F, which places the computer in Open Firmware mode. The firmware version will be listed at the top of the screen.

Before installing Mac OS X, you must update your computer's firmware if an update is available. For a list of the firmware versions required by Mac OS X, and links to the necessary updates, refer to Knowledge Base document 86117, "Mac OS X: Chart of Available Firmware Updates."

NOTE ▶ Older firmware updates do not run in Mac OS X; they run only in Mac OS 9. Firmware updates must be done from a writable partition. Review the update instructions for system requirements.

▶ Update Third-Party Products

Updating your computer's firmware does not ensure that all of your existing peripherals and software will be compatible with Mac OS X. Therefore you should also check with the manufacturers of any devices you use with your computer to find the latest software updates for those devices. Likewise, you should check with the publishers of any third-party software you use to determine if updates are necessary for compatibility with the version of Mac OS X you intend to install. Some updates must be performed prior to upgrading to Mac OS X, and others require that Mac OS X be installed first.

Upgrade to Mac OS 9.2 or Later

It is not necessary to have Mac OS 9 installed when upgrading to Mac OS X; Mac OS 9 is required only if you wish to run Classic applications in Mac OS X. In that case, you must install Mac OS 9.2 or later, either before or after installing Mac OS X.

If you are using a Macintosh that will boot Mac OS 9, you should first install Mac OS 9 and then install any print drivers and fonts that you will use in the Classic environment in that System Folder. Use the Software Update control panel to make sure you have updated to the latest version (9.2.2 as of this writing). On newer computers that cannot boot Mac OS 9, you will need to copy over a licensed Mac OS 9.2 or later System Folder from another machine.

After you install Mac OS X, you will use Classic preferences to configure your computer to run your Mac OS 9 applications. For more information on Classic, see Appendix D, "The Classic Environment."

If you are upgrading from one version of Mac OS X to another, it is likely that your hardware and software will simply continue working as they always have. However, if you are upgrading from Mac OS 9, you must run your existing programs in Classic mode (which runs Mac OS 9 within Mac OS X), or switch to native Mac OS X alternatives (Safari for browsing, Mail for email, iCal for appointments, etc.), many of which are included with the new operating system.

Choosing a Partition Method

Partitioning divides a disk into sections, or volumes, each of which works like a separate disk. However, because you must erase a drive to split it into partitions, you should make the decision to partition early in the configuration process to avoid the laborious process of backing up data, partitioning, and then restoring.

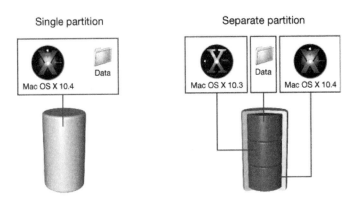

You can install different versions of Mac OS X on separate partitions of the same volume. Furthermore, Mac OS X and Mac OS 9 can inhabit the same volume without any problems, and you can switch between them as needed, provided your computer is capable of booting Mac OS 9. The following table discusses the pros and cons of keeping the two together on a single volume (or partition) versus on separate partitions.

Partition Method Issues

Options	Pros	Cons
Single partition	Requires minimal preparation.	If you use both Mac OS 9 and Mac OS X, you can mistakenly delete Mac OS X files while working in Mac OS 9.
Separate partition	Easy to upgrade, reinstall, or uninstall each operating system. Easy to organize your information in a logical manner.	More preparation is required, such as partitioning the disk. If you partition the disk, you will need to back up data.

One of the advantages of having two separate partitions is that if the operating system on the main partition becomes corrupted and unbootable, you can use the Startup Manager to boot from the operating system on the second partition. If you press the Option key while the computer boots, the Startup Manager will scan each partition on any connected drive and display an icon representing the operating system last used on that partition, if one exists. Select an icon, and the computer will boot using the selected System folder.

> **NOTE ▶** Some Macintosh computers start up only in Mac OS X and cannot boot Mac OS 9. For more information, refer to Knowledge Base document 86209, "Macintosh: Some Computers Only Start Up in Mac OS X."

If you install Mac OS X and Mac OS 9 on the same partition, the hard disk must be formatted as Mac OS Extended (Journaled). If you are installing Mac OS X on its own partition, Mac OS Extended is the recommended hard disk format, but you can also use UNIX File System (UFS) if, for example, you want to develop UNIX-based applications within Mac OS X.

> **NOTE ▶** Although applications running in the Classic environment can read and write files from a UFS partition, the Classic environment can only start from a Mac OS 9 System Folder located on a Mac OS Extended partition. Also, you will be unable to read files from a UFS partition if you boot Mac OS 9.

Based on the preceding information, determine if you want to install Mac OS X on its own partition, or if installing it alongside Mac OS 9 is acceptable. If you need to partition the drive, you can use Disk Utility (included on the Mac OS X Install DVD), but you should know that partitioning a drive is a time-consuming process that necessitates a full backup before starting if you want to retain your files.

> **NOTE ▶** With software such as Coriolis Systems' iPartition (www.coriolis-systems.com) or Prosoft Engineering's Drive Genius (www.prosofteng.com), you can repartition volumes without requiring erasure. Use any third-party utilities at your own risk.

Performing the Mac OS X Installation

You can start the Mac OS X installation process by booting from the Mac OS X Install DVD (with the disc in the drive, press the C key during startup) or by launching the Install Mac OS X application in the Finder, which will restart the computer and boot the computer from the disc.

> **NOTE ▶** If you are installing Mac OS X on a PowerBook or an iBook, the computer needs to be plugged into an AC power source to avoid exhausting battery power before the installation is complete.

The Installer is largely self-explanatory. When in doubt, let the onscreen instructions guide you. After selecting your language, continue through several screens that welcome you, explain the requirements, and then request your agreement to the software license terms. It's only when you select where and how Mac OS X is installed that you need to think carefully about your choices.

Selecting the Destination

In the Select Destination window, you select which volume will receive the operating system installation. Mac OS X can only be installed onto Mac OS Extended or UFS volumes. If you have multiple volumes from which to choose, keep in mind the pros and cons discussed previously in "Choosing a Partition Method."

Choosing the Installation Type

If you wish to perform the default installation method, click Continue after selecting the destination. Otherwise, click Options to see your installation options. (The Options button appears only after a destination volume is selected.) The following table discusses the pros and cons of the three installation methods.

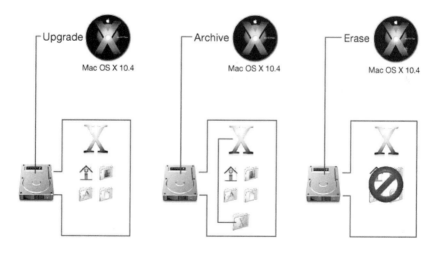

Installation Type

Options	Pros	Cons
Upgrade Mac OS X	Updates Mac OS X 10.2 or later, maintaining preferences, fonts, applications, and files.	Requires that Max OS X 10.2 or later is installed. Existing problems may not be fixed, so this is not recommended for troubleshooting.
Archive and Install	Same as update, except creates a new /System and /Library, updates invisible folders, and creates a new /Previous System folder.	New /System and /Library will not have any custom files from current installation, so some applications and device drivers may need to be reinstalled.
Erase and Install	Provides a clean start. Can install on any partition with enough available space.	Erases all data on selected partition.

The Archive and Install option is similar to the Clean Install option in Mac OS 9—the existing System folder is archived into a Previous System folder, and a fresh version of the operating system is installed. If Mac OS X is not already present and configured, Archive and Install is not available as an option.

> **NOTE ▶** You can't start your computer using the Previous System folder if you want to undo your new installation. The Previous System folder is retained only so that you can manually restore specific files as needed after installation. If you do not need the contents of the Previous System folder for troubleshooting, you should discard the folder after you have determined that the new installation is working properly.

Even though you won't be using the Previous System folder, you can retain many of your user and network settings. In the Installation Options sheet, select the "Preserve Users and Network Settings" checkbox to automatically import existing users, home folders, and network settings during installation. (If you select this option, the Setup Assistant will not appear after the installation.)

The following settings are *not* preserved after an Archive and Install:

▶ Whether or not a network time server is used

▶ The computer's time zone (stored in the file /etc/localtime)

▶ The list of configured printers (stored in the file /etc/printers.conf)

▶ The resolution of your display(s) and—if more than one display is connected—settings such as arrangement (stored in the com.apple.windowserver.plist in /Library/Preferences and in ~/Library/Preferences/ByHost)

▶ Sharing preferences (stored in /etc/hostconfig)

> **NOTE** ▶ The /etc directory does not appear when browsing in the Finder. For information on accessing hidden directories, see Lesson 4, "File Systems."

If you choose the Erase and Install option, you must specify whether to reformat the destination volume as either Mac OS Extended or UNIX File System.

▶ Mac OS Extended, which is considered the "native" Macintosh volume format, has been used by Macintosh computers since Mac OS 8.1, and provides support for forked files. (Forked files are explained in Lesson 4, "File Systems.") If the drive will be accessed by a computer running Mac OS 9 or earlier, or by applications running in the Classic environment, you will need to use Mac OS Extended as the volume format and ensure that you install the Mac OS 9 drivers. Mac OS X 10.3 and later support Mac OS Extended (Journaled), which helps protect the file system against power outages or other cases in which the system is restarted or shut down prematurely.

▶   UNIX File System (UFS) is the volume format frequently used by other UNIX-based operating systems. You might consider using the UFS volume format in the following instances:

•   If you are installing Mac OS X on an external drive that will be later connected to another computer running UNIX

•   If you will be compiling and running UNIX applications that rely upon UFS features such as case-sensitivity

NOTE ▶ Keep in mind that Mac OS Extended is the recommended volume format for Mac OS X. If you do have a need for UFS, consider creating two partitions: a Mac OS Extended partition for Mac OS X and Mac OS applications, and a UFS partition for UNIX applications.

MORE INFO ▶ Refer to Knowledge Base document 25316, "Mac OS X 10.2 or Earlier: Choosing UFS or Mac OS Extended (HFS Plus) Formatting."

Customizing the Packages

By default, after selecting the destination and choosing the installation type, the installation proceeds with the Easy Install configuration, which installs the following packages:

▶   Essential System Software — The base system software

▶   Printer Drivers — Drivers for some third-party printers

▶   Additional Fonts — Additional fonts that expand the choices when writing in languages other than English

▶   Language Translations — Base Mac OS X support in languages in addition to your primary language

This additional package is not installed by default:

▶   X11 — Software to enable X11 applications to run on Mac OS X

If you click the Customize button, the Installer shows you a list of packages to be installed. Some packages are optional, such as Printer Drivers and Additional Fonts, but are selected for installation by default. If a checkbox contains a minus sign (–), the package is made up of smaller packages, and not all subpackages will be installed. Click the disclosure triangle next to the package to list the subpackages.

Once installation has begun, the Installer shows the percentage completed. The time required to complete the installation depends upon the options chosen, the speed of your computer, and the speed of its optical drive. It is not uncommon for the Installer to require over an hour to complete the entire process. If the screen goes blank during the installation process, press any key. *Do not* interrupt the process, or the computer may be left inoperable with only a partially installed operating system.

Completing the Installation

When the Mac OS X Installer has finished, the bulk of the installation process is complete; but you should perform a few recommended steps to ensure an optimal user experience with the new operating system.

Configuring with Setup Assistant

When the installation is complete, the Installer restarts the computer and Setup Assistant opens to gather information necessary to register Mac OS X and create a new user account. If Mac OS X was installed previously, Setup Assistant will not run automatically because the user accounts and configurations are kept from the original installation.

For the purpose of following the exercises in this book, you should make the selections explained on these pages. However, if you are comfortable with the installation process and know what you are doing, feel free to configure Mac OS X differently.

NOTE ► If you don't type anything in the Setup Assistant, after a few minutes you'll hear instructions on how to use VoiceOver to set up your computer. VoiceOver, new in Mac OS X 10.4, is available only in English. For more information on VoiceOver, see "Mac OS X Accessibility Support" in Lesson 6, "Application Environments."

1   At the "Welcome" screen, select United States, then click Continue.

2   Select "Do not transfer my information," then click Continue.

    If you want to transfer information from another computer, see the "Transferring Information with Migration Assistant" section later in this lesson.

3   Select the appropriate keyboard layout, then click Continue.

4   Select the wireless network you wish to join, then click Continue.

    This step appears only if your computer has an AirPort Card or AirPort Extreme Card installed.

5   If the networking settings aren't supplied automatically by DHCP, enter the information necessary to establish an Internet connection, then click Continue.

    This information is usually provided by your ISP or network administrator.

6   When asked for your Apple ID, click Continue.

    If you already have an Apple ID or create a new one, the system will be configured to use your Apple ID for tasks such as buying songs from the iTunes Music Store. For purposes of this book, it's not necessary to enter an Apple ID.

7   In registration, press Command-Q, then click Skip when prompted to skip the remaining registration and setup process.

There's no need to register Mac OS X for purposes of following the exercises in this book; but if you fill out this screen, your information is sent to Apple along with some basic system configuration details to be used for statistical purposes. You can read more about Apple's privacy policy by visiting www.apple.com/legal/privacy.

8 At the "Create Your Account" screen, enter the following information:

▶ Name: *Apple Admin*

▶ Short Name: *apple*

▶ Password: *apple*

NOTE ▶ The passwords used in this book are *not* good examples of secure passwords. They are used only for simplicity's sake. Use a more secure password if your computer contains sensitive information.

Create Your Account

Every person who uses this computer can have a user account with their own settings and a place to keep their documents secure.

Set up your user account now. You can add accounts for others later.

Name: Apple Admin

Short Name: apple
This will be used as the name for your home folder and cannot be changed.

Password: ••••••••

Verify: ••••••••

Password Hint: (optional)

Enter a word or phrase to help you remember your password.

Go Back   Continue

If you are on a network that uses NetInfo directory services, you are prompted to use your account information from a server or to create a new local account. If your network does not use NetInfo, you are prompted to create a local account. The initial local account is an administrator account that allows you to change settings in System Preferences, install applications, and use certain utilities. For purposes of following along with the examples in this book, use Apple Admin as the name of your new administrator account.

NOTE ▶ Information about creating and managing additional user accounts is presented in Lesson 3, "User Accounts."

When you create a local account, a short name is derived from the account name you entered. You can change the short name now if you like; however, once you create the account, the short name is permanent and you cannot change it without resorting to a third-party utility such as ChangeShortName. The short name is commonly used for command-line login, File Transfer Protocol (FTP) or ssh login, and email accounts. The short name is typically eight lowercase characters. However, with Mac OS X 10.3 and higher, the short name can be up to 255 bytes in length. (The number of characters can vary depending upon the language used, but using two bytes per character is a safe rule of thumb.) The short name cannot contain spaces or special characters ($< >$ ""* {} [] () ^! # | & $? ~). You can use either the user name or the short name to log in to Mac OS X.

9   Click Continue.

10 Select your time zone, and click Continue.

11 If prompted, set the time and date. Click Continue.

12 Click Done, and the Finder appears.

Welcome to Mac OS X! You can now eject the Mac OS X Install DVD.

You can quit the Setup Assistant after you have created the first user account, but you will need to complete the Mac OS X configuration, including network settings, using other utilities.

Transferring Information with Migration Assistant

Mac OS X 10.4 includes the Migration Assistant, which automates the migration of user information from any Mac OS X volume or partition, whether in another Macintosh or on an external drive.

To transfer information from a Macintosh computer running Mac OS X version 10.1 or later, first start your older computer and press the T key until the FireWire logo appears on screen, indicating the computer is in Target Disk Mode. Using a standard FireWire cable, connect the older computer to the newer computer. Launch Migration Assistant (/Applications/Utilities) on the newer computer and follow the onscreen prompts to transfer your home folder data, applications, user accounts, and most preferences from the older computer to the newer one. For more information, refer to Knowledge Base document 25773, "Mac OS X 10.3: Transferring data with Setup Assistant frequently asked questions (FAQ)."

> **NOTE ▶** Migration Assistant does not transfer all data from the older computer. Some preferences and File Vault–protected user accounts are not transferred. Also, you might need to upgrade or reinstall some transferred applications before they will function correctly on the new operating system and computer.

Configuring System Preferences

After you have used Setup Assistant to complete the initial configuration of Mac OS X, you can further configure the operating system using System Preferences. System Preferences is located in the main Applications folder, but it can also be opened by choosing it from the Apple menu or by clicking its icon in the Dock.

System Preferences displays a collection of icons, each representing a collection of settings that can be configured. By default, the icons are grouped into four categories: Personal, Hardware, Internet & Network, and System. If you prefer, you can change System Preferences to display the icons in alphabetical order by choosing View > Organize Alphabetically. The View menu also provides a complete list of the panes, allowing you to go directly from one System Preferences pane to another. Be aware that the System Preferences window may look different from the following screenshot if the user has added third-party preference items.

When you make changes in System Preferences, Mac OS X stores your settings in individual .plist files. If a System Preferences pane displays an icon of a lock in the lower-left corner, it means that particular preference affects all users. As such, to make changes to that setting, you must first authenticate as an administrator. Systemwide preference files are stored in /Library/Preferences. Conversely, panes without the lock icon control settings specific to the currently logged-in user, and changes are stored in ~/Library/Preferences.

Finding System Information

You can choose Apple > About This Mac to find basic system information such as the operating system version, amount of memory installed, and the processor type and speed. Click the version number to display the Apple engineering build number; click it again to display the computer's serial number.

NOTE ► Earlier Macintosh computers, such as Power Mac G3 (Blue and White), are unable to display the computer's serial number.

Click the More Info button to launch System Profiler, which provides detailed system information.

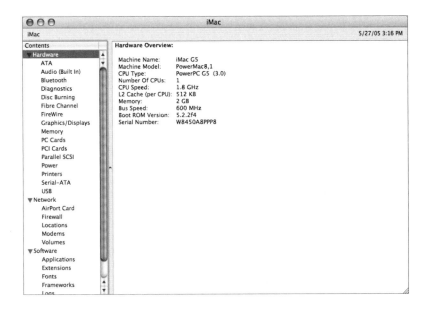

Updating System Software

After you install Mac OS X, Software Update will run automatically, if you have a working Internet connection. (If Software Update does not run automatically, choose Apple > Software Update.) This process checks Apple's software download site for the latest updates for Mac OS X and lists available updates. When you select an update from the list, Software Update displays information about the update. Usually the information includes a URL you can click to see additional details.

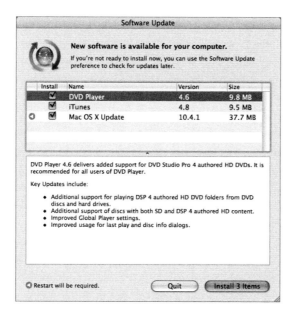

Software Update provides options for how you want to process an update. If you don't want to install a specific update (if, for instance, you don't have an iPod and don't need iPod updates), you can select the update in the list and then choose Update > Ignore Update. In the future, Software Update will not display that update. However, when a later version of that update is posted, it will be added to the updates to install. If you need to update multiple computers running Mac OS X, you may want to download the update by choosing Update > Download Only. Then, instead of installing, the update package will be downloaded to /Library/Packages. You can copy downloaded packages from this location to other computers as needed, where they can be opened and installed manually.

> **NOTE ▶** Sometimes an update will be available only after a prior update has been installed. To ensure that you have a fully up-to-date system, after you complete an update of your system, you should run Software Update a second time to see if any newer updates are available.

To verify whether a software update was installed successfully, look for its receipt in the folder /Library/Receipts. The Installed Updates pane of Software Updates preferences also lists the updates that have been installed. Clicking "Open as a Log File" displays the installer log file in the Console utility, which lists installed updates and any errors encountered.

Checking Console Logs

The Console utility lets you see technical messages from the Mac OS X system software and Mac OS X applications. Processes that do not have a graphical interface will output messages to Console as well as to the system log. Most of the information sent to Console is captured in the system log. Opening the Console utility while you are troubleshooting will give you a better sense of what is happening on Mac OS X, because the Console utility displays information and errors from processes you may not know are running.

Lines displayed in Console are usually made up of a date stamp, the name of the process, and the message. For instance:

Feb 28 18:45:08 localhost SystemStarter: Startup complete.

This message is simply informational. It shows that this computer completed startup at 6:45 P.M. on February 28, 2005.

Using Console to View Installation Log

During installation, any errors and informational messages are stored in a log file. After installing, or if you are experiencing problems that you think may be related to installation, check the installation log to see if any errors occurred.

1 Open Console (/Applications/Utilities).

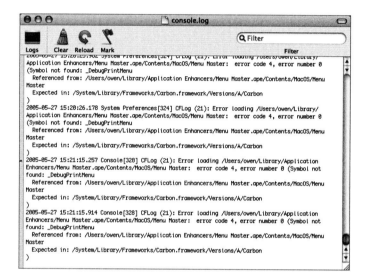

2 If the list of available log files is not listed on the left side of the Console window, choose View > Show Log List.

3 Click the disclosure triangle next to /var/log to see the list of log files in that folder.

NOTE ▶ In general, UNIX tools store their logs in /var/logs, whereas Apple utilities and third-party applications store their logs in ~/Library/Logs or /Library/Logs.

4   Select install.log. This is the log file created during installation.

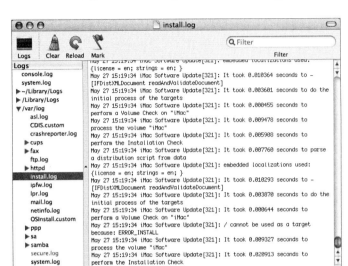

Look for any errors that may have occurred during installation.

You can use the Filter field at the top right to truncate the log display. For example, if you type *error* in that field, you will only see log entries that include that word. Try a few different terms, such as *error* and *finish*.

5   Quit Console.

Troubleshooting Mac OS X Installation

If your computer meets the Mac OS X system requirements but you're unable to complete the installation, you can troubleshoot the problem using the knowledge, tools, and processes you've learned in this lesson.

As you've learned, installing Mac OS X is a process that involves transferring the packages of system software from the Mac OS X Install DVD to the hard disk of your computer. Very generally speaking, this process has three phases. These phases represent potential points of failure:

▶   Reading packages from the Mac OS X Install DVD

▶   Processing the packages in RAM using the CPU

▶   Writing the packages to the destination volume

Problems with the Mac OS X Install DVD

During the installation process, the Installer attempts to verify the integrity of the DVD. If you are certain your disc is clean and has no smudges or scratches, you can skip this verification step. If the Installer indicates that there's a problem with the DVD, try using the disc on another computer. If you experience the same symptom on two computers, the disc could be the problem. If your Mac OS X Install DVD is unusable, call Apple for replacement. If the disc works on another computer, the problem could be with your computer's optical drive.

Problems Processing the Packages

The CPU is very unlikely to be the source of an installation problem, especially if the computer starts up successfully. However, marginal-quality third-party memory can contribute to installation issues, issues that might not otherwise be apparent in day-to-day computer tasks. You might need to remove third-party RAM from your computer.

> **TROUBLESHOOTING** ▶ During an installation, Mac OS X boots from the Mac OS X Install DVD, and is unable to use Virtual Memory. If you have a limited amount of physical RAM available, the speed of your installation might be affected, and if RAM is very limited, you might encounter errors if you are transferring a large amount of data using the Archive and Install option.

Problems Writing the Packages

To test for problems with the hard disk drive to which you are installing, start the computer with the Mac OS X Install DVD, choose Utilities > Disk Utility, click First Aid, then click Verify Disk. After verification or any necessary repair, try the installation again.

> **TROUBLESHOOTING** ▶ An Erase installation often succeeds where installations without erasing fail. You should make sure you have a working backup of your important data before erasing the volume. Due to the extreme nature of this solution, you might wish to try all other options first.

Other Troubleshooting Tips

If you encounter problems during the installation of Mac OS X or any software updates, there are a few simple things you can try that will help you resolve or gain more information:

▶ Make sure your computer meets the minimum requirements for Mac OS X 10.4, including the correct version of firmware.

▶ Check the installation log in the Installer by choosing File > Show Log, or use Console to view /var/log/install.log. Error messages listed there can help you troubleshoot the problem.

▶ Turn off the Screen Saver and Energy Saver in System Preferences so they do not activate while you are downloading or installing.

▶ If you are installing Mac OS X on a portable computer, make sure that it is plugged in to AC power while you are installing Mac OS X or downloading updates.

▶ Try restarting the computer and installing the update again. Since some installation issues are not reproducible, you may succeed the second time.

▶ If the issue persists, disconnect any other devices you may have connected to your computer and retry the installation. Other devices could affect your installation. Disconnect or remove anything that did not come with your computer. If removing all non–Apple memory leaves you with insufficient memory to install Mac OS X, then remove everything but the memory. If your problem persists, you may have an issue with your non–Apple memory.

NOTE ▶ If your installation does not work, or you feel that you need to undo a System Update, you should not try to delete some system files and run an installation from an older Mac OS X Install Disc. That can introduce a wide range of problems, including unlinked application frameworks that require another reinstallation to repair. If an installation or upgrade does not go smoothly, back up all user data and perform an Archive and Install with a current Mac OS X Install Disc, then run Software Update to get up-to-date, and reinstall all third-party applications and drivers.

For more tips, refer to Knowledge Base document 106692, "Mac OS X: Troubleshooting installation and software updates."

What You've Learned

▶ Mac OS X uses standards throughout the operating system. These standards enable Macintosh computers to integrate into networks and share data and peripherals with other computers.

▶ Mac OS X 10.4 can install on any Macintosh computer with a G3 processor or later that also has a DVD drive, built-in FireWire, a minimum of 256 MB of memory, and 3 GB of available disk space.

▶ Before you install Mac OS X, you need to make key decisions about how you want to configure the system, including if you want to partition your drive or not. If you are upgrading from Mac OS 9, you should also note your network configuration information so that you can use it when you configure Mac OS X.

▶ After using Setup Assistant to do the initial configuration, you can use System Preferences to perform additional system configuration.

▶ To ensure that your system is up-to-date, you should check for updates on a regular basis by choosing Apple > Software Update, or using Software Update preferences.

▶ Use Knowledge Base to research known installation issues.

References

The following Knowledge Base documents (located at www.apple.com/support) will provide you with further information regarding installing Mac OS X.

Apple Software Restore

▶ 42929, "Using Restore Discs with Mac OS X 10.2 through 10.3.1"

▶ 106451, "Using Apple Software Restore to install or reinstall parts without erasing (Mac OS X 10.1.5 or earlier)"

Firmware Issues

▶ 42642, "To continue booting, type 'mac-boot' and press return" Message"

▶ 58492, "Differences Between the Mac OS ROM and bootROM"

▶ 60351, "Determining BootROM or Firmware Version"

▶ 86117, "Mac OS X: Chart of Available Firmware Updates"

Installation Issues

▶ 25404, "Mac OS X: How to reinstall a prior version"

▶ 25773, "Mac OS X 10.3: Transferring data with Setup Assistant frequently asked questions (FAQ)"

▶ 75187, "Mac OS X: Software installations require administrator password"

▶ 106163, "Mac OS X: System Requirements"

▶ 106178, "Startup Manager: How to Select a Startup Volume"

▶ 106235, "Mac OS X: Disk Appears Dimmed (or Grayed Out) in the Installer"

- 106442, "Mac OS X 10.0, 10.1: Installer Does Not Display Hard Disk"
- 106464, "Your Mac won't start up in Mac OS X"
- 106692, "Mac OS X: Troubleshooting installation and software updates"
- 106693, "Mac OS X: Troubleshooting installation from CD or DVD"
- 106694, "Mac OS X: Troubleshooting the Mac OS X Installer"
- 106695, "Troubleshooting Automatic Software Update in Mac OS X"
- 106704, "Mac OS X: Updating your software"
- 107120, "Mac OS X: About the Archive and Install feature"

Miscellaneous

- 2238, "Macintosh: How to Reset PRAM and NVRAM"
- 86209, "Macintosh: Some Computers Only Start Up in Mac OS X"
- 86246, "Using the Software Install and Restore DVD with PowerBook G4 (12-inch)"
- 107249, "Mac OS X: About file system journaling"

UFS and Mac OS Extended

- 25316, "Mac OS X 10.2 or Earlier: Choosing UFS or Mac OS Extended (HFS Plus) Formatting"

Lesson Review

Use the following questions to review what you have learned:

1. What are the different configuration choices when installing Mac OS X?
2. What things should you do before you upgrade Mac OS 9.x to Mac OS X?
3. What is the purpose of the local account?
4. What are the quick fixes to consider when troubleshooting an installation problem?

Answers

1. Mac OS X can be installed on a single partition along with Mac OS 9.x.
    You can also install Mac OS X on one partition or volume while
    Mac OS 9.x is installed on another. Mac OS X can also be installed by
    itself, without Mac OS 9.x. You can also choose to update a previous
    version of Mac OS X to Mac OS X 10.4.

2. Before installing Mac OS X, you should make a backup of the data on
    your hard disk, read the Read Before You Install document, collect net-
    work configuration information from Mac OS 9.x, upgrade firmware (if
    necessary), and upgrade to Mac OS 9.2.2 (if you plan on using Classic
    applications).

3. The initial local account is automatically an administrator account with
    which you can change settings in System Preferences, install applications,
    and use certain utilities.

4. Check the installation log; confirm that firmware is up-to-date;
    restart/reinstall; check for disk problems; disconnect nonessential
    hardware; and turn off Energy Saver and Screen Saver preferences.

3

Time   This lesson takes approximately 1 hour to complete.

Goals   Create, configure, and manage user accounts in Mac OS X

Understand security issues involved with user accounts and passwords

Troubleshoot user account issues

Lesson 3
User Accounts

Mac OS X is a true multiuser operating system, which means that the computer can be used by more than one user, and that every resource, file, and program is associated with a user on the system.

In Mac OS 9, the Multiple Users control panel allowed you to configure the system for more than one user. This feature was added to the operating system to give each user a unique workspace. Microsoft Windows implements multiple user accounts with functionality similar to Mac OS 9. UNIX, on the other hand, was designed to be a multiuser environment because most computers in existence at the time UNIX was developed were large computers that had to be shared by many users.

This lesson introduces you to the three types of user accounts in Mac OS X; how to create and manage user accounts; and your options for increasing account security.

Understanding User Types

There are tens of millions of Macintosh users in the world today, performing a wide variety of tasks from accounting to layout to writing. However, in the context of Mac OS X, there are only three types of users: standard, administrator, and System Administrator.

Your user type doesn't dictate the tasks you can perform with the Macintosh, but it does determine the level of privileges you enjoy for changing how the Mac operates.

You can configure three types of users in Mac OS X:

▶   A standard user can use a basic set of applications and tools and is limited to making configuration changes that affect only the user's account, such as what applications and files are opened when the user logs in and what picture is displayed as the user's background pattern. A standard user cannot make changes to any settings that are system-wide (Security, Energy Saver, Print & Fax, Network, Sharing, Accounts, Date & Time, and Startup Disk preferences). A standard user is also restricted from using Directory Setup and NetInfo Manager to change configurations.

   If a standard user attempts to make a system-wide modification, the user must authenticate with the user name and password of an administrator user before the changes can be made.

▶   An administrator user, or admin user, has basic use of the tools to configure and customize Mac OS X. The initial local account configured in Setup Assistant is an administrator user.

   One of the most powerful attributes of an administrator is that this user type can change settings on any of the panes in System Preferences. (If a pane displays an icon of a lock in the lower-left corner, it means that particular preference affects all users and requires authentication as an administrator to change.) An administrator can make changes using utilities such as NetInfo Manager. An administrator also can install applications and resources that may be used by all users on the system.

▶ A System Administrator (also called superuser or root) has read and write access to all settings and files on the system, including hidden system files that a regular administrator account cannot modify.

By default, System Administrator is disabled. The user exists, but you can't log in using that account. Mac OS X was configured this way to help secure the computer and avert unintentional deletion of important files and folders. System Administrator can be enabled using either NetInfo Manager or the command line. When viewing items owned by System Administrator in the Finder, the Info window will usually show the owner as "system."

NOTE ▶ There can be multiple standard and administrator users on any Mac OS X system, but only one System Administrator. Also, unlike other user types, the System Administrator does not have a home folder in Users.

Every user has certain attributes: long name, short name, password, and unique numeric user identification (UID). Although UID numbers aren't displayed in the user interface, Mac OS X uses the UID internally to identify users. These numbers can be viewed in NetInfo Manager or the command line. Each user account also has its own home folder in Users and owns any files that are created when someone is logged in as that user.

TIP ▶ While the initial account created on Mac OS X is an administrator account, it is a good idea to create a standard account for performing daily activities, even if you are the sole user of the computer. This way if someone gains physical access to the computer when you step away for a moment, they will not have administrative privileges.

Creating and Editing User Accounts

Both administrator and standard users use Accounts preferences to manage user accounts. Although standard users can change their own account information, such as the login password, only administrator users can add or delete user accounts. Throughout this lesson, we assume that you are initially logged in as an administrator using an account named Apple Admin. If you prefer to continue using your existing account, that's fine, as long as it's an administrator account. Whenever the Apple Admin account is discussed in the book, substitute your administrator account instead.

To create a new account, click the Add User (+) button. You then provide a long name, a short name, a password, and an optional password hint for the user.

Accounts preferences is divided into four panes:

> **NOTE** ▶ Login Items is only available when you are configuring your own account, and Parental Controls is only available when you're editing standard accounts.

▶ Password — You enter the user's full name and short name. Selecting the "Allow user to administer this computer" checkbox changes the account type from standard to administrator. You also enter the user's password and an optional password hint.

> **TIP** ▶ You can create a user account without a password, but doing so is strongly discouraged for security reasons. An alert is displayed when no password is entered.

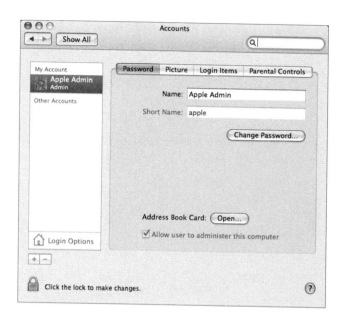

When a user account is created in Mac OS X, a home folder is created for that user in Users. The home folder has the same name as the user's short name. You can quickly access your home folder by clicking the home icon in the Sidebar at the left of the Finder window. The short name can be as long as 255 Roman characters. However, if a short name is longer than 32 characters, Classic applications (as well as some Mac OS X applications) might give errors while saving files. In such a case, you can save the files in a folder that has a name less than 32 characters in length, and then move them later, using the Finder.

NOTE ▶ When creating a new user account, think carefully about the user's short name. After you create an account you can easily change a user's long name, but changing the short name is a complicated procedure. Renaming the home folder does not change the user's short name because that information is stored in the local NetInfo database (/var/db/netinfo/local.nidb).

MORE INFO ▶ Refer to Knowledge Base document 106824, "Mac OS X: How to change user short name or home directory name."

▶ Picture — You select a login picture. This picture is also used as your Address Book picture and as the default picture in iChat. You can upload a custom picture by clicking Edit and then Choose.

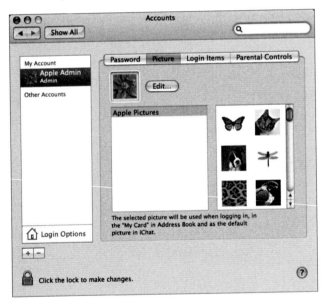

▶ Login Items — If you are modifying your own account, you can specify which items to open automatically when you log in. This pane was called Startup Items in previous versions of Mac OS X.

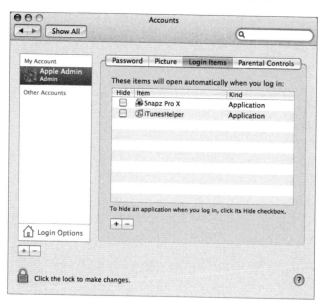

▶ Parental Controls — For modifying a standard user account, the Parental Controls pane (called Limitations in previous versions of Mac OS X) allows administrators to limit what a standard user can do on the computer with applications such as Mail, Finder & System, iChat, and Safari. For example, you can allow or deny iChat requests and emails from specific people, limit access to System Preferences, and prevent Finder tasks such as burning CDs or DVDs. You can also specify a limited set of applications that the user can open.

NOTE ▶ The accounts list identifies non-administrator accounts as either Standard or Managed, depending upon the Parental Controls settings. This book uses the term "standard user" to refer to both types of non-administrator accounts, regardless of their Parental Controls settings.

To apply your changes, switch to another pane, add a new user, or quit System Preferences.

Setting Login Options

The Login Options pane in Accounts preferences is used to set options that affect how users log in as well as what they can do once they are logged in. To access the Login Options pane, select a user in the list at the left, then click Login Options at the bottom left.

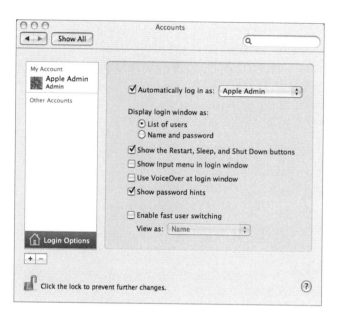

If you are an administrator user, you can configure the computer to log in as a particular user every time it starts up or restarts. Select the "Automatically log in as" checkbox, and choose a user from the corresponding pop-up menu. You will be prompted for that account's password (if any). The next time the computer boots, Mac OS X will automatically log into that account. This option is best for computers with only one user account in a secure environment.

You can configure the login window to display a list of user accounts with a login picture for each one or a prompt for the user name and password. The latter is the best choice for computers with several user accounts, and it also provides an extra measure of security because users must know a valid name and password to log in. If you have selected Network Startup in Startup Disk preferences, you can enter a local user account in the login window, or click Other and enter a network user name and password.

You can also choose whether or not to show the Restart, Sleep, and Shut Down buttons. This security feature can keep a user from restarting in an insecure mode, short of using the reset or power buttons on the computer itself. This security feature is useful in managed environments such as kiosk-type installations, where you want to prevent a user from restarting the computer with a modifier key pressed.

New in Mac OS X 10.4 are the options for showing the Input menu in the login window (necessary for proper input of passwords if users of the computer use different keyboards or language mappings), using VoiceOver at the login window (good for visually-impaired users), as well as whether to show password hints in the login window (recommended only in environments where security is not a priority).

Finally, you can enable fast user switching (discussed later in this lesson). This feature lets multiple users share a computer without quitting applications and logging out. For the purposes of the following exercises, make sure fast user switching is enabled.

Creating a Standard User Account
This exercise guides you through the process of creating a standard user account:

1   Open System Preferences and click Accounts. If necessary, unlock Accounts preferences by clicking the lock icon and authenticating as an administrator.

2 Click the Add User button (the plus sign beneath the accounts list), and enter the following information:

▶ Name: *Chris Johnson*

▶ Short Name: *chris*

▶ Password: *changeme*

▶ Verify: *changeme*

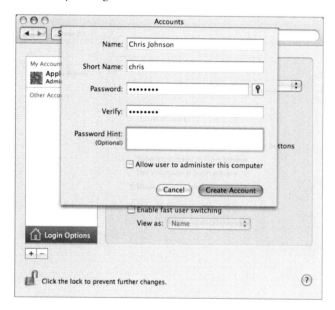

3 Click Create Account.

You have created a local user account for Chris.

4   Verify that the Chris Johnson account is in the Other Accounts list at the left.

5   Repeat steps 2 and 3 to create another standard user:

▶   Name: *Martha Flowers*

▶   Short Name: *martha*

▶   Password: *marflo*

▶   Verify: *marflo*

Test the New User Account

Log in using Chris Johnson's user account to verify that the user account was created correctly.

1   Choose Log Out Apple Admin from the Apple menu.

2   In the dialog asking if you are sure, click Log Out.

3   In the login window, select Chris Johnson.

4   Enter Chris Johnson's password: *changeme*

5   Click Log In.

You are now logged in as Chris Johnson.

6   Log out of the Chris Johnson account.

7   Log in to the Apple Admin account.

Switching Between Users

Mac OS X 10.3 introduced a new feature, fast user switching, which lets multiple users share a computer without quitting applications and logging out. When one user logs in to his or her own account, other accounts remain active in the background with applications running and documents still open.

Although the UNIX-based security model in Mac OS X helps keep data and applications secure, enabling fast user switching can introduce some potential security risks. For example, an encrypted disk image currently opened under one account would be potentially accessible from another account if both accounts are currently logged in with fast user switching. For this reason, you should not enable fast user switching on a computer where you do not know and trust all of the users (such as in a computer lab or a kiosk).

When you activate fast user switching in the Login Options pane of Accounts preferences, a new menu appears on the right side of the menu bar. You can use this menu to switch between accounts. If you switch to an active user account (an account that is logged in), you'll see the account in the same state in which it was last left, with any applications running. This feature enables you to keep each account's user environment distinct and intact without wasting time.

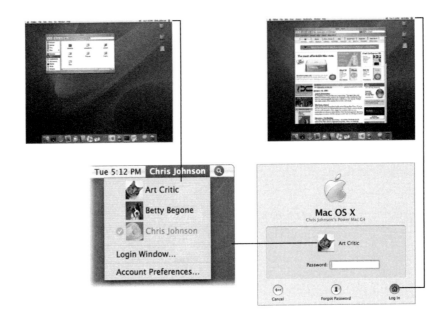

When using fast user switching, keep in mind that you might encounter resource conflicts. Many peripherals cannot be shared among multiple users on the same computer simultaneously. For example, if a user opens a scanner application and then switches out, a second user logging in may not be able to access the scanner. In some cases, applications that control peripherals will release control of the device when a user switches out.

Some applications have issues when two or more people attempt to use the application at the same time. Mac OS X includes a list of versions of applications that are known to have issues when opened by more than one user. When a second user attempts to open the application, the system will warn the user that the application is already in use and cannot be opened. If you encounter an application that has problems being opened by multiple switched users, contact the application's developer—a more recent version may have fixed the problem.

MORE INFO ▶ Refer to Knowledge Base document 25619, "Mac OS X 10.3, 10.4: Some applications only work in one account at a time."

You can also experience conflicts in accessing documents. A user with the right permissions can open the same document that a previous user was editing, and can make changes to it, even if the first user left the document open. This can result in conflicts. Therefore, you should coordinate work on shared documents with other users of the system to avoid problems.

Also, only one account at a time can use the Classic environment. If one account has a Classic application open, other users on that Mac OS X computer will not be able to run Classic applications until the first user quits the running Classic application and stops the Classic environment.

> **NOTE ▶** If fast user switching is turned on, an administrator user cannot select or edit the account of any user that is currently logged in (the account name appears dimmed in Accounts preferences).

Deleting User Accounts

As an administrator user, you can use Accounts preferences to delete any user account. However, you cannot remove all the administrator users because there must be at least one.

To delete an account, select it, then click the Delete User (minus sign) button. The system will prompt you to put the contents of the user's home folder in a disk image (.dmg) file in the /Users/Deleted Users folder or to delete the home folder contents immediately.

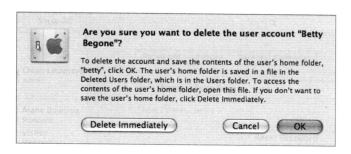

If you click OK, the user's home folder will be moved into a disk image file in /Users/Deleted Users. If the files need to be transferred to another user account, an administrator user can move the disk image to that user's home folder. The user can then mount the disk image and retrieve the needed files. (Disk images are covered in Lesson 4, "File Systems.")

> **NOTE** ▶ If you click Delete Immediately, the user's home folder will be deleted and cannot be recovered. It is not put in the Trash, so this command should be used with caution.

> **TIP** ▶ When deleting a user that has FileVault configured, be sure that you first turn off FileVault for the user and then delete the user account.

Deleting a User Account

The following steps walk you through deleting a user account:

1   In Accounts preferences, select the Martha Flowers user account.

    If you are still logged in as Chris Johnson, you must first click the lock icon then authenticate using the Apple Admin account before you can make changes in Accounts preferences.

2   Click the Delete User button (the minus sign).

    A dialog appears, informing you that the contents of the user's folder will be put in the Deleted Users folder.

    You have two options when deleting a user account: you can save the contents of the user's home folder in a disk image, or you can immediately delete the user's home folder.

3   Click OK.

4   Verify that Martha Flowers is no longer listed in the Other Accounts list.

5 Quit System Preferences.

6 Open the Users folder in the Finder.

Verify that the folder martha has been deleted and that a martha.dmg file has been placed in the Deleted Users folder.

Restoring a Deleted User's Files

The contents of the martha home folder have been stored in the martha.dmg disk image. (Disk images are covered in Lesson 4, "File Systems.") The following steps show you how to open the disk image and restore its contents:

1 Navigate to /Users/Deleted Users.

2 Double-click martha.dmg.

The martha volume will be mounted on your desktop and its contents displayed in a new window. You should be able to view the folders and files from the old Martha Flowers home folder.

If you need to have another user take over the files from the Martha Flowers account, you could copy the disk image to the new user's home folder, and that user could mount the disk image and copy any needed files.

3 Create a new folder in Users named *martha*.

4 Copy the contents of the mounted image into the folder /Users/martha.

5 Unmount the martha volume from the desktop.

6 Open System Preferences.

7 Click Accounts.

8 Unlock the Accounts pane by authenticating as Apple Admin.

9   Add a new user, Martha Flowers (Short Name: *martha*, Password: *marflo*). A dialog appears stating that a folder in the Users folder already has the name "martha."

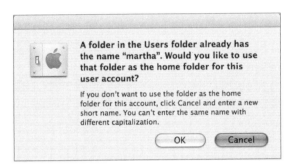

10 Click OK to use that folder as the home folder for the new account you are creating.

11 Quit System Preferences.

12 Use the user accounts menu at the top right to switch user accounts, and log in as Martha Flowers (Password: *marflo*).

13 Log out of the Martha Flowers account.

14 Log in to the Apple Admin account.

Securing Your Macintosh

With its UNIX core, Mac OS X has many robust built-in security features that restrict attempts to compromise the system, either intentionally or accidentally. However, as with any security system, there are ways to bypass or override the controls. In the end, to secure your machine, you must control physical access to the computer as well as user access to the files on the computer.

There are various types of passwords used in Mac OS X, although some of these are optional:

▶ Login password — Each user should have a single login password that is used in the login window and prevents other users from accessing his or her files. (Administrators' login passwords also allow them to change system-wide settings.)

▶ Open Firmware password — The computer itself can be protected by a single password that prevents unauthorized users from altering the startup process.

▶ Master password — An administrator must create a single master password before users can protect their home folders with FileVault. The master password acts as a back door for resetting passwords on FileVault-protected accounts.

▶ Resource passwords — Users may create or enter passwords as needed in Web sites, servers, applications, folder archives, and encrypted disk images. For example, to retrieve email, your email client will require the password provided by your Internet service provider.

▶ Keychain password — This password unlocks a user's keychain, a Mac OS X feature that simplifies the storage and automatic retrieval of resource passwords as they are needed.

To maintain a secure company or departmental network and a safe network environment for your users, you must ensure that everyone on your network uses only high-quality passwords.

Creating Passwords

Whenever you create a password, it is important to pick one that will be easy to remember but difficult for other people to guess. If you allow users to transcribe passwords, the written passwords should be stored in a secure place to prevent unauthorized access to the accounts.

The passwords used in this book are *not* good examples of secure passwords. They are used only for simplicity's sake. However, Mac OS X 10.4 includes a tool called Password Assistant that determines the quality ("strength") of specific passwords and suggests good passwords. To access Password Assistant, click the small icon of a key that appears in Accounts preferences, Security preferences, Keychain Access, and other Mac OS X 10.4 utilities.

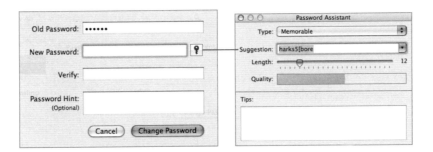

If you choose Memorable from the Type pop-up menu, Password Assistant will generate a password of the specified length, composed of uppercase and lowercase letters, punctuation, and numbers. Such passwords are designed to be easy to remember but not vulnerable to *dictionary attacks*. A dictionary attack is a common intrusion attempt, where an intruder or intrusion tool simply tries to authenticate with common usernames and words that can be found in a dictionary for the passwords (for example, jsmith as the username and workbook as the password.)

High-quality passwords would be SuP3rM@n!, not superman; l%%k@meNøw, not lookatmenow; and E2B3Two®, not earlytobedearlytorise. Enter these passwords into Password Assistant and watch the Quality indicator. For even stronger passwords, choose a different setting from the Type pop-up menu, or increase the length of the password. A standard user can change his or her own login password, but before doing so the user must enter the current password for authentication. If a user forgets a password, any administrator user on the computer can change the password using Accounts preferences. A password for any account, including the System Administrator, can be changed by booting from the Mac OS X Install DVD and choosing Utilities > Reset Password.

NOTE ▶ Be warned that resetting a login password allows a user to log in with a new password, but changing passwords this way does not reset keychain passwords, master passwords, or network passwords used in a directory service environment.

Setting an Open Firmware Password

You can set an Open Firmware password that must be entered whenever anyone attempts to alter the normal startup procedure by pressing a modifier key (such as Option to choose a different startup disk). For instructions, refer to Knowledge Base document 106482, "Setting up Open Firmware Password Protection in Mac OS X 10.1 or later."

Encrypting Home Folders with FileVault

Although login passwords provide some protection from users gaining access to documents stored in another user's home folder, other users can still gain access to those files. For example, anyone with a Mac OS X Install DVD or an administrator account on the computer can reset a password and log in to the account. Even without changing passwords, someone with System Administrator access can access any file on the system, including those in another home folder.

You are now ready to turn on FileVault protection.

WARNING: **Your files will be encrypted using your login password. If you forget your login password and you don't know the master password, your information will be lost.**

Once you turn on FileVault, you will be logged out and FileVault will encrypt your entire home folder. Depending on how much information you have, this could take a while. You will not be able to log in or use this computer until the initial setup is completed.

You can't log in to this account from another computer to use it for Windows file or printer sharing.

☐ Use secure erase   (Cancel) (Turn On FileVault)

FileVault enables users to encrypt the contents of their home folders, allowing file access only when the user is logged in. When a user enables the FileVault feature, the user's entire home folder is transferred into an encrypted sparse disk image (which is covered in more depth in Lesson 4, "File Systems").

> **NOTE** ▶ A sparse image is a special kind of disk image that can automatically resize as needed. However, like any file system, a sparse image can become damaged after an abrupt system restart or power outage. Use Disk Utility to repair damaged or corrupted sparse images and disk images.

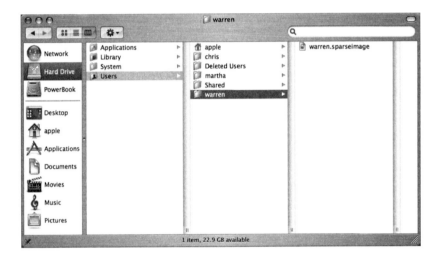

When the user logs in to the computer locally (not via ssh or Remote Access), the disk image is decrypted and mounted in the Users folder, allowing the user to use his or her home folder. When the user logs out, the disk image is unmounted and re-encrypted, leaving only the disk image file in place of the user's home folder contents. Other users, including administrators, may access the disk image file, but because the disk image file is encrypted, they can't access the contents without the password. The time necessary to encrypt and decrypt the home folder depends upon the size of the folder and the speed of the computer.

NOTE ▶ When turning FileVault on or off for an account, there must be disk space available equal to or greater than the size of the user's home folder. If there is not enough disk space, the account cannot be converted.

TIP ▶ FileVault is not a good choice for home folders with large amounts of data. If you need to encrypt large amounts of data, you should put it in an encrypted disk image on an external FireWire drive or other storage device.

One of the drawbacks of encrypting data is that if the user forgets his or her password, access to the files in the home folder is lost. If an account has FileVault enabled, an administrator user cannot use Accounts preferences to change that account's password, nor can the administrator user turn off FileVault for the account; only the user can do that.

Because users often forget passwords, Mac OS X provides a master password feature to allow passwords on FileVault-protected accounts to be reset. The master password is used only as a back door for recovering FileVault-encrypted accounts. If during login a user enters three incorrect passwords for his or her FileVault-encrypted account, the account's password hint is displayed along with a Reset Password button. After the user clicks Reset Password and enters the master password (obtained from the administrator), he or she can set a new login password.

If you forget the master password, you can reset it, but you must know the passwords for any accounts with FileVault enabled:

1   As an administrator user, delete the master password keychain file (/Library/Keychains/FileVaultMaster.keychain). When the master password keychain is deleted, Mac OS X assumes that no master password is set yet.

2   In Security preferences, set a new master password.

3   Log in to each account that has FileVault turned on, and use Accounts preferences to reset the password for each account.

NOTE ▶ Do not forget the master password! Although it is possible to reset the master password, it still requires all users with FileVault-protected accounts to know their passwords. If a user has forgotten his or her login password, and you have forgotten the master password, there is no way to recover the user's data.

Setting the Master Password

If you want to use FileVault to encrypt your home folder, you must first set the master password for the computer in Security preferences. This password is different from the password you set in Accounts preferences.

To set the master password:

1   Log in as Apple Admin.

2   Open System Preferences and click Security.

3   Click Set Master Password.

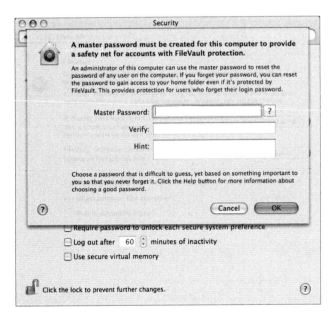

4   Authenticate as Apple Admin if requested.

5   Type *applemp* in the Master Password and Verify fields.

6   Click OK.

The master password is set for the computer. You can change it later if you want to by clicking the Change button in Security preferences.

7   Quit System Preferences.

8   Choose Apple > Log Out Apple Admin.

Encrypting a Home Folder

To encrypt a home folder using FileVault, create a new user for this exercise and then encrypt the home folder:

1   Open Accounts preferences.

2   Unlock the Accounts pane by authenticating as Apple Admin.

3   Add a new user, Warren Peece (Short Name: *warren*, Password: *peece*).

4   Log out of the Apple Admin account.

5   Log in to the Warren Peece account.

6   Open Security preferences.

7   Click the lock icon at the bottom left of the window, then authenticate as Apple Admin.

8   Click Turn On FileVault.

9   Type Warren's password (*warren*) in the Password field and click OK.

A warning message appears asking you if you are sure you want to turn on FileVault.

10 Take a moment to read the warning message, and then click Turn On
FileVault.

The system logs out Warren and displays a message indicating that the
system is encrypting Warren's home folder and displays a progress bar.
The system creates a sparse disk image, copies the home folder into the
image, and deletes the old home folder. When the system is finished
encrypting Warren's home folder, the login window appears.

Verifying the Home Folder Encryption

Once a home folder is encrypted, the contents of the home folder are inaccessible unless the owner of the home folder logs in. Do the following to verify
that the system encrypted Warren's home folder:

1 Log in as Apple Admin.

2 Go to /Users/warren.

You should see a file named warren.sparseimage. This is the disk image
file where Warren's home folder is stored. If you double-click the disk
image file, the system prompts you to enter a password. If you enter
Warren's password, the disk image mounts.

3 Click Apple Admin in the menu bar, and choose Warren Peece from the
user accounts menu.

4 Log in using Warren's password.

5 Go to /Users/warren.

Notice that Warren can access the contents of his home folder.

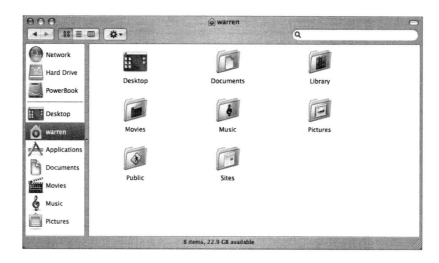

6   Choose Apple > Log Out Warren Peece.

Resetting a User's Password
If Warren forgets his password, the contents of his home folder are inaccessible,
unless his password is reset using the master password.

1   In the login window, select Warren Peece.

2   In the Password field, type *ABC*.

3   Click Log In.

Because ABC isn't Warren's password, the window will shake.

4   In the Password field, type *123*.

5 Click Log In.

Again, access will be denied.

6 In the Password field, type *xyz*.

7 Click Log In.

Because logging failed three times, the login window will request the master password.

8 In the Master Password field, type *applemp*.

9 Click Log In.

An alert appears explaining that the user's old keychain will be saved and a new one created.

10 Click OK.

11 In the New Password and Verify fields, type *peece*.

This will be Warren's new password.

12 Click Log in.

The computer will then log in Warren.

13 Choose Apple > Log Out Warren Peece.

Setting Security Options
You've just learned how to set a master password and turn on FileVault in Security preferences. This pane has a collection of other options to help protect your system from unauthorized use.

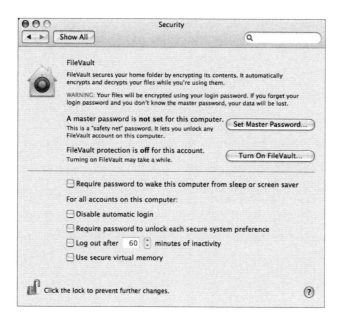

You can specify that a password is required to wake the computer from sleep or from a screen saver. You can also disable automatic login to force users to authenticate, require users to enter a password to unlock a secure system preference, and log out a user after a specific number of minutes of inactivity.

A new feature in Mac OS X 10.4 is the use of secure virtual memory. This addresses a rare issue in which private information could be obtained by searching the information left over in the virtual memory scratch files. Select the "Use secure virtual memory" checkbox to take advantage of this feature.

> **TIP** ▶ While the default installation of Mac OS X has automatic login enabled, most corporate environments would want this feature turned off, as well as requiring a password to wake a system from sleep. For additional security, consider using secure virtual memory, FileVault, and the Open Firmware Password utility.

Using Keychains

Beyond the user login password, a user has to keep track of passwords for many other resources, such as Web sites, servers, and applications. When you connect to a server or Web site or open a keychain-aware application, the password used can be stored in the keychain. The next time you access those resources, the password is read from your keychain automatically.

The user's default keychain is automatically created at the same time the account is created. That keychain is named "login" and is stored in ~/Library/Keychains. By default, the login keychain is protected by the user's original login password. A system-wide keychain named "System" is also created by default and is shared by all users on the system. Since the keychain is not "tied" to the computer, it can be copied to other computers. For example, when a user upgrades to a new computer, he or she can copy the keychain from the old computer to the new one.

You can use Keychain Access (/Applications/Utilities) to create additional keychains for each user, based on types of resources or on particular locations. Users can also use Keychain Access to manage their keychains, including what passwords are stored in a keychain and what password is used to unlock the keychain. Keychain Access also includes Keychain First Aid (located under the Keychain Access menu), which can be used to verify and repair keychain settings and permissions.

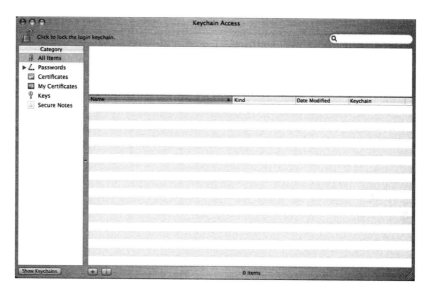

You can change the password to unlock a keychain at any time, however, if you want your default keychain to be unlocked automatically when you log in, make sure your keychain password is the same as your Mac OS X login password. If an administrator changes a login password, the keychain password for that account does not get changed as well. As a result, the user can log in with the new password, but the keychain will not automatically open.

Synchronizing Login and Keychain Passwords

When users change their own login password using Accounts preferences, their keychain password is updated with the new password information if the keychain's existing password is the same as the user's existing login password. If a user's login password is changed by an administrator or by the Reset Password utility on the Mac OS X Install DVD, the user's keychain is still protected by the user's old password and needs to be synchronized with the new login password.

This exercise will guide you through resetting a user's keychain password, creating a keychain entry, then synchronizing the login and keychain passwords.

1   Restart using the Mac OS X Install DVD.

2   At the first screen, select "Use English as the main language" then press Return.

3   Choose Utilities > Reset Password.

4   In the Reset Password window, select the volume icon that represents your startup disk.

    The "Select a user of this volume" pop-up menu will change to list the user accounts on that volume.

5   Choose Chris Johnson from the pop-up menu.

    New users do not yet have data in the keychain, so changing their passwords has few consequences.

6   In both password fields, enter *f00tba11* (f-zero-zero-t-b-a-one-one).

7   Click Save.

8   Click OK in the Password Saved dialog.

    You have changed Chris Johnson's login password. Because the new login password does not match the original login password also used for the keychain, Chris is at risk of losing his keychain data. If a user forgets his or her keychain password when his or her login and keychain passwords are out of sync, the keychain cannot be unlocked and might need to be recreated.

9   Quit Reset Password.

10 Quit Installer.

11 Click Restart.

12 Log in as Chris Johnson (password: *f00tba11*).

13 Open Accounts preferences.

14 Click Change Password.

15 Enter the password you just reset: *f00tba11*

16 Enter a new password: *chris*

17 Quit System Preferences.

Chris Johnson's keychain does not contain any data. We will now attempt to create an entry in the keychain.

18 Launch Disk Utility (/Applications/Utilities).

19 Choose File > New > New Blank Image.

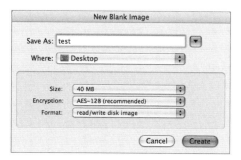

20 Choose AES-128 from the Encryption pop-up menu.

21 Enter *test* as the file name.

22 Click Create.

23 In the Authenticate window, enter *test* in the Password and Verify fields, select the "Remember password (add to Keychain)" checkbox, and click OK.

Disk Utility attempts to add this disk image's password information to your keychain. Because the keychain is locked, you must authenticate with the keychain password.

24 When prompted for your keychain password, enter *f00tba11* and click OK.

Because the keychain is protected by the original "changeme" password, the request fails.

At this point, Chris has no access to his keychain data. If Chris forgot his keychain password, he would not be able to access his keychain data even though his login password could be reset.

25 In the Password field, enter *changeme* and click OK.

Because you entered the password that protects the keychain, Disk Utility is able to create the encrypted disk image and save its password to the keychain.

26   Unmount the test disk icon from the Finder desktop.

27   Open Keychain Access (/Applications/Utilities).

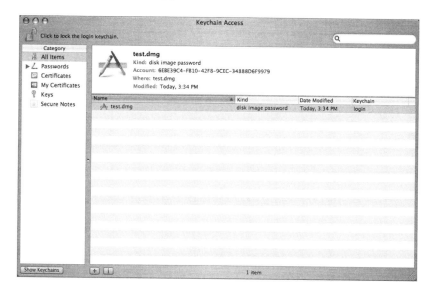

28   Click Show Keychains at the bottom left.

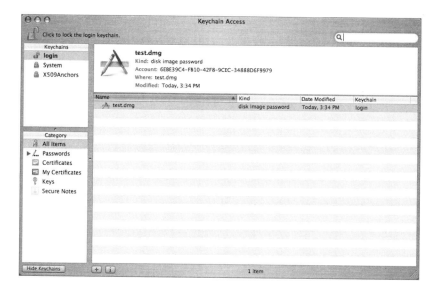

29 Lock the keychain by clicking the lock icon above the list of keychains.

30 Double-click the disk image entry.

31 In the Attributes pane, select the "Show password" checkbox.

Because the keychain is now locked, you are prompted for the keychain password.

32 In the Password field, enter *changeme* and click OK.

The keychain will unlock.

33 In the Password field of the "Confirm Access to Keychain" dialog, enter
changeme and click Always Allow.

This grants the Keychain Access application the permission to retrieve the
encrypted disk image password. Notice that the disk image password (*test*)
is now visible.

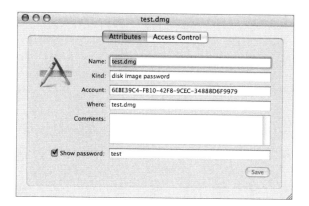

34 Close the test.dmg window.

Because the keychain password is not the same as the login password,
mounting the test disk image will always require Chris to enter the disk
image password. Let's synchronize the keychain password with the login
password so that the disk image is automatically opened when double-clicked.

35 In Keychain Access, verify that the login keychain is unlocked.

36 Choose Edit > Change Password for Keychain "login."

37 In the Change Keychain Password dialog, enter the following information:

▶ Current Password: *changeme*

▶ New Password: *f00tba11*

38 Click OK to save the new password.

Chris' keychain password is now synchronized with the login password. If Chris changes his login password again, the keychain password would also be changed because the login password and the keychain password are now the same.

39 Quit Keychain Access.

Troubleshooting User Account Issues

Here are some basic user account troubleshooting topics and solutions:

▶ If you are unable to log into a computer because the administrator login passwords are lost, boot from the Mac OS X Install DVD and choose Utilities > Reset Password. If you can log in using an administrator account, you can reset a user's password in Accounts preferences.

NOTE ▶ If an account is protected by FileVault, the only way to reset its login password is to first enter the master password. If you forget your master password in addition to your account's login password, there is no way to recover the data that was encrypted by FileVault.

▶ Whenever you have a problem with your computer, one troubleshooting technique is to log in with a different user account and see if the problem is reproducible. If the problem does not occur with the other user account, you can focus on the things that are user-specific, such as permissions and preferences.

▶ If a user's login password is changed by an administrator or by the Reset Password utility on the Mac OS X Install DVD, the system does not change the old password stored in the keychain to the new one. To fix this problem, the user should use Keychain Access to change the keychain password to match the login password.

▶ When using fast user switching to switch to another account, you might not be able to access certain resources. To determine if fast user switching is the cause, turn off fast user switching.

▶ If you can't make changes to certain System Preferences such as Network, Sharing, and Energy Saver, or you cannot install applications in the Applications folder, it's because you are a standard user and not an administrator. As a standard user, you are limited to making configuration changes that affect only your account, such as what applications and files are opened when you log in and what picture is displayed as the background pattern. You cannot make changes to system-wide settings without first authenticating as an administrator.

▶ You can get information such as Mac OS version, build number, serial number, date/time/time zone, and machine name by clicking the text field under Mac OS X in the login window.

What You've Learned

► There are three types of users—standard, administrator, and System Administrator—and each user has different capabilities.

► Creating and managing users is done in Accounts preferences.

► Security preferences provides options to increase user account security.

► How users are able to log in, including enabling the fast user switching option, is managed in the Login Options pane of Accounts preferences. Other available options include whether or not a list of users is displayed in the login window, and which account, if any, the computer should automatically log into.

References

The following Knowledge Base documents (located at www.apple.com/support) will provide you with further information regarding user accounts in Mac OS X.

Fast User Switching

► 25619, "Mac OS X 10.3, 10.4: Some applications only work in one account at a time"

User Access

► 93460, "iMovie: Using FileVault Can Affect Performance"

► 106156, "Mac OS X: Changing or resetting an account password"

► 106824, "Mac OS X: How to change user short name or home directory name"

► 107180, "Mac OS X: How to manage user access to applications, system preferences, and disc burning via 'Capabilities,' 'Limitations,' or 'Parental Controls'"

► 107297, "How to get files from a previous home directory after Archive and Install (Mac OS X)"

Open Firmware Password

▶ 106482, "Setting up Open Firmware Password Protection in Mac OS X 10.1 or later"

Lesson Review

Use the following questions to review what you have learned:

1. What are the three types of user accounts in Mac OS X?

2. What tool do you use to create, edit, or delete users?

3. What are some considerations when changing a user's login password?

4. What is the master password?

Answers

1. Standard, administrator, and System Administrator.

2. Accounts preferences is used to create, edit, or delete users.

3. If a user changes his or her own login password using Accounts preferences, his or her keychain password will also be updated. If the login password is changed from a different administrator account or from the Mac OS X Install DVD, the keychain password will not be updated.

4. The master password provides a back door for recovering data encrypted by FileVault. If a user is unable to log in to his or her account after three successive attempts, the user can enter the master password, which allows him or her to reset the login password.

4

Time

This lesson takes approximately 1 hour, 30 minutes to complete.

Goals

Manage the Mac OS X file system

Format a hard drive on Mac OS X

Archive, compress, and encrypt files in Mac OS X

Describe and implement Mac OS X support for securely erasing files

Describe how the file system handles bundles, packages, and forked files

Describe search paths, hidden folders, and system-related folders

Lesson 4
File Systems

This lesson discusses several features of the file systems on your Mac OS X computer.

First, this lesson describes how to format, partition, and repair disk drives. You will look at drive configuration and the file system layout after installing Mac OS X. You will then contrast the underlying files installed on the disk with how the Finder displays these files, and review how the file system uses search paths.

After learning about the file system, you will explore how users interact with the file system. This includes what's involved with naming and opening files, including the Finder mechanism that associates a file with applications that can open that file. You will explore file data and metadata, including how Spotlight searches for specific files. Finally, you'll learn about archives, packages, disk images, and burning folders to optical media.

Setting Up Disk Drives, Partitions, and Volumes

Disk drives come in all shapes and sizes, from large and fast fixed internal devices, to externally connected FireWire drives, iPods, and even USB–based devices like the iPod shuffle, which can serve as a disk drive. Regardless of the connection method, all disk drives are formatted into software partitions called volumes. To ensure data is preserved and the file system is properly updated, mounted volumes on removable media must be ejected before the removable device is disconnected.

> **NOTE ▶** All volumes in the Finder are mounted, whether they are shared network volumes or partitions on physical drives. Volumes on removable drives (FireWire disks or USB keychain drives) are unmounted using the File > Eject command in the Finder or with the Unmount button in Disk Utility. If all volumes on a physical drive are not unmounted before the drive is disconnected, if the drive is abruptly disconnected, or if there is a power outage, the disk catalog on those volumes might be damaged, which could result in data loss.

Whether a physical disk drive is formatted as one or more partitions, or whether external drives are connected, all mounted volumes appear as separate drives in the Finder, as shown here.

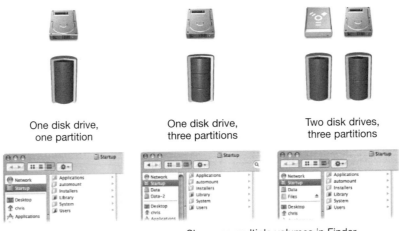

One disk drive, one partition

One disk drive, three partitions

Two disk drives, three partitions

Shows as one volume in Finder

Shows as multiple volumes in Finder

Choosing Mac OS X Volume Formats

Mac OS X is designed for compatibility with non-Macintosh volume formats, so you will find that Disk Utility, the Mac OS X formatting utility, offers a wide range of formatting options. The exact formatting options for your drive will vary, depending upon factors that can include the size of the drive, the drive geometry, the size of the partition you are formatting, and previous formatting used on the drive.

The most common drive formats that you will use for your volumes are:

▶   Mac OS Extended — Previously called HFS Plus, this is the format most familiar to Apple customers; it is used by both Mac OS X and Mac OS 9.

Mac OS X Server 10.2.2 introduced a new Mac OS Extended file-system feature known as journaling, which helps protect the file system against power outages or unforeseen failures in server components, reducing the need for repairs. While Mac OS Extended is still supported in Mac OS X 10.4, Mac OS Extended (Journaled) is the default and is recommended for most users.

MORE INFO ▶   Refer to Knowledge Base document 107249, "Mac OS X: About file system journaling."

The original Mac OS Extended file system is case-preserving, but case-insensitive, which means if you name a file File1, the Mac OS Extended file system will retain the upper-case letter F whenever you view the file. You cannot, however, put files called file1 and File1 in the same folder because Mac OS X doesn't distinguish between the two names. In Mac OS X 10.4, Disk Utility has the ability to format volumes using case-sensitive versions of Mac OS Extended or Mac OS Extended (Journaled). Case sensitivity was designed to support developers and other specialized users. Because case sensitivity can be confusing for users, it should be used only if needed.

▶ Mac OS Standard (HFS, or hierarchical file system) — This is an older file system that Mac OS X can access, but you can't install Mac OS X on an HFS volume. Furthermore, HFS is somewhat inefficient in its use of available storage space; Mac OS Extended allows more information to be stored on the same volume and is therefore preferred.

▶ UNIX File System (UFS) — This format is compatible with other UNIX-like operating systems. It is case-sensitive, so you can create files called file1 and File1 in the same folder. UFS volumes are not visible in the Classic environment, so this is not an appropriate volume format if you need to use Classic. However, UFS may be preferable when developing UNIX-based applications within Mac OS X.

▶ MS-DOS file system (FAT, or file allocation table) — This is the format used by Microsoft Windows. Files on a Windows formatted drive are usable by the Windows operating system as well as Mac OS X. Due to the physical drive geometry and other factors, the MS-DOS formatting options available in Disk Utility depend heavily upon whether the disk is currently formatted in a Windows format. Unless you have a specific need to create a partition in MS-DOS (FAT) format, you will seldom use this option.

You can mount MS-DOS volumes in Mac OS X, but Mac OS X does not support that format for startup volumes. Mac OS X can also mount volumes in the Windows NT (NTFS) format. Disk Utility cannot create volumes in NTFS format. NTFS volumes cannot be mounted in read-write mode, but you can access files on NTFS volumes mounted read-only.

▶ Free space — This is blank space on a drive that is not formatted specifically for any volume format. You might configure a drive with a free space partition if you need to copy files onto it from a computer running Linux.

MORE INFO ▶ Refer to Knowledge Base document 25316, "Mac OS X 10.2 or Earlier: Choosing UFS or Mac OS Extended (HFS Plus) Formatting."

Working with Disk Utility

Disk Utility is a very useful tool for working with volumes. Beginning with Mac OS X 10.3, Disk Utility includes the functionality provided by Disk Copy in previous versions of Mac OS X. Disk Utility's user interface has changed to accommodate the feature set of both programs. This section discusses the various features of Disk Utility.

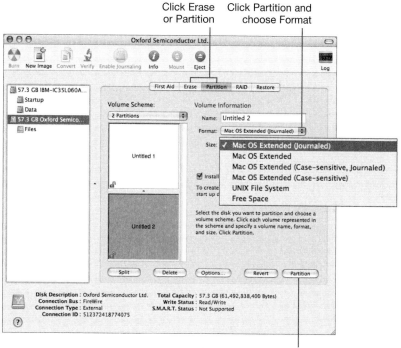

Disk Utility is the primary tool you will use for volume and disk management. You will find Disk Utility on the Mac OS X Install DVD and at /Applications/ Utilities. You can run Disk Utility before an installation to perform a number of tasks: to check, repair, partition, and format drives; to create images of existing data; or to mount or unmount and restore existing partitions. Disk Utility can also be used as a diagnostic tool. Note that you cannot erase or partition the startup disk.

You will immediately notice disks and partitions in the list at the left when you open Disk Utility. If you select a disk, you can use the Partition pane to create partitions. You cannot partition a partition; so the Partition pane is only accessible if you select a disk. In the Erase pane, you can erase the contents of a partition or drive and change its format. You can also use this utility to erase CD-RW and DVD-RW discs.

If you plan to boot into Mac OS 9, and your computer supports it, you must select the Install Mac OS 9 Disk Drivers checkbox when you partition your hard disk. This formatting option places Mac OS 9 startup drivers on the disk. If these drivers are not present, you will not be able to start up the computer in Mac OS 9. This option is not required for using the Classic Environment in Mac OS X, because Classic can access drives in the standard Mac OS Extended formats.

> **NOTE ▶** The Mac OS 9 driver option is hardware dependent and does not appear on systems that do not start up in Mac OS 9, such as the Mac mini.

Getting Information

There are two easy ways to get in-depth information about the drives and volumes connected to your computer: System Profiler and Disk Utility. Each provides very complete information about your drives and volumes, although the information is presented in different contexts.

System Profiler (/Applications/Utilities) is bus-oriented, and when it provides information about storage devices, it identifies them in the context of the bus on which they are located. When you select the drive bus on the left, you see all devices on that bus (including hard drives, optical drives, and other connected devices).

System Profiler is a reporting tool rather than a utility that edits your disks and partitions, so it provides no information about unmounted partitions on a particular disk.

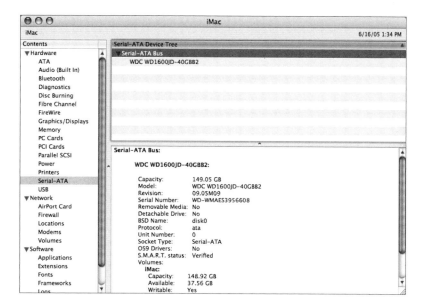

Disk Utility is drive-oriented, so the left column in Disk Utility contains a list of all connected drives. Beneath each drive is an indented list of partitions on that drive. Starting with Mac OS X 10.3, CDs recorded with multiple sessions are displayed correctly as separate partitions in the left column of the Disk Utility window. Unmounted partitions are dimmed, and information about them cannot be gathered.

When a drive or partition is selected from the list in Disk Utility, you can click
Info to display detailed information about the drive, such as the drive's capacity
and bus type.

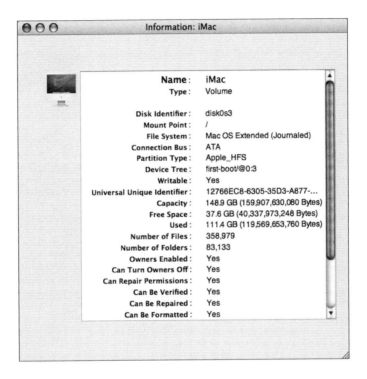

Applying First Aid

The First Aid pane of Disk Utility can repair permissions issues and disk format
problems. Unusual behavior, such as inability to mount disk images, copy files,
install applications, or spool print jobs, could be caused by incorrect file permissions. Missing files and folders could be caused by disk format problems.

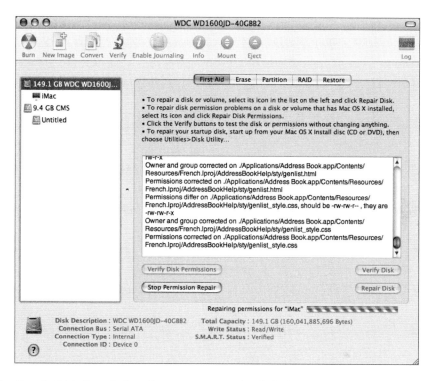

The Repair Disk Permissions button restores the default permissions of Mac OS X system files and applications in the Applications folder on the startup disk only. Disk Utility restores the default permissions of items installed by the Apple installer based on information in the installation receipt packages stored in /Library/Receipts. However, many third-party installers do not store installation receipts. This means many applications installed with third-party installers, and any applications installed by drag-and-drop, will not be affected by the Repair Disk Permissions feature. While Disk Utility does not fix permissions on those files, it is easy to manually correct file permissions, as you will see in later lessons.

The Repair Disk feature verifies and repairs the folder structure of a volume, using the BSD tool fsck. Disk Utility can perform repairs on partitions in all of the formats that it can create: UFS, Mac OS Standard, Mac OS Extended, and MS-DOS (FAT).

Because you cannot repair your startup disk while your computer is booted from it, you would normally use Repair Disk from your Mac OS X Install DVD. You could also repair your startup disk using a second computer, with your computer connected in Target Disk Mode.

If Disk Utility indicates that it discovered problems after you click Repair Disk Permissions or Repair Disk, repeat the process until you get a clean bill of health.

Remember, the options available in the First Aid pane are just that—your first line of defense against minor disk injuries. For more serious trauma cases, you'll want to rely on more powerful third-party tools.

Using Secure Erase

The Erase pane in Disk Utility allows you to securely erase free space or an entire volume. If you wish to ensure that files previously placed in the Finder's Trash are completely erased, start by clicking the Erase Free Space button. If you wish to erase an entire drive or partition, start by selecting it and clicking the Security Options button.

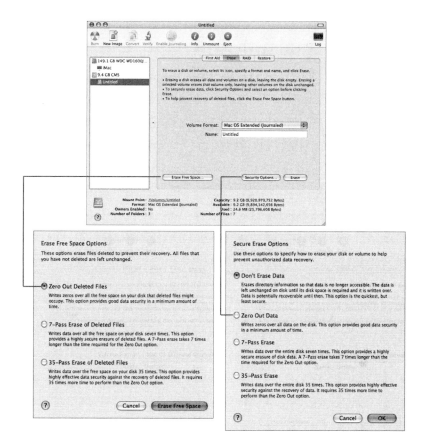

Whether you are securely erasing free space or an entire volume, Disk Utility's options are fairly straightforward. In both methods, you can select Zero Out Data, 7-Pass Erase, or 35-Pass Erase. Zero Out Data writes a single pass of zeros over the portions of the disk being erased, while 7- or 35-Pass will write and delete random zeros and ones for the specified number of passes.

While the multipass erase options take time to run, they provide a highly secure mechanism for ensuring that the data on a drive cannot be restored. This is very useful when retasking a computer or transferring a drive between employees with different levels of security access, or clearing a home machine for a change of ownership. Allocate plenty of time for a multipass erase.

NOTE ▶ 7-Pass Erase meets current U.S. Department of Defense security requirements. Use 35-Pass Erase for very sensitive data.

NOTE ▶ The Finder also supports a Secure Empty Trash option that performs a 7-Pass Erase on items in the Trash. Files erased this way do not need to be erased again with Erase Free Space unless you wish to apply more erase passes to the files.

Configuring RAID

Disk Utility provides a tool to configure a software RAID in Mac OS X. Redundant Array of Independent Disks (RAID) is used to configure multiple hard disks so that they appear as one volume in the operating system (sort of the opposite of partitioning, which makes one hard disk look like multiple volumes). You can configure the RAID scheme to use concatenation or striping (RAID 0), which stores data across the disks, or mirroring (RAID 1), which stores the same data on all disks. With RAID 0 selected, a single volume will display the drive capacity as the total amount of all drives being used in the array.

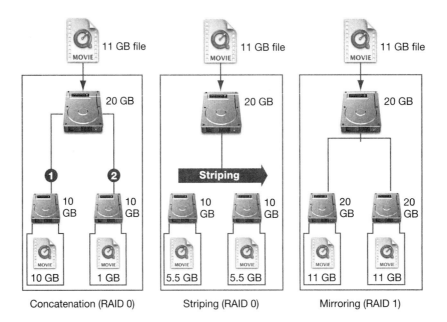

This illustration explains how an 11 GB file is saved to disk under the different RAID schemes. At the left, two 10 GB drives act as one regular-speed 20 GB volume with concatenation. Center, two 10 GB drives act as one fast 20 GB volume with striping. Right, two 20 GB drives act as one 20 GB mirrored volume. As always, all disks in a RAID should be the same size, as RAID will use the lowest-common denominator size (30 GB and 20 GB striped together would make a 40 GB volume).

NOTE ▶ New in Mac OS X 10.4 is the ability to use partitions in creating a RAID.

▶   Concatenation (RAID 0) — The most basic form of RAID 0. This form allows multiple drives to be treated as a single volume, although without performance benefits or redundancy. In the Finder, two concatenated 10 GB drives appear as a single 20 GB volume. Data written to this volume is written to the first drive until it is full, and then written to subsequent drives in the RAID as needed. Concatenated RAID volumes are often referred to as "JBOD" (Just a Bunch of Disks).

▶   Striping (RAID 0) — Allows multiple drives to be treated as a single volume, although data is striped across all disks. This allows performance improvements because each drive can access the bus separately, improving throughput.

▶   Mirroring (RAID 1) — Stores the same data on all disks, allowing redundant data storage. However, although RAID 0 drives are added together to create the full volume size available in the Finder, a mirrored RAID will appear in the Finder to be the size of the smallest physical disk.

NOTE ▶ Each RAID format has risks and advantages. Keep in mind that mirroring is the only RAID format that provides data redundancy.

Exploring Disk Utility

In this exercise, you will explore the features available in Disk Utility.

1   Log in as Chris Johnson.

2   In the Finder, choose Go > Utilities (Command-Shift-U).

3   Open Disk Utility.

4   Select the entry in the list that represents your main hard disk.

   The disk entry usually has the manufacturer name visible. Do not select the formatted drive partition, the entry that is indented beneath the drive entry. Note that the Partition button is available when you select a disk.

   The bottom of the screen displays details about the disk drive, such as its total capacity and its connection bus.

5   Note the capacity of your main disk drive.

6   Note the connection bus used for your computer.

   Your connection bus would depend upon the computer you are using, but would most likely be either ATA or Serial ATA. Less likely buses would be SCSI, FireWire, or USB.

7   Select the partition entry beneath the disk drive entry.

   Now that you have selected a partition, the Partition button is no longer available, because you cannot partition a partition. Also notice that the information at the bottom of the screen has changed to display details for the selected partition. Disk Utility displays the number of files on the partition, the partition's format, and where in the file system the partition is mounted. If you have selected the boot partition, the mount point is /. If you had selected a non-boot partition, the mount point would be /Volumes/name, where "name" is the name of the partition.

8   Click the First Aid button.

The First Aid pane allows you to verify and repair disk permissions and the disk itself. Because you have selected the partition from which you are booted, the Verify Disk and Repair Disk buttons are dimmed. In order to repair your main hard drive, you would need to boot using another disk, such as the Mac OS X Install DVD.

On the other hand, the Verify Disk Permissions and Repair Disk Permissions buttons are only available when you have selected a boot volume.

9   Click the Erase button.

The Erase pane allows you to erase free space on a partition or completely erase a disk or partition. In this case, you have selected your boot volume, so the Security Options and Erase buttons are dimmed. You could erase free space.

10   Click the RAID button.

The RAID pane is used to combine two or more volumes into a RAID volume.

11   Click the Restore button.

The Restore pane is used when you want to restore applications and files from a disk image.

Understanding the File System Layout

Awareness of low-level details of disk drives is helpful for troubleshooting, but most users simply format their drives, install software, and use the computer to do things. The thousands of Mac OS X system files are irrelevant to them, and they do not need to know where the operating system stores files for its own use.

Mac OS X shields users from this complexity in several ways. First, while there may be thousands of files installed with the OS, the average user only sees the interpreted view the Finder provides of those files. This includes displaying a user-friendly layout of the file system, despite the fact that the underlying representation is considerably more complicated.

Second, the Finder has mechanisms in place to link files with applications that can open them with a double-click. The Finder manages system resources during this process, such as identifying the user's preferred applications for opening particular files, and locating fonts for displaying the information inside a word-processing file.

Understanding the Finder's role in simplifying the user's interaction with the file system will help you troubleshoot file system issues.

Examining Top-Level and Home Folders

Mac OS X permissions distinguish between system files and files that can be configured and modified by users and administrators. This gives greater protection to important system files.

Folders are often denoted in terms of the path to their location, which establishes their position in the file system hierarchy relative to /, known as "root" due to its position at the top of the file system hierarchy. (The term *root* comes from the file system metaphor of an inverted tree, where the root structure is at the top.) A folder called /Applications, for example, is located in the highest level of the file system, and is found in /. A folder called /Applications/Utilities is found in /Applications.

The main top-level folders in Mac OS X are Applications, Library, System, and Users. If you have installed the developer tools, you will also have a top-level folder called Developer. If you have installed Classic on the same volume, you will also have the top-level folders Applications (Mac OS 9), Desktop (Mac OS 9), and System Folder.

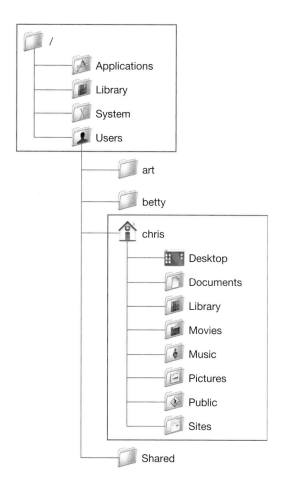

When you create a user account (see Lesson 3, "User Accounts"), Mac OS X creates a home folder for that user within Users. This location is where that new user stores personal documents. Other users do not have write permissions for your home folder. Items in the active user's home folder are often described with ~/ before the name, because that is how you could identify them at the command line (see Lesson 7, "Command-Line Interface").

By default, the following subfolders appear under each user's home folder:

▶   Desktop — Any item on the Mac OS X desktop

▶   Documents — Default folder for the user's documents

▶   Library — User-specific application support, fonts, preference files, and so on

▶   Movies — Folder for movie files such as QuickTime videos

▶   Music — Folder for music files such as MP3s

▶   Pictures — Picture files to be used by applications such as iPhoto

▶   Public — Shared folder for Mac OS X Personal File Sharing

▶   Sites — Folder for Mac OS X Personal Web Sharing

> **NOTE** ▶ Mac OS X structures a new user's home folder by duplicating the appropriate language's user template (/System/Library/User Template).

With the exception of the ~/Library folder, you needn't keep any of the other home folders if you don't want them. Also, there is nothing that prevents you from placing MP3 music files in the ~/Documents folder, or storing MPEG movies in the ~/Pictures folder. Keep in mind that some applications expect to find documents in specific places, so deleting these folders or placing your documents in other folders may cause problems.

In Mac OS X, core operating system files reside in a folder called System. To secure the integrity of the core system against malicious or accidental removal of files, System is marked read-only for all users. Editing system files requires administrator authentication, whether you access the files via the command line or use an administrative utility.

> **NOTE** ▶ Deleting files from System can cause major problems, some of which may require that you reinstall Mac OS X. End users should be instructed to leave the contents of System undisturbed.

System-wide resources that are not installed by the operating system are added to the Library folder. For example, many third-party utilities install startup items in /Library/StartupItems. The Library folder is accessible to administrator users. Administrators should add resources to Library, not to System.

Since Mac OS X is a multiuser system, each user has separate resources, such as personal fonts. These resources are stored in each user's home folder—specifically, in the ~/Library folder. For example, the Mail application stores all of a user's mail in the ~/Library folder. This system ensures that user-specific information is stored in each user's home folder, protecting that information from other users, and making it easy to back up and restore all of the documents and preferences for each user.

Viewing Hidden Folders

Some folders do not ordinarily appear in the Finder. Most of these folders are used by the system and are not useful to ordinary users. To see these folders in the Finder, you can choose Go > Go to Folder, enter the path, then click Go.

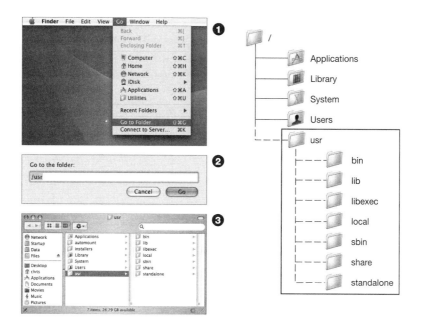

Hidden top-level folders include private, cores, etc, tmp, var, Volumes, bin, dev, sbin, and usr. Permissions for these hidden folders are set to allow only the root user to write to them. An administrator can read the files but cannot make changes without authenticating as root.

In addition, any folder or file with a name beginning with a period (.) will not appear in a Finder listing. You can go to a folder with a name beginning with a period if you navigate to it with Go to Folder. You can also use the Finder's Find command to identify invisible files by searching for the invisible attribute.

> **NOTE** ▶ Files and folders that are hidden in the Finder are visible at the command line, as you will see in Lesson 7, "Command-Line Interface."

Following Search Paths

Mac OS X puts resources such as fonts, frameworks, and preference data in various places. When Mac OS X needs those resources, it searches known locations in a specific order until it locates the resource. This is called the *search path*. Understanding the system search path is invaluable when troubleshooting system problems.

The order in which Mac OS X searches for resources is

1. User (~/Library)
2. Local (/Library)
3. Network (/Network/Library)
4. System (/System/Library)
5. Classic (/System Folder)

> **NOTE** ▶ The search order above is comprehensive, but the Network and Classic paths are skipped if not available, as is the case in many circumstances.

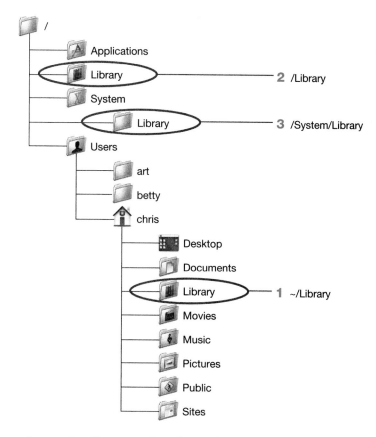

A good example of how search paths work involves fonts, which can reside in many locations. If you have multiple fonts of the same name installed, Mac OS X will load the first one it finds in the search path, depending upon the application requesting the resource. This order also applies to preferences and other resources in the Library folders.

> **MORE INFO** ▶ Refer to Knowledge Base document 106417, "Mac OS X: Font Locations and Their Purposes."

Using Font Book to Understand Search Paths

For an example of resource paths, look at how Mac OS X uses fonts and how Font Book makes it easy for you to install fonts in public or private locations. Anyone can use the Finder to drag fonts into ~/Library/Fonts and make those fonts available to their user account, but fonts installed in that location are not available to other users on the computer. This may be exactly how you intend for those fonts to be installed: you might want to install licensed fonts for only one specific user. However, most fonts are licensed for a computer system, so you might want to install them in a location that is accessible to all users.

An administrator user can install fonts in all of the system search path locations, but the /System/Library/Fonts folder is reserved for system fonts, so most of the time you will place fonts in /Library/Fonts or ~/Library/Fonts. Font Book makes it simple to install fonts in these central locations, so it's an effective tool for installing new fonts or troubleshooting font problems.

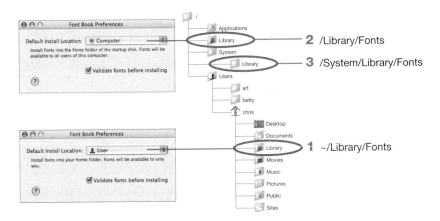

When Font Book reads your fonts, it queries all locations in the search path for valid resources of that type. If you encounter problems with a corrupt or damaged font, you can track back through the search path to identify the problem font. First, remove all fonts from ~/Library/Fonts, because that is the first location in the search path. If that does not resolve the problem, remove all fonts from /Library/Fonts. When you find the font store with the corrupt font, perform split-half searches to identify the problem font. You will learn about split-half searches in Lesson 14, "Troubleshooting."

Removing a Font

You can use the Font Book utility to watch what happens when you move a font to the Trash.

1   Log in as Apple Admin.

If you are still logged in with another account using Fast User Switching, log out from that account so the only account currently logged in is the Apple Admin account.

2   Quit all applications to ensure that no fonts are in use.

Note that you cannot quit Dashboard, so it will remain active in the Dock.

3   Open Font Book (/Applications).

It may take a while for Font Book to display the list of fonts since it must first compile them by looking in all the locations of the search path. The User collection is listed as "Off" since there are no fonts installed solely for the active user in ~/Library/Fonts.

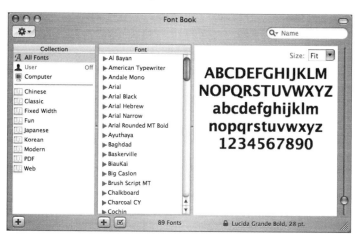

4   In the Collection column, click Computer.

Font Book displays all fonts installed for all users of the computer in /Library/Fonts.

5   In the Font column, click Arial.

6   Choose File > Export Fonts, and use the defaults to save to the Documents
folder with the name of Exported Fonts.

This creates a backup copy of the Arial font.

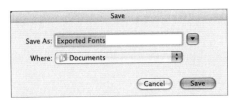

7   Choose File > Show Font Files (Command-R).

This opens a Finder window revealing the current location (/Library/Fonts)
of the selected Arial font. Position this window so that you can see both the
Finder window and the Font Book window simultaneously.

8   Returning to Font Book, choose File > Remove "Arial" family, then click
Remove when asked if you are sure.

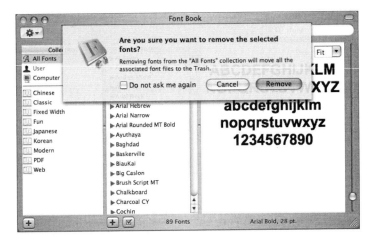

The Arial font disappears from the Font Book window as well as the Finder window. It is no longer available to users of this computer, unless they have their own copy installed in their home folder, as shown in the following steps.

Adding a Font to Be Used by One User Only

You can use Font Book to install a font in your own Fonts folder.

1   In Font Book's Collection column, click User.

2   Choose File > Add Fonts (Command-O).

3   In the dialog that appears, navigate to the Exported Fonts folder created in step 6 of the previous exercise.

4   Double-click Arial.

    Arial should now appear in the User's font list.

5   Choose File > Show Font Files (Command-R).

    This opens a Finder window revealing the current location (~/Library/Fonts) of the selected Arial font.

Confirming That the Font Is Unavailable to Other Users

If you log in as a different user, you don't have access to the fonts in user Apple Admin's Fonts folder.

1   Log in as Martha Flowers.

2   Open TextEdit (/Applications).

3   Choose Format > Font > Show Fonts (Command-T).

4   Confirm that the Arial font is not in TextEdit's Font pane.

5   Log in as Apple Admin.

6   In Font Book's Collection column, click User.

7   Select Arial, choose File > Remove "Arial" family, then click Remove when asked if you are sure.

8   In Font Book's Collection column, click All Fonts, choose File > Add Fonts, then choose the exported copy of Arial.

Once you have confirmed that Arial is once again available to all users, you can delete the Exported Fonts folder.

Learning File Management

An original design goal of the first Macintosh was to make using a computer easy. The first Apple file system engineers worked to find techniques to allow more "human" file names, and built a file system that did not require file extensions for files to open properly.

The Macintosh file system was based on the concept of a type and a creator. The type refers to the document type, such as PDF or JPEG, while the creator specifies the application used to create the document. Type and creator were used for opening files under the original Mac OS.

As computers became more interconnected and the Internet developed, it became clear that users needed to easily transfer and use files across different operating systems. These files had to work smoothly across multiple platforms and application types. Corporations set up local area networks with a variety of servers, including file servers, which users of any platform could use for storing or sharing files. The Macintosh file system was a seamless client in multiplatform environments.

File system design has evolved, from enabling end users to name and use files easily to incorporating dynamic search technologies and providing advanced file system features for modern needs. Modern users need access to file types used years ago on early computers, but must be able to efficiently manage and find specific files on large disks in a timely manner. Now you will learn about file management features in Mac OS X, and new features in Mac OS X 10.4.

Examining File Forks

In early versions of the Macintosh operating system, Apple file system engineers devised a binary file format and a disk-based catalog to associate files with the applications that could open them. The disk-based catalog was called the desktop database. That binary file format is still supported in Mac OS X 10.4: on a Mac OS Standard or Mac OS Extended volume, each file can have two parts known as forks—a data fork and a resource fork.

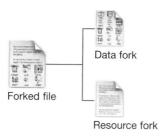

Forked file — Data fork — Resource fork

A data fork is similar to a file on any operating system—it contains a chunk of data. A resource fork historically was used to store additional information relevant to the file itself, such as a custom icon, or individual file preferences, or the last location of a palette. In Mac OS X, much of that information is stored within the data fork for the file. Data that is useful for the file system, such as details you see in the Info window, and the file type, are stored in the HFS catalog. The HFS catalog in Mac OS X is different from the old desktop database, but is just as essential in matching files with applications that can open them.

Resource forks are useful to provide backward compatibility, but they do not move smoothly to other file systems. When you move these files to non–Macintosh file systems, the resource forks might be discarded, potentially stripping the file of important information. In today's computing environments, files move from platform to platform as email attachments or through file servers, which can introduce other complications. Traditionally, to preserve all of the file data, Mac OS files had to be encoded into a flat file format before transfer. BinHex was a common format (its name means "binary hexadecimal"), but it was not user-friendly at all. In Mac OS X, to ease cross-platform file transfer, more portable file formats have been developed—one of the most useful is the *package,* discussed in the next section.

UFS volumes handle forked files differently. UFS doesn't have a catalog to help with file and application matching. To accommodate that, the file manager service in Mac OS X creates a shadow file for every binary file on the UFS volume. To help the Macintosh work seamlessly with UNIX-formatted volumes, this shadow file, in a format called AppleDouble, contains three things:

▶ HFS catalog data for the file

▶ Resource fork data, if any

▶ Extended attribute data, if any (Extended attributes can be set in Mac OS X Server 10.4. Mac OS X 10.4 supports them, but cannot set them.)

Opening Packages

Mac OS X includes a mechanism to aid compatibility with the rest of the networked world, but at the same time provide a way to store resources and structured information in what appears to users to be a single file. The solution is called a package. The Finder presents and treats the package as a single file, although in reality it is a specially marked folder that can contain files and other folders. An application bundle in Mac OS X is one example of a package. Another example is a Keynote 2 file, which appears to the user as a single file, although it is really multiple files in a package.

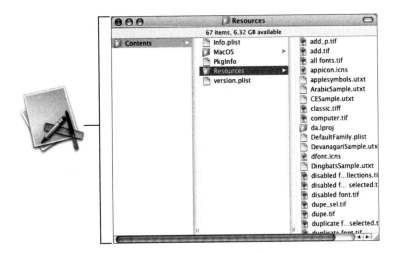

The average user typically does not need to know about packages, just as the typical Mac user may never have been aware of resource forks. However, in the same way that a power user might have used ResEdit to edit the resource fork of a file in Mac OS 9, an administrator may need to view the contents of a package in Mac OS X. You can see the contents of an application package by Control-clicking its icon in column or icon view.

You gain the real benefit of packages when you transfer packages to non–Macintosh file systems for storage, such as UFS or FAT, then copy those packages back to a Macintosh. The transfer to those file systems takes place as though the package is a folder, and the file is stored on the nonnative file system as a folder. When you copy that folder back to a Macintosh, the package flag ensures that the folder contents are copied like a folder, but the Mac user sees a package after the copy is complete.

Using the Finder to Open Files

User files (documents) are typically associated with particular applications, so you can simply double-click a file to open it with its associated application. In Mac OS X, applications keep track of the types of files they can read. When there might be several applications that can open a specific type of file, how does Mac OS X select the application to open when a document is double-clicked? To do this, Mac OS X has a LaunchServices process that keeps a record of which applications can be used to open various types of files. Two examples of this are as follows:

▶ JPEG files — Mac OS X includes Preview, Safari, and QuickTime, all of which can all open JPEG files. The default setting is for JPEG files to be opened with Preview.

▶ HTML files — Mac OS X includes Safari and TextEdit, both of which can open HTML files. The default setting is for HTML files to be opened with Safari.

> **NOTE** ▶ To see the default application for a given document type, Control-click the document in the Finder, then select Open With in the contextual menu that appears. Pressing the Option key with this menu open changes "Open With" to "Always Open With."

As new applications are installed, the Installer updates the HFS catalog with new document types, and populates the LaunchServices database with new default bindings. This is how, after you install a third-party accounting application, Mac OS X is able to properly open the accounting application when you double-click its files.

The LaunchServices databases are stored in /Library/Caches, named com.apple.LaunchServices.*userID-based value*.csstore. (The userID-based value will change from computer to computer.) There are databases for each user who has logged into the computer, because that file holds the "trusted bit" for applications. (The first time an application opens, an alert notifies the user, asking if it's OK to proceed. If so, the application's trusted bit is set and the alert won't appear again.) Each user also has a LaunchServices.plist file in his or her local ~/Library/Preferences folder that contains user-set bindings. User-set bindings override the default LaunchServices bindings, but only for that user.

Overriding Default Preferences for Opening Files

Most documents are identified by type or extension. A file extension consists of a period (.) followed by several characters that identify the type of file. The Finder is set by default to display the full file name with extension, although you can change that setting for individual files in the Info window, and in many Save dialogs. A file works the same whether its extension is visible or hidden.

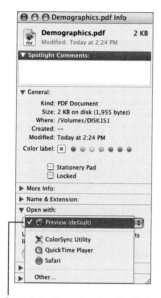 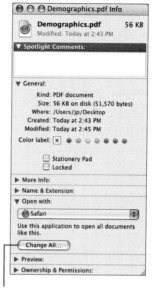

Sets default application for file by
making change to document's
"resource fork"

Sets default application for all files of that
type by making change to ~/Library/
Preferences/com.apple.LaunchServices.plist

You can also change the application associated with a file using the Info window.

1   Select a document in the Finder.

2   Choose File > Get Info (Command-I).

3   In the Info window, click the "Open with" disclosure triangle.

4   Choose an application from the "Open with" pop-up menu.

The next time the selected file is opened in the Finder, it will be opened
with the chosen application.

5   If you want all files of the same type to be opened with the chosen application, click Change All.

When making changes to a specific file, the change is stored in the file itself. When using the Change All button, it updates the binding for the active user, and stores it in ~/Library/Preferences/com.apple.LaunchServices.plist. In other words, if one user changes the application association for a specific set of files, those changes do not affect other users on the computer.

If you need to reset the system-wide bindings, discard the database (named com.apple.LaunchServices-*userID-based value*.csstore) from /Library/Caches and restart the computer. You can delete the user-set bindings file as well.

Opening Documents That Do Not Have Default Settings

Traditionally, Mac OS applications have supported types and creators. However, on the Internet, and in other operating systems, file extensions are used to determine which applications open specific files. In most cases, a file extension is a multicharacter suffix preceded by a period, such as .pdf or .jpg.

To be a good client and support both types of historical behavior, the Finder looks at file extensions as well as creator and type to determine how to open a file. If you double-click a file, the Finder first looks for a creator entry and if it finds one, uses it to determine which application opens the file. If there is no creator, it looks at the extension and finds an application that can open files with that extension. If there is no creator or extension, it looks at the file type and finds an application that can open that file type. If there is no creator, extension, or file type, the Finder will prompt you to choose an application that will become the default application to open the file.

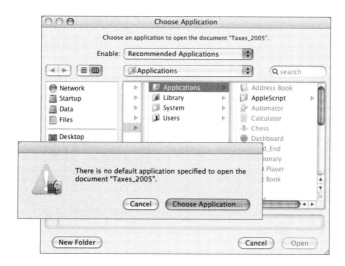

To recap, this is the order of precedence the Finder uses when opening a new file that wasn't previously known:

► Creator

► Extension

► Type

► Ask user

> **NOTE** ► This is the same mechanism used by some web browsers. Certain Helper applications can be configured to open certain document types, identified by the file extensions, such as .mov, .hqx, or .sit.

Finding File Data and Metadata

Along with opening files, a common task when using any computer is locating the right files to open. In Mac OS X, a search can cover two types of file information: data and metadata.

▶ Data — The file's contents. In the case of a letter written using a word processor, this is the actual text of the letter. For a spreadsheet, this is the actual numbers and formulas included in the spreadsheet. Data is what users typically associate with the contents of their user files, in the form of documents, music, pictures, or video.

▶ Metadata — Information about a file. Examples of metadata might include creation date, label, type of file, or author. Some kinds of metadata can be changed easily, such as file name or label. Other types of metadata are set automatically, such as date modified or image size. Still other kinds of metadata can be set within the application that created the file, such as the caption of a photograph or the author of a word-processing document. Types of metadata associated with a file vary according to the type of file. An MP3 file might have metadata that includes information about the name of the song, the artist, genre, duration, and how the song was encoded. A JPEG image file will often include metadata that relates to the size of the image or the camera settings used to take the photograph. The Finder's Info window reveals only some of the metadata available in a typical document.

Both data and metadata are important when looking for files, and Mac OS X 10.4 includes new functionality for indexing and searching for data and metadata.

Searching for Files Using Spotlight

Mac OS X 10.4 uses a new feature called Spotlight to search for data in files throughout your system. Spotlight creates and stores metadata indexes in an invisible folder named .Spotlight-V100 at the root level of each locally connected volume. Indexing takes place in the background while you are working.

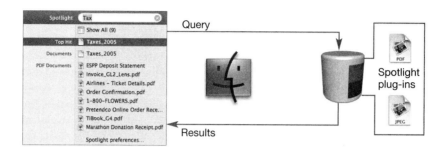

On startup, Mac OS X 10.4 looks for index files stored on each connected volume. If it does not find them, it creates a new index. Any time you connect to a new volume locally, Spotlight indexes its content. The Mail application maintains its own content index at ~/Library/Mail/Envelope Index. If this index is removed, Mail will create a new index the next time it is launched.

> **NOTE ▶** If you remove a metadata index, Spotlight rebuilds it the next time you restart. While Spotlight may seem to continue working properly, it will not be able to find or store any new data until you restart and Spotlight rebuilds the index files.

File permissions are one of the metadata components that Spotlight indexes. So although all the content is indexed, Spotlight will filter its results to show only those files that the current user has permissions to access.

Spotlight metadata for files in a FileVault-enabled user account is stored in ~/.Spotlight-V100. It is less secure to keep metadata outside the encrypted FileVault, so Spotlight automatically keeps the index for these files safely inside the encrypted home folder.

To find and store metadata associated with the various file types on a typical Mac OS X system, Spotlight uses plug-ins to gather metadata and save it in a way that Mac OS X and Spotlight can search quickly.

When you save a file, the plug-in examines its content and stores metadata about that content in the indexed database. This allows you to search for the metadata with Spotlight and quickly find the path of every file that matches your criteria.

Many kinds of metadata, such as file size, creation date, and modification date, are common to all files. Mac OS X also includes plug-ins for metadata in common file formats used by specific applications. Applications that use the generic file formats can use the plug-ins supplied with Mac OS X. Applications with custom file formats will need to use their own plug-ins for Spotlight to index and search their metadata and contents.

Mac OS X includes Spotlight plug-ins for several file formats and bundled applications. The plug-ins index most common Apple and third-party applications, such as Address Book, iCal, iTunes, Keynote, Mail, Microsoft Office, Pages, and Preview, as well as common generic formats such as PDF, RTF, and QuickTime.

NOTE ▶ Plug-ins for common file formats and bundled applications are located in /System/Library/Spotlight. Although Mac OS X does not include AppleWorks, Keynote, Microsoft Office, or Pages as bundled applications, plug-ins for these applications are included and are located in /Library/Spotlight.

Plug-ins created by developers other than Apple can be stored in multiple locations. They will take the form of a bundle or plug-in stored inside the application that references the data. Third party plug-ins can also be stored in ~/Library/Spotlight or /Library/Spotlight.

NOTE ▶ Mac OS X does not index content or metadata on inserted optical media such as CDs or DVDs. If you burn a CD or DVD in Mac OS X, the burned disc does not contain a Spotlight-V100 folder and does not store content or metadata indexes.

Using Archives and Disk Images

Everyone should know that backups are a critical component of every desktop environment, and there are several backup packages you can use, including the .Mac Backup utility. However, Mac OS X has built-in tools that you can use to manage your desktop working environment. The Archive feature in the Finder helps you organize data and manage your files so that they take up less space, and Disk Utility can create compressed disk images with entire file systems that you can easily burn to CD or DVD. This provides day-to-day benefits for you and your end users.

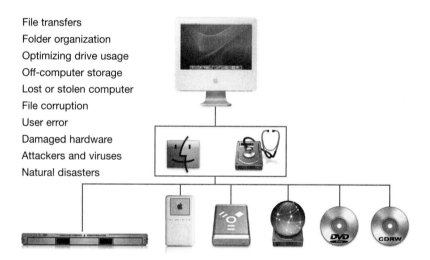

File transfers
Folder organization
Optimizing drive usage
Off-computer storage
Lost or stolen computer
File corruption
User error
Damaged hardware
Attackers and viruses
Natural disasters

Archives and disk images do not replace a backup strategy, but they can be an effective component, making backups more effective by reducing file counts and organizing files that can be removed from your drive.

The Mac OS X tools for archiving and transferring files, which we will explore next, are an essential part of computer maintenance. Time spent organizing and archiving with these tools will pay dividends, so that you can smoothly recover from any kind of data loss or hardware problem.

If you wish to incorporate automated backups or use advanced backup components such as tape libraries, there are several third-party options available, but they are beyond the scope of this book.

Creating Archives from the Finder

The Finder can archive files and folders without additional software. Archived files take up less disk space, so archiving is useful for making backup copies of your data and transferring large folders across a network.

To archive files or folders, select an item or items in the Finder and choose File > Create Archive. Whether you archive a single file or a folder full of files, the archive is created with the name of the file or folder and a .zip extension. If you archive several selected items, the archive file is called Archive.zip. When you double-click an archive in Mac OS X, it expands automatically. If the archive was made from a folder, that folder will appear and the files inside it will be decompressed.

NOTE ▶ The original files are not changed or deleted when you create an archive. If you want to create free disk space, be sure to drag the originals to the Trash after you've confirmed that the archive was properly created.

Zip files have traditionally been archives of flat files. However, starting in Mac OS X 10.3, the Finder's archives support file forks using the AppleDouble format. When a current Mac OS X computer archives a forked file, the forks are split, and then seamlessly rejoined when the file is decompressed. It is important to note that a Windows client might see two files when it decompresses a Mac OS X archive that includes forked files: one file with the original name containing the data fork, and a second file beginning with ._, representing the resource fork.

NOTE ▶ If you give an archive to Windows users and they are unable to open it, they may be using an older version of the PKZIP application or they have several copies of PKZIP installed, and an older one is trying to open the archive. You can suggest that they upgrade to the latest version of PKZIP (www.pkware.com), specifically use the Open command in the latest version of PKZIP they have installed, or use a third-party utility that can decompress more up-to-date archive formats.

Creating Disk Images with Disk Utility

A disk image is a file that you can mount on your desktop as if it were a separate volume with its own file system. Disk images are useful for many reasons: you might need to transfer files over the Internet or on media such as CD or DVD, or you might need to ensure that you distribute an exact representation of a file and folder structure. Disk images are very useful for that because they are bit-for-bit copies of the files in the original folder structure copied into a single file.

There are two common types of disk images:

▶ Disk Utility images — Normally carry the extension .img or .dmg. A Disk
   Utility image icon looks like a hard disk on a blank document.

   Disk Utility is included with Mac OS X and can create disk images.
   Depending on the settings of a downloaded disk image, the Finder may
   open it automatically on the desktop as a plain, white volume icon. If the
   disk image is not set to open automatically, you can double-click to manually mount it. Like a removable drive, the disk image is mounted until you
   drag the volume icon to the Trash or restart the computer.

   Mac OS X 10.2.3 introduced Internet-enabled disk images, which are
   identical to regular disk images, except that when the disk image mounts,
   its contents are copied to the hard drive and the disk image itself is moved
   to the Trash.

▶ Self-mounting images — Normally have an .smi extension. The icon for
   a self-mounting image file looks like a blue floppy disk on top of a white
   diamond.

   This type of volume can mount on any Macintosh. However, .smi files,
   originally created for Mac OS 9, require Disk Utility to open.

Creating a disk image is a good way to archive or transfer a set of files and
hierarchical folders, because it stores them in a single flat file that can be compressed to save space. Compression is useful for speeding up file transfers or
saving disk space. You can also create disk images of bootable CDs and hard
disks, and encrypt your images for additional security.

The panes in Disk Utility allow you to select the destination folder, format,
and encryption type for your disk image. You can create an image from a drive
or folder, or create an empty image of a specific size that you can copy files
into when it is mounted. Image formats include read/write, read only, compressed, and DVD/CD master. Encryption types include none or AES-128.

> **NOTE** ▶ You can resize or split disk images at any time using the
> command-line utility hdiutil. You will read more about command-line
> utilities in Lesson 7, "Command-Line Interface."

Disk Utility can use Apple Software Restore (ASR) to restore an entire hard drive. This allows you to very quickly restore everything from a backup image or configure new computers as a part of large deployments. To use the restore feature, click the Restore tab in the Disk Utility window and follow the onscreen instructions. Always observe licensing restrictions when you use this feature, and be careful when restoring to ensure that you do not accidentally overwrite data.

Creating a Disk Image File with Disk Utility

In addition to managing and repairing disk drives, you can use Disk Utility to create disk images. The following steps will guide you through using Disk Utility to create a compressed disk image.

1   Open Disk Utility (/Applications/Utilities).

2   Choose File > New > Disk Image from Folder.

3   Navigate to the /Library/Fonts folder.

4   Click Image.

5   Verify that Fonts is entered in the Save As field.

6   Choose Desktop from the Where pop-up menu (Command-D).

7   Verify that "compressed" is chosen from the Image Format pop-up menu.

8   Verify that "none" is chosen from the Encryption pop-up menu.

9   Click Save.

10   When prompted, enter an administrator user's name and password.

   A Disk Utility Progress window appears. When Disk Utility is finished, the image file Fonts.dmg appears on the desktop.

11   Quit Disk Utility.

Mounting and Using a Disk Image File

The disk image file format is useful for software distribution. Images can be mounted and used like a drive volume.

1   Double-click the Fonts.dmg file on your desktop to mount it.

You will see a drive volume icon on your desktop. Open it to reveal all of the individual font files.

2   Eject the Fonts volume.

3   Delete the Fonts.dmg file.

Burning CDs or DVDs

If your Macintosh comes with a built-in CD or DVD burner, Mac OS X can burn optical discs using the Finder or Disk Utility. Disk Utility is designed to burn a disk image file to disc, while the Finder is designed to allow easy ad hoc disc burning. If you use Disk Utility to burn disk images onto optical media, each disk image can be burned as a separate session.

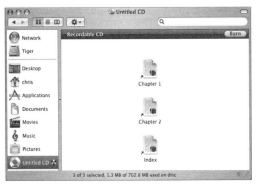

Untitled CD.fpbf

Untitled CD.fpbf

You can use the Finder to burn files directly to a blank disc in a single session. New in Mac OS X 10.4 is the ability to create a burn folder. Previous versions of Mac OS X used a multistep burning process, in which Mac OS X created a disk image file during the initial copy stage, and then used it to burn the disc. This method required that your startup drive had enough free space available to create this disk image behind the scenes.

A burn folder can be created from the Finder's File menu and can be saved and reused over time. When copying items to the burn folder, only an alias to the original item is copied. This allows you to change items in the Mac OS X file system; the resulting burn folder will reflect these changes automatically. For example, you can create a burn folder of your ~/Documents folder and burn it to a CD every week. The contents of the burn folder will always accurately reflect your ~/Documents folder, including any changes you made during the week. This feature is very useful to archive a static folder organization where the folder contents change frequently, such as with financial records.

> **NOTE ▶** Though the terms are sometimes interchanged, "disc" refers to optical storage media, such as CD-ROM, CD-R/W, or DVD-R, while "disk" refers to most other storage media or devices, such as floppy disks or hard disk drives.

> **NOTE ▶** For maximum compatibility burning optical media, use the optical drives Apple ships in its computers, such as a Combo drive for burning CDs or a SuperDrive for burning CDs or DVDs. When considering third-party optical drives for burning discs, check with the manufacturer to ensure that it is fully compatible with Mac OS X 10.4. For example, some third-party DVD burners can burn discs on a Macintosh when using Disk Utility or DVD Studio Pro, but not when using iDVD.

Ignoring Volume Ownership

The permission to access removable media such as optical discs is determined by the ownership, just like any other Mac OS X volume. You can use the "Ignore ownership on this volume" checkbox in the Info window to gain access to a removable volume that is otherwise inaccessible due to ownership.

> **NOTE ▶** This feature was designed for convenience when using removable media. However, you can also use it to ignore ownership on disk partitions other than the boot volume, which means that file ownership alone is not sufficient to protect files on a nonroot partition. Users with more stringent security needs should use other techniques, such as encryption, to protect files.

1   In the Finder, select the volume and choose File > Get Info (Command-I).

2   Click the disclosure triangle next to Ownership & Permissions.

3   Select the "Ignore ownership on this volume" checkbox.

Troubleshooting the File System

When troubleshooting file system problems, try these suggestions:

▶   If you are having problems accessing files on a local hard drive, use Disk Utility's First Aid to verify and repair any problems with the disk drive.

▶   If a computer becomes unbootable, a corrupted or deleted system file might be the cause. To fix these problems, try the following:

   1.   Put the computer in Target Disk Mode by pressing the T key while starting up the computer until the FireWire logo appears. In Target Disk Mode, the computer acts as a FireWire drive and can be connected to another computer, allowing you to run diagnostics, examine the drive contents, and recover and back up the files on the drive, even though the drive is unbootable. Now the computer's internal startup disk acts as an external FireWire drive that can be connected to another computer, allowing you to run diagnostics, examine the drive contents, and recover and back up the files on the drive, even though the drive is unbootable. You can also enter Target Disk Mode using Startup Disk preferences. Finally, you can "bless" the drive by using the bless command from the command-line interface (for instructions on its use, enter man bless).

2. Reinstall the operating system to replace the missing files. When the operating system version on the Mac OS X Install DVD is older than the one on the hard drive (as would be the case if you applied any system software updates), you'll need to use the Archive and Install option, which will enable you to install the older operating system without erasing the drive. You'll still need to apply updates to make the operating system version current.

What You've Learned

▶ Mac OS X 10.4 is a flexible, powerful operating system that provides support for legacy drive formats and modern file systems. Mac OS X integrates well with the Internet, and provides utilities you can use to troubleshoot and manage your storage devices.

▶ Mac OS X supports several volume formats. Mac OS Extended and UFS are the primary formats. The Mac OS Extended volume format supports file forks and packages.

▶ Mac OS X allows you to securely erase files so that they cannot be recovered.

▶ Mac OS X uses paths to indicate the location of files and folders. The file system has a standard layout. Some folders are hidden until you navigate to them in the Finder by choosing Go > Go to Folder.

▶ Mac OS X has standard top-level folders and standard folders within each user's home folder. System files installed by the operating system are stored in /System. Mac OS X searches for resources in multiple locations in a specific order, known as a search path. Fonts are an example of a resource that uses a search path.

▶ Disk Utility allows you to configure, verify, and repair hard disks.

▶ Disk image files are useful for archiving a folder and its contents. File compression and encryption allow you to conserve storage space and make your images more secure.

References

The following Knowledge Base documents (located at www.apple.com/ support) will provide you with further information regarding file systems in Mac OS X.

Backup

▶   106941, "Mac OS X: How to back up and restore your files"

Fonts

▶   106417, "Mac OS X: Font Locations and Their Purposes"

▶   106737, "Mac OS X: How to Add or Remove Classic Fonts"

Disk Utility/fsck

▶   25668, "About disk optimization with Mac OS X"

▶   106214, "Using Disk Utility and fsck for file system maintenance in Mac OS X"

▶   107250, "Mac OS X: fsck reports benign errors when journaling is turned on"

▶   107333, "Mac OS X: How to create a password-protected (encrypted) disk image"

Mac OS Extended File System (HFS)

▶   107249, "Mac OS X: About file system journaling"

▶   25316, "Mac OS X 10.2 or Earlier: Choosing UFS or Mac OS Extended (HFS Plus) Formatting"

Burning CDs and DVDs

▶   61339, "Mac OS X: About burning data onto CDs"

▶   42718, "SuperDrive: About Rewriteable DVD Discs"

Lesson Review

Use the following questions to review what you have learned:

1. List some top-level folders in Mac OS X.

2. What kind of hardware must your computer have in order to burn optical media?

3. What two quick fixes are appropriate to consider when troubleshooting local file system issues?

Answers

1. /Applications, /Library, /System, and /Users.

2. Apple has two internal optical drives for burning media, a SuperDrive and a Combo drive. The Combo drive can be used for burning CDs or reading DVDs. The SuperDrive can be used for reading or burning DVDs or CDs. There are various third-party CD and DVD burners on the market, although you should check their compatibility before purchasing. For example, some third-party DVD burners may work with Disk Utility or DVD Studio Pro, but not iDVD.

3. Repair with Disk Utility; use Target Disk Mode to verify/install OS.

5

Time   This lesson takes approximately 1 hour to complete.

Goals   Control access to applications and data files with file and
folder permissions

Troubleshoot permissions issues

Lesson 5
Permissions

Mac OS X is designed as a multiuser operating system, with a number of features that help multiple users work on the same computer while maintaining unique files and settings. In fact, with fast user switching and remote login, you can even have more than one user logged in simultaneously. In Mac OS X, to ensure internal security on your computer, the file system uses permissions to limit access.

Imagine that your computer is a set of filing cabinets in an office with a private filing cabinet for each employee. Each employee's private cabinet is locked, unless they specifically grant different access to drawers inside their cabinet. Each employee's private cabinet can have a public in box where coworkers can leave files and a public out box where coworkers can take files. An open "shared" cabinet that anyone can access is available to place files everyone can use.

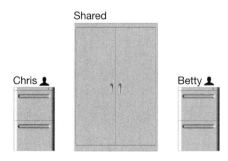

There are three categories of users for each filing cabinet:

▶ The owner

▶ Group members and guests who have access to one or more drawers inside the cabinet

▶ Others who have access to the in box and out box, but no access to the owner's drawers

You use these categories to define permissions, such as Read & Write access, Read Only access, or No Access.

In this lesson you will learn about file access and permissions issues. The topics will include theoretical and practical information about the Mac OS X user-based permissions model, some examples of permissions in context, and how to troubleshoot file permissions issues.

Understanding the Mac OS X User–Based Access Model

For security and ease of use, each user on your computer stores files in his or her home folder. Unless these files are explicitly placed in a publicly-accessible folder, they can only be opened and edited by the Owner or the System Administrator. Other files, such as applications in Applications and system files in System, are located outside your home folder because they are intended to be shared by all users of your computer.

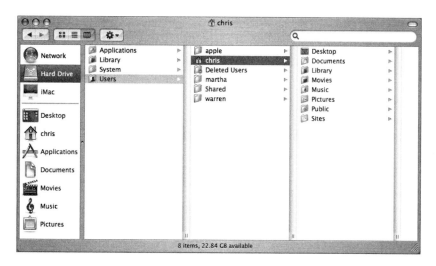

By default, folders in a home folder have the No Access permission for Group and Others, and Read & Write access for Owner. There are only two exceptions: the Sites folder, which is used for web pages, and the Public folder.

If you want to share files with other users on your network, but you do not wish to grant them physical access to your computer, you can use the Public folder, located in your home folder. If you have not set up file sharing for other folders, a file sharing client connecting to your computer as a guest will open the Public folder by default.

> **NOTE** ▸ When you create a new folder, by default it is Read Only for Others, so other people can read its content if they can navigate to it. For this reason, it is best to keep your files and subfolders in your Documents folder; otherwise other users may have access to the files.

Storing Files Based on Access

This exercise demonstrates how you can restrict access to files and applications based on where you save the file.

Creating Two Files

The following steps will walk you through creating two files and storing them in two separate locations:

1   Log in as Chris Johnson.

2   Open TextEdit.

3   Create a file, name it Secret, and save it in Chris's Documents folder.

4   Create another file, name it Shared, and save it in Chris's Public folder.

5   Quit TextEdit.

Testing Access to the Files

Follow these steps to test your access to the files you just created:

1   Switch to Martha.

2   Open a Finder window.

3   Go to the Users folder.

4   Go to Chris's home folder.

    You should not be able to see the contents of the Documents folder, so you have no access to the Secret document therein. However, you should be able to open Chris' Public folder and access the Shared file therein.

5   Log out Martha.

Using the Shared Folder

Along with the Public folder available in each user's home folder, Mac OS X includes a specific location where you can place files that are to be shared among all local users on the computer. This shared location is /Users/Shared. The /Users/Shared folder has permissions set so that any local user can add files or folders that any other local user can access. While /Users/Shared would not be available to guest users across the network, it is the recommended place for storing files shared among local users.

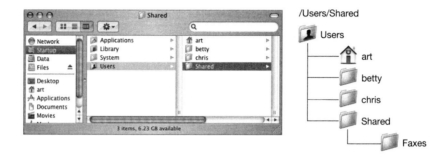

The permissions for new files and folders created in /Users/Shared are set to Read & Write for Owner, and Read Only for Group and Others. This means files and folders in this location can be opened by any user account. The /Users/Shared folder also has a setting called the *sticky bit,* which ensures that only the owner of a file or folder can delete it. (You can read more about the sticky bit at the command line by entering *man sticky* and pressing Return. See Lesson 7, "Command-Line Interface," for more information.) The /Users/Shared folder is ideal for local sharing, because any user can view shared files, but only the owner can delete the original file from the shared location.

Setting File and Folder Permissions

In multiuser operating systems like Mac OS X, at the operating system level, *permissions* control user access to particular files and folders and protect core operating system files from inadvertent edits. At the user level, permissions determine whether other users are allowed to access the files and folders that you create.

Each file and folder in the file system is automatically associated with an owner and a group when it is created. At any time, however, the owner or an administrator can choose File > Get Info (Command-I) in the Finder to set permissions. It is useful to remember that permissions limit access to the *contents* of the file or folder, which can lead to unexpected access issues. You will learn more about access limits later in this lesson.

Files and folders have different permissions, because folders are containers for files. The access levels for files are Read & Write, Read Only, and No Access. If you have Read & Write access to a file, you can open the file and change its contents. If you have Read Only access to a file, you can open the file but cannot change its contents. No Access indicates that you cannot open the file.

Folders have four assignable access levels. The access levels you can set for a folder are Read & Write, Read Only, Write Only (Drop Box), and No Access. If you have Read & Write access to a folder, you can change the contents of the folder by adding, removing, or renaming files within the folder. If you have Read Only access to a folder, you can open the folder and see what it contains but you cannot add, remove, or rename files in the folder. Write Only (Drop Box) access indicates that you can add files to the folder but cannot see the folder's contents. No Access, of course, means that you cannot add files to the folder nor can you see the contents of the folder.

For example, the Public folder in your home folder has Read & Write permissions for Owner, and Read Only for Group and Others. The Drop Box folder within the Public folder has Read & Write permissions for Owner, and Write Only for Group and Others.

To view and set the permissions on a file or folder, select the file or folder in the Finder and choose File > Get Info (Command-I). Click the Ownership & Permissions disclosure triangle, and then click the Details disclosure triangle to reveal the current permissions. Use the pop-up menus in this area to change the permissions for Owner; Group, non-owners who belong to a defined group; and Others, non-owners who do not belong to the group. (As a result, you can assign permissions so that Others have a higher access level than the Owner!) Once permissions have been set for a folder, the same permissions can be set on all items in the folder by clicking the "Apply to enclosed items" button.

Although not represented in the Info window, there is also an *Execute* permission. The Execute permission tells Mac OS X to run a set of instructions in a file or on a package's contents. The system opens applications by executing the application bundle when you double-click the application file's icon in the Finder. The Execute permission also makes a folder work properly as a container for files. When you view a folder in the Finder, the Finder must perform a file system operation to display the folder contents, with the Finder interpreting the result of your command. The Execute flag on a folder allows the Finder to perform this task.

This is an important consideration, because if an application won't launch, you must remember that an application bundle is a special type of folder. If an application does not open, it could be due to a missing Execute permission on the application itself, or it could be due to an incorrect permission on a file inside the application bundle. In either case, the Repair Disk Permissions feature in Disk Utility might help.

> **NOTE** ▶ Permissions can be improperly changed, such as when creating files using Mac OS 9. To help you fix permissions problems on bootable Mac OS X volumes, Disk Utility includes a Repair Disk Permissions feature that uses permissions from application and operating system receipts in /Library/Receipts. Open Disk Utility, select the volume, then click the Repair Disk Permissions button in the First Aid pane to fix problems with items that have receipts. For more information, refer to Knowledge Base document 106712, "Troubleshooting permissions issues in Mac OS X."

> **NOTE** ▶ Sometimes you may find that a particular application doesn't seem to respect the file permissions. It may be able to modify a file, even though the file was marked Read Only. Some applications don't modify files directly. Instead, they duplicate the file and modify the copy. When you use the Save command, the application then deletes the original file and renames the duplicate to match the original file.

Groups

In Mac OS X, every user account is a member of at least one group, and every file and folder has group permissions assigned. Groups give permissions to sets of users who are able to perform similar functions. Mac OS X does not provide an application to easily create and manage groups. Instead, it uses some preset groups to give users permissions and functionality. If you need to create and manage groups, you will need to use Mac OS X Server.

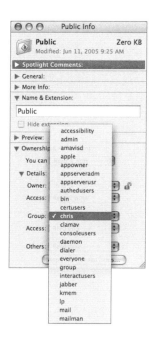

One preset group that you commonly see in Mac OS X is admin. All users with administrative privileges are automatically added to this group so that they can make system-wide changes. Users who do not belong to the admin group cannot change ownership or permissions on files other than their own, unless they first authenticate as an administrative user. In most cases, unless you are specifically trying to establish a very limited set of access permissions, you should use default group assignments. However, if you intend to grant access to any administrator user, you can change the group assignment to the admin group, and if you want to limit access to only a specific user, you can change the group assignment to the automatically-created group for that user, as shown here.

Assessing Folder and Document Permissions in Context

Folder and document permissions can present complicated challenges. For example, consider the scenario in the following illustration. If you assign the indicated permissions to a folder and a file within it, can you safely assume that no harm can come to your file?

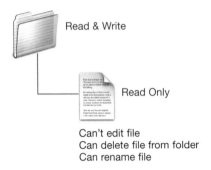

Read & Write

Read Only

Can't edit file
Can delete file from folder
Can rename file

At first glance, the document appears safe, and it is certainly true that the contents of the file cannot be changed. However, the document can be deleted or renamed because the folder permissions are Read & Write. Consequently, a user could delete the file and replace it with a file of the same name but with different contents.

Take a look at the set of permissions in the following illustration. What, if any, modifications can you make to the document?

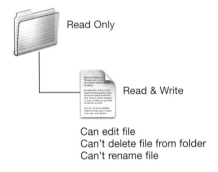

Read Only

Read & Write

Can edit file
Can't delete file from folder
Can't rename file

You can change the contents of the file using applications that rewrite document data in place, such as command-line tools. However, applications that
attempt to make backup copies or require "Save As" when saving documents
cannot edit the file in this location because the Read Only folder permissions
prevent you from adding files to or removing files from the folder. You could
save the edited file to another location, of course. Similarly, you cannot rename
the file.

This set of permissions on a containing folder is useful when you are sharing a
set of templates or need to make a set of files available to your users but do not
want them to be able to change your folder organization.

The permissions in the following illustration are somewhat more complicated.
The containing folder is still Read Only, meaning that you cannot rename, add,
or delete enclosed files. However, as you saw in the preceding illustration, you
could still edit those files in place.

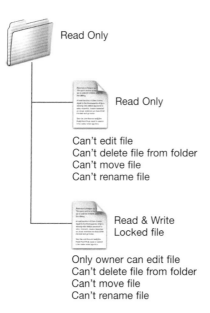

Read Only

Read Only

Can't edit file
Can't delete file from folder
Can't move file
Can't rename file

Read & Write
Locked file

Only owner can edit file
Can't delete file from folder
Can't move file
Can't rename file

To prevent editing in place, the first file has been set to Read Only. This limitation prevents editing in place, and retains the limitations of the containing folder. Also, because you cannot write to the file, you cannot use the Finder to move, rename, or delete it.

To show a different limitation on editing in place, the second file has been set to Read & Write, but has been locked by the owner. In addition to permissions, files have a locked attribute that you can set in the Info window. Locking a file overrides some permissions for Group and Others, because locked files cannot be edited, deleted, or moved by anyone but the Owner.

Folder and document permissions interact in potentially surprising ways. For example, you may have Read & Write access to a file but still not be able to open the file because the file resides in a folder to which you have no access. The combinations presented here are not always apparent to your end users, but you should know how to manage permissions so that you limit access in the manner that works most effectively for your organization.

One effective method for limiting access is cascading permissions. By nesting less-protected folders inside more-protected folders, and by shrewdly placing files within your folder hierarchy, you can achieve almost any access design for your storage system.

Setting Permissions on Files and Folders

Permissions can be set on both files and folders, thereby controlling who can access or modify these items. In this exercise, you will modify and compare permissions on three files and three folders on your computer, then see how those permissions interact.

Change the Permissions on Three Folders

1   Log in as Chris Johnson.

2   Go to Chris's home folder.

3 Open the Public folder.

4 In the Public folder, create three folders (Command-Shift-N) with the following names:

   ▶ Read Only

   ▶ Read Write

   ▶ Write Only

5 Select the Read Only folder and open the Info window by choosing File > Get Info (Command-I).

6 Expand the Ownership & Permissions disclosure triangle, and then expand Details.

7 Confirm that the access permissions for Group and Others is Read Only.

8 Select the Read Write folder and open the Info window.

9 Expand Details.

10 Change the access permissions for Group and Others to Read & Write.

11 Close the Info window.

12 Select the Write Only folder and open the Info window.

13 Expand Details.

14 Change the access permissions for Group and Others to Write Only (Drop Box).

15 Close the Info window.

Change the Permissions on Three Files

You will now create three text files and change their access permissions.

1   Open TextEdit (/Applications/TextEdit).

2   Create three documents and save them in Chris's Documents folder:

▶   NoAccess

▶   ReadOnly

▶   ReadWrite

3   Quit TextEdit.

4   Open Chris's Documents folder.

5   Select the NoAccess.rtf file, and change the permissions for Group and Others to No Access in the Info window.

6   Select the ReadOnly.rtf file, and confirm that the permissions for Group and Others are Read Only in the Info window.

7   Select the ReadWrite.rtf file, and change the permissions for Group and Others to Read & Write in the Info window.

8   Open a new Finder window and navigate to Chris's Public folder.

9   Put the NoAccess.rtf file in the Read Write folder.

10   Put the ReadOnly.rtf file in the Write Only folder.

11   Put the ReadWrite.rtf file in the Read Only folder.

Test the Folder and File Permissions

These steps will demonstrate the effect of different permissions on files and folders.

1   Switch to Martha's account.

2 Open a new Finder window (Command-N) and navigate to the Read Only folder in Chris's Public folder.

3 Open the ReadWrite.rtf file with TextEdit.

4 Add some text to the document and try saving.

Note that you cannot save the ReadWrite.rtf file to the Read Only folder, and a standard user cannot delete this file unless that user first authenticates as an administrator user.

NOTE ▶ This behavior is counterintuitive. TextEdit, like most other applications, creates temporary files when you try to modify and save a file. Because the folder is Read Only, you cannot add a temporary file. Thus, any attempt to save the file fails. However, if you were to use an application that does not create a temporary file, modifying your file would be allowed.

5 Use the Save As command to save the ReadWrite.rtf file to the Read Write folder. (Do not change the name of the file.)

6 Open the Read Write folder and open the ReadWrite.rtf file with TextEdit.

7 Add some more text to the document and try saving.

You can save the ReadWrite.rtf file to the Read Write folder because both the file and folder allow Read & Write access.

8 In TextEdit, try opening the NoAccess.rtf file in the Read Write folder.

You cannot open the NoAccess.rtf file with TextEdit because the permissions on the enclosing folder are set to Read & Write, but the permissions of the file itself are set to No Access.

You can delete the NoAccess.rtf file from the Finder because the permissions on the folder are set to Read & Write, which allows changes to how files are stored in the directory.

9 In the Finder, try opening the Write Only folder.

When you try to open that folder, access to the folder is denied.

In the Finder, you can move the ReadWrite.rtf file from the Read Write folder to the Write Only folder.

10 In TextEdit, try opening the Write Only folder.

You cannot see the files in the Write Only folder.

11 Quit TextEdit.

12 Log Martha out.

Troubleshooting Permissions Issues

When you encounter problems with permissions, the first step is to determine the scope of the problem. You must determine if your issue is a single problem file or a folder full of files with the same problem.

Permissions issues can be a challenge. For example, you might encounter system instability or erratic behavior due to incorrect permissions. You may also have a functional need to bypass permissions, or might need access to files that are owned by a user whose account has been deleted. Here are some basic troubleshooting techniques for permissions issues:

▶ Sometimes incorrect file permissions cause erratic system behavior, such as inability to mount disk images or add files to the Applications folder as an administrator user. The First Aid pane in Disk Utility has a button that will scan and restore the permissions of Mac OS X system files and Apple–installed software.

> **MORE INFO** ▶ Refer to Knowledge Base document 106712, "Troubleshooting permissions issues in Mac OS X."

▶ If you have problems accessing a specific file due to incorrect permissions, you can often use an administrator account to fix the permissions manually. Use the Get Info command (Command-I) in the Finder, and authenticate as an administrator to override the ownership permissions.

▶ Changing ownership for a large number of files can be a problem. If you need to reassign ownership for a number of files, for example when you restore a deleted user, the easiest method is to create a new user account and copy the deleted user's disk image file into the Drop Box of the new user account. After the user logs in with the new user account, the user can mount the .dmg file. The Finder will automatically change ownership of the files when the user copies the files from the disk image to the user's new home folder.

You can also use the command line to perform large-scale permissions changes. This will be covered in Lesson 7, "Command-Line Interface."

What You've Learned

▶ Permissions are used to grant different access levels to your files and folders. You can share them as Read Only, or you can give users Read & Write access, or simply deny other users access to your files and folders.

▶ Mac OS X provides a common folder for all local users at /Users/Shared.

▶ Folder permissions and file permissions can be combined to limit access in very sophisticated ways.

References

The following Knowledge Base documents (located at www.apple.com/support) will provide you with further information regarding users and permissions in Mac OS X.

Files

▶ 106237, "Unable to move, unlock, modify, or copy an item in Mac OS X"

Permissions

▶ 25751, "About Disk Utility's Repair Disk Permissions feature"

▶ 25554, "Mac OS X: File can't be moved if locked"

▶ 106712, "Troubleshooting permissions issues in Mac OS X"

▶   107031, "Mac OS X 10.2, 10.3: Clicking 'Apply to enclosed items' copies permissions but not owner or group"

▶   107039, "Mac OS X 10.2: How to Change Ownership & Permissions Using the Finder"

Trash

▶   106272, "You can't empty the Trash or move a file to the Trash in Mac OS X"

Lesson Review

Use the following questions to review what you have learned:

1.   What are permissions and why are they important?

2.   What kinds of symptoms might you see if an application's permissions are not set properly?

3.   What tools are most useful when troubleshooting permissions issues?

Answers

1.   Permissions provide security to keep one user from modifying or viewing another user's files. They are important because Mac OS X was designed to be used by more than one person.

2.   If an application's permissions are not set properly, the application may not launch, it may not be able to save files, it may not be able to open specific types of files, and files created by the application may have problems.

3.   The Verify Disk Permissions and Repair Disk Permissions buttons in Disk Utility's First Aid pane, the Finder Info window, and the Terminal application for file system view of file permissions.

6

Time   This lesson takes approximately 1 hour to complete.

Goals   Install, run, and troubleshoot native Mac OS X applications

Use Activity Monitor to monitor processes

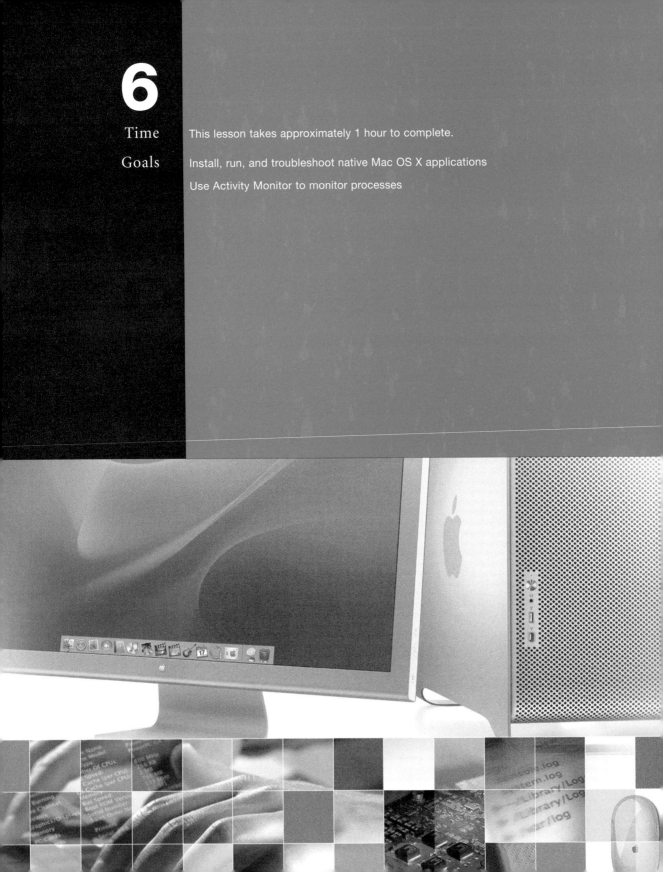

Application Environments

An application environment consists of the libraries, library resources, application programming interfaces (APIs), and services that you need to run applications developed with those APIs. The application environments depend on the underlying layers of the system software: the core services (Quartz, OpenGL, QuickTime, and so on) and the core operating system (the kernel environment called Darwin).

In this lesson, you'll learn about the many application environments available to Mac OS X users. Those environments support programs created for present and past versions of Mac OS, as well as applications created for Java and UNIX environments.

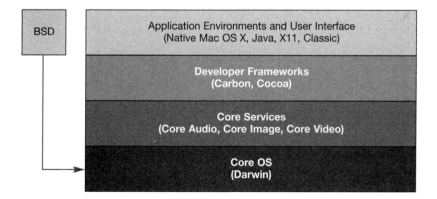

Identifying Macintosh Application Environments

The following types of applications can run in Mac OS X:

▶ Native Mac OS X

▶ Classic

▶ Java

▶ BSD

All application environments are accessible through the Aqua graphical interface. This is true even for some BSD tools and applications, which provide a graphical user interface either through native applications such as Network Utility or through the X11 graphical system. However, to directly use pure BSD-only tools, you need to use a command-line interface utility such as Terminal.

Native Applications

Native applications are designed specifically to be used with Mac OS X. They can take full advantage of Mac OS X features such as preemptive multitasking and 64-bit memory management.

Native applications usually are stored in Applications. If you want to install an application so that only a specific user can use it, you can install it into ~/Applications. In addition, applications often place support files in /Library/Application Support and ~/Library/Application Support.

Mac OS X originally provided two development environments for creating native applications: Carbon and Cocoa. When Mac OS X first shipped, the term Carbon referred to applications that were based on the existing procedural programming APIs used with Mac OS 9 applications and that could be used to develop an application that ran on both Mac OS 9 and Mac OS X. Cocoa referred to an entirely new object-oriented development methodology to develop applications that only ran on Mac OS X. Over time, these development environments began to share capabilities and developers could (and often did) support both within the same application.

When looking for applications to run on Mac OS X 10.4, you should not be concerned with whether the application uses Carbon or Cocoa. Just look for an application with the "Built for Mac OS X" icon. For a list of applications developed for Mac OS X, visit the Macintosh Products Guide at http://guide.apple.com.

> **NOTE ▶** While this book does not include introductory information on using built-in native applications such as Address Book, Mail, Safari, and Sherlock, .Mac members can find tutorials for these products and Mac OS X in the .Mac Learning Center. Visit www.mac.com for information on the .Mac Learning Center.

Classic

The Classic environment supports legacy applications—applications designed to be used with Mac OS 9 or earlier. Using the Classic environment, you do not need to upgrade all of your applications immediately after upgrading to Mac OS X. To use the Classic environment, however, you must install Mac OS 9.2 or later in addition to Mac OS X.

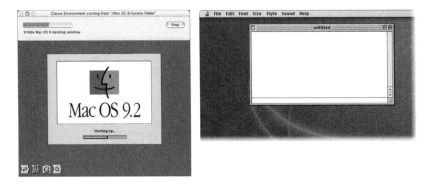

For more information, see Appendix C, "The Classic Environment."

Java

Using the Java application environment, you can develop and run Java applications and Java applets on Mac OS X.

You can use Safari or other web browsers to run Java applets. Just type the URL for the applet location. Applet Launcher is no longer a separate application in Mac OS X 10.4.

Java Web Start (/Applications/Utilities/Java) runs full-featured Java applications that are downloaded and launched by your web browser. Web Start applications are launched by clicking a web page link that downloads a small .jnlp file and launches it. If the application is not present on the computer, the Java Web Start utility automatically downloads the necessary Java class files (that are stored in a Web Start cache in ~/Library/Caches) and starts the application. Once running, the application is independent of the browser, which allows you to quit the browser or surf to another page. If you launch the same application a second time, Web Start will allow you to convert the .jnlp file into a standalone application that you can double-click and run without having to use the Web Start utility.

> **MORE INFO** ► For more information about Java Web Start, visit http://developer.apple.com/java/javawebstart.

BSD/X11

Because Darwin uses BSD 5.0 UNIX, you can write and run UNIX shell scripts to use any of the command-line interfaces in Mac OS X. You can also run UNIX-style applications and tools that have been ported to Mac OS X. The BSD layer provides yet another platform for professional developers and scripters.

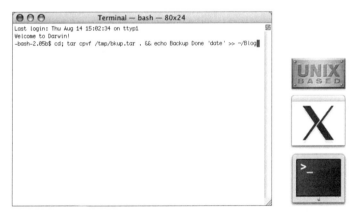

You will learn how to use the command-line interface in Lesson 7, "Command-Line Interface."

> **MORE INFO** ► To learn more about BSD, visit www.bsd.org. For more information about the Darwin kernel, visit www.opendarwin.org.

Initially, applications running on UNIX-based operating systems were limited to the command line. Later, the X Window System, more commonly called X11, allowed developers to create more sophisticated user interfaces for their applications. X11 for Mac OS X is a complete X Window System implementation for running X11-based applications on Mac OS X.

X11 for Mac OS X is included with the Mac OS X Install DVD, but it's not installed by default. (To install it, click the Customize button in the Installer. X11 will appear in /Applications/Utilities.) X11 for Mac OS X includes the full X11R6.6 technology including a window server, libraries, and basic utilities such as xterm.

> **NOTE** ▸ You can launch an installed X11 application by double-clicking its icon in the Finder.

Monitoring Process Management

A *process* is a running program or set of threads, and an address space. A *thread* is a set of instructions that can be assigned independently to the CPU. Therefore, different threads of a single process can run on one processor at different times, or at the same time on different processors. This is called *symmetric multiprocessing*. The job of a process is to manage memory and other resources related to the execution of its threads. Processes can run without an explicit user interface: for example, some applications and most system-level processes, called *daemons* (pronounced "demons"), run in faceless mode.

Activity Monitor (/Applications/Utilities) allows you to view and monitor every application and process that is running on the computer. As stated in Lesson 3, "User Accounts," every program (and therefore every process) is owned by a user. Activity Monitor tells you who owns each process, its status, how much of the CPU is being used to run the process, and how much memory is used by the process. You can identify the process by its ID number, which appears in the Process ID column. Each process ID (PID) is unique.

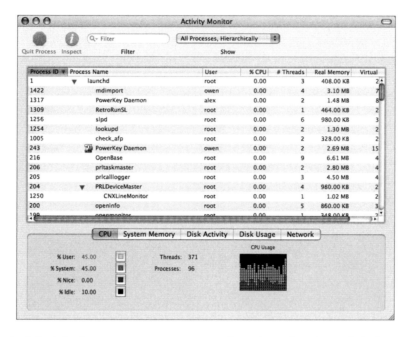

In Activity Monitor, you can sort processes by column heading. Click the column heading to select it, and click it again to sort up or down. You can also filter the process list by choosing which processes to show from the pop-up menu in the Activity Monitor toolbar, or by typing a partial process name into the filter field.

Although it might seem easy to match a process to a running application, don't always make that assumption. For instance, if Classic is running, its process is actually called TruBlueEnvironment and all of the applications running in Classic are merely threads of that process. Also, Activity Monitor displays some Carbon applications as LaunchCFMApp, rather than listing their individual application names.

To see more information about a process, including memory usage, statistics, and open files, select the process in the Activity Monitor window and click the Inspect icon in the toolbar.

To quit a process, select it in the Activity Monitor window and click the Quit Process icon in the toolbar, or choose View > Quit Process. This is just like using kill at the command line. You can also use Force Quit, which is equivalent to the kill command, but with a more abrupt halt of the process (kill -9 at the command line). You will read more about quitting applications in "Troubleshooting Applications in Mac OS X," later in this lesson.

The bottom pane of Activity Monitor contains buttons you can click to see system-wide information about the CPU, system memory, disk activity, disk usage, and network statistics.

Using Activity Monitor to Force a Process to Quit

Activity Monitor is just one of several tools you can use to force quit an application; it's particularly handy for force quitting a process that is running in the background, such as the Dock.

1   Open Activity Monitor (/Applications/Utilities).

    Activity Monitor displays a list of all processes currently running.

2   Choose Windowed Processes from the pop-up menu at the top of the window.

3   In the Finder, open Safari (/Applications).

4   Switch back to Activity Monitor.

    Notice that a new entry for Safari has been added to the process list.

5   Select the Safari entry in the process list.

6   Click the Quick Process icon in the toolbar.

7   In the Quit Process dialog, click Quit.

    The Safari entry disappears from the process list. The application remains closed until reopened manually.

8   In Activity Monitor, select the Dock entry in the process list.

You can scroll through the list to locate it, or you can narrow down the list by typing the beginning of the name in the Filter field.

9   Choose View > Quit Process.

10 In the Quit Process dialog, click Force Quit.

The Dock disappears and then reappears almost immediately, as Mac OS X automatically reopens it.

11 Quit Activity Monitor.

Understanding Protected Memory

Protected memory is a memory scheme in which each process gets its own address space. This memory space is protected because the operating system prevents processes from trying to use memory outside of their allocated space, which is a frequent cause of system crashes on other systems.

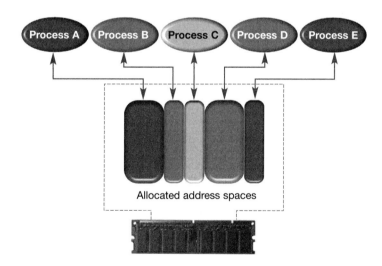

Allocated address spaces

The operating system manages the protected memory space of a process. It allocates the amount of memory that processes requests. Practically speaking, the process has a nearly endless amount of memory to work with, but the operating system is really only giving it as much as it needs at any given time. This means that you do not need to assign memory to applications in Mac OS X as you had to in Mac OS 9.

Virtual memory uses a swap, or temporary, file on the hard disk to help ensure that there is always enough physical memory for every process running. Data that is stored in RAM but not needed immediately is transferred to the hard disk so that more physical memory can be made available to the next process that needs it. Mac OS X manages virtual memory without the need for user configuration. This also means that users do not need to quit applications when they no longer need them, because inactive applications use little memory and no processor time. Virtual memory can't be turned off in Mac OS X as it could in Mac OS 9; it is always on.

Mac OS X 10.4 introduces two new features for virtual memory. The new virtual memory manager uses a 64-bit process model, allowing the operating system to set up an extremely large access space. Users can also enable encrypted virtual memory so that their on-disk virtual memory partition is secure. To do so, open Security preferences and select the "Use secure virtual memory" checkbox.

Viewing Applications in System Profiler

Sometimes it's handy to know the applications that are installed on a system. System Profiler creates reports about how a system is configured, including a list of applications installed in the Applications folder. System Profiler is located in /Applications/Utilities. You can also open System Profiler by choosing Apple > About This Mac, then clicking More Info.

Mac Seventeen			
Mac Seventeen			2/8/05 3:02 PM

Contents	Application Name	Version	Last Modified
▼ Hardware	Activity Monitor	1.4	1/22/05 4:39 PM
ATA	Address Book	4.0	1/31/05 9:18 PM
Audio (Built In)	AirPort Admin Utility	4.1.1	1/31/05 6:13 AM
Bluetooth	AirPort Setup Assistant	4.1.1	1/31/05 8:38 PM
Diagnostics	Apple Graphing Calculator	1.0	1/18/05 5:21 AM
Disc Burning	AppleScript Utility	1.0	1/31/05 6:09 AM
Fibre Channel	Audio MIDI Setup	2.1	1/31/05 4:39 AM
FireWire	Automator	1.0	1/31/05 9:22 PM
Graphics/Displays	Bluetooth File Exchange	1.6	1/31/05 9:20 PM
Memory	Calculator	4.0	1/31/05 6:16 AM
PC Cards	Chess	2.1	1/31/05 5:43 AM
PCI Cards	ColorSync Utility	4.4	1/31/05 7:26 AM
Parallel SCSI	Console	2.1	10/5/04 2:41 PM
Power	Dashboard	1.0	1/29/05 5:49 PM
Printers	Dictionary	1.0.0	1/20/05 5:02 PM
Serial-ATA	DigitalColor Meter	3.4	1/31/05 7:29 AM
USB	Directory Access	1.8	1/6/05 9:04 PM
▼ Network	Disk Utility	10.5	1/31/05 5:54 AM
AirPort Card	DVD Player	4.5	1/31/05 9:05 PM
Firewall	Folder Actions Setup	1.1	1/31/05 5:35 AM
Locations	Font Book	2.0	1/20/05 2:49 PM
Modems			
Volumes			
▼ Software			
Applications			
Extensions			
Fonts			
Frameworks			
Logs			

Activity Monitor:

```
Version:         1.4
Last Modified:   1/22/05 4:39 PM
Get Info String: 1.4, © 2002-2004 Apple Computer Inc. All Rights Reserved.
Location:        /Applications/Utilities/Activity Monitor.app
Kind:            Native
```

To see a list of the applications installed on your startup drive that are available to all users with appropriate permissions, open System Profiler and, in the Contents pane on the left, select Applications under Software. System Profiler scans the Applications folder and its subfolders to create a list of applications. System Profiler presents the list of found applications at the right, listing each application's name, version number, and date of last modification. When you select an application in the list, System Profiler displays information about the application in the lower pane.

> **NOTE** ▶ With Mac OS X 10.4, System Profiler now displays information on installed fonts, Apple and third-party preference panes, and loaded startup items, as well as a more complete list of log files. There is also an option to send System Profiler reports to Apple, so that your computer's configuration will be on file if you contact AppleCare for technical support.

NOTE ▶ When booted from the Mac OS X Install DVD, you can choose Utilities > System Profiler, but be aware that it will report on software located on the disc, not the local hard drive. This might be confusing when looking at the lists of applications, extensions, frameworks, logs, or startup items.

Enabling Mac OS X Accessibility Support

Some users have difficulty using the standard display, keyboard, and mouse to interact with the computer. You can use Universal Access preferences to provide easier access to all applications system-wide.

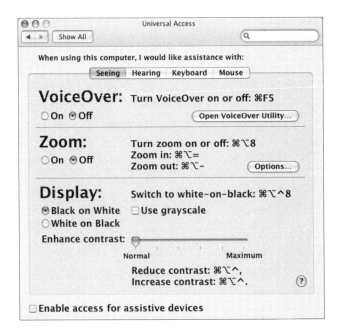

Universal Access preferences are divided into four panes:

▶   Seeing — Options for users who need assistance with viewing the display, such as zooming the display to the location of the pointer.

▶   Hearing — Options for setting the screen to flash whenever an alert sound occurs.

▶   Keyboard — Options for users who need assistance with keyboard operations, such as pressing multiple keys simultaneously.

▶   Mouse — Options for users who need assistance with mouse operations, such as configuring the keypad to control the pointer.

Everyone can take advantage of and benefit from Universal Access features. Some users prefer to navigate their computer's interface with the keyboard instead of the mouse. Others use the zoom feature to get a closer look at something, while others like to hear email messages and chats read aloud. For people learning to read, hearing the computer read aloud can help them learn. The VoiceOver Utility lets you specify how much description you hear.

> **NOTE** ▶ VoiceOver is a new Mac OS X 10.4 feature in the Seeing pane of Universal Access preferences that provides a spoken description of all interface elements. Used in combination with the Keyboard Shortcuts pane of Keyboard & Mouse preferences, VoiceOver allows sight-impaired users to navigate the computer by reading aloud every button and menu. Because VoiceOver is fully integrated into the operating system, every application, including third-party applications, should support these features.

If you want to use special software or peripheral devices to control the computer, in the bottom of the Universal Access preferences window select the "Enable access for assistive devices" checkbox. This lets other applications control the user interface. Because of the possible security risk of using third-party software to control your computer, this option must be explicitly enabled for some accessibility software to work. GUI Scripting, which was introduced in Mac OS X 10.2, also requires this checkbox to be selected (enabling GUI Scripting in the AppleScript Utility automatically selects this checkbox in Universal Access preferences).

Troubleshooting Universal Access

When troubleshooting issues with Universal Access, consider the possibility that its preference file is corrupt. In ~/Library/Preferences, locate com.apple.universalaccess.plist and move this file to the desktop, then log out. The system will replace the preference file with a new default file when you next log in. If the Universal Access problem does not reoccur, the old preference file was probably at fault. If so, you can delete the copy you moved to the desktop.

Because Universal Access features change how the interface works, they can be confusing if they are activated when they are not needed or intended. Here are descriptions of symptoms that may be related to Universal Access features, along with the keyboard shortcuts that may have inadvertently enabled the features:

Symptom Description	Question to Ask	Keyboard Shortcuts
My keypad doesn't work.	Check the Mouse pane of Universal Access preferences. Is Mouse Keys turned on?	Press the Option key five times.
A weird symbol appears on the screen and I hear a noise every time I press Shift, Option, Command, or Control.	Check the Keyboard pane of Universal Access preferences. Is Sticky Keys turned on?	Press the Shift key five times.
Letters do not appear unless I hold the key down. I also hear a noise when I type.	Check the Keyboard pane of Universal Access preferences. Is Slow Keys turned on?	none

Symptom Description	Question to Ask	Keyboard Shortcuts
All the colors on my screen are reversed, and there's an orange glow on gradients.	Check the Seeing pane of Universal Access preferences. Is Display set to White on Black?	Command-Option-Control-8
My screen is black and white, although Millions is chosen in the Colors pop-up menu in Display preferences.	Check the Seeing pane of Universal Access preferences. Is the "Use grayscale" checkbox selected?	none
My screen is zoomed in, and moves around when I move the pointer.	Check the Seeing pane of Universal Access preferences. Is Zoom turned on?	Command-Option-8
My computer keeps talking to me.	Check the Seeing pane of Universal Access preferences. Is VoiceOver turned on?	Command-F5

Troubleshooting Applications in Mac OS X

Because Mac OS X applications use the entire operating system, troubleshooting an application that doesn't work correctly can potentially be a complex task. However, there are some simple steps you can take to fix application-level problems.

If you can't open a document, the first step is to isolate the cause of the problem:

▶   Try opening a different document within the application.

▶   Try logging in as a different user. If the problem disappears, the problem could be improper preference settings or application support files in the other user account. If the problem still occurs, the application or its support files could be corrupted.

If you are unable to open a Mac OS X application, a file used by the application might have been deleted or corrupted. Try the following to fix the problem:

▶   Try removing the application's files from the Application Support folders in /Library and ~/Library. Instead of deleting these files during troubleshooting, first move them to an alternate location to see if this fixes the problem. If this does not help, you can then move the files back to their original location and continue with other troubleshooting steps.

▶   Try deleting and reinstalling the application to restore the application files that have been corrupted or deleted.

Force Quitting Applications

If an application stops responding, you can force quit the application using the Force Quit Applications window or the Dock. Press Command-Option-Esc or choose Apple > Force Quit to open the Force Quit Applications window. Select the application in this window and click Force Quit.

> **NOTE** ▶ You will lose all unsaved changes to open documents when you Force Quit an application.

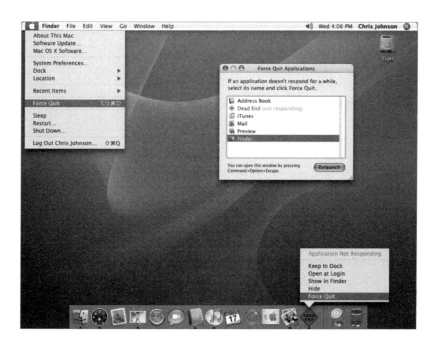

You can also Control-click an open application's icon in the Dock to see a contextual menu (or simply hold the mouse button down on the icon until the menu appears). Quit usually appears at the bottom of the menu, and the names of open documents or windows usually appear at the top of the menu. However, if the program is hung, the topmost menu item is Application Not Responding, in which case you should press the Option key to change Quit to Force Quit. Choosing Force Quit from this menu has the same effect as clicking Force Quit in the Force Quit Applications window.

> **NOTE ▶** If you Option-click the active application's icon in the Dock, the application's open windows and menu are hidden. If you Option-click the icon again, everything reappears.

Due to protected memory, the Force Quit command affects only the selected application. The only exception to this is with Classic applications. Force quitting Classic applications might impact other Classic applications, but does not affect applications running in Mac OS X. If the Force Quit command fails for an individual Classic application, the entire Classic environment will shut down. As such, before attempting to force quit a Classic application, be sure to save any open documents in all other Classic applications.

> **NOTE ▶** You should always restart Classic if you force quit a Classic application. Classic memory is managed as a block, and other problems might be present.

If you select the Finder in the Force Quit Applications window, the Force Quit button changes to Relaunch. You cannot quit the Finder, but you can force it to quit as needed, and it will relaunch automatically. You can also use Activity Monitor to quit applications, as explained in "Process Management" earlier in this lesson.

Force Quitting an Application

If an application becomes unresponsive, you can use the Force Quit Applications window or the Dock's contextual menu to force the application to quit.

1   Open TextEdit (/Applications).

2   Press Command-Option-Esc.

   The Force Quit Applications window appears.

   You can also open the Force Quit Applications window by choosing Apple > Force Quit.

3   Select TextEdit from the list.

4   Click Force Quit.

5   In the confirmation dialog that appears, click Force Quit.

The system will force TextEdit to quit, and it should no longer appear in the Force Quit Applications window.

6   Close the Force Quit Applications window.

7   Open TextEdit.

8   Click the TextEdit icon in the Dock and hold down the mouse button.

9   Press Option to change Quit to Force Quit in the contextual menu.

10   Choose Force Quit.

The system will force TextEdit to quit, and it should no longer appear in the Dock.

Using Safe Launch

Applications in Mac OS X usually store user-modifiable settings in preferences files that end in ".plist" (an abbreviation for "property list"). These files are usually stored in /Library/Preferences and ~/Library/Preferences, although some applications have their own preferences folders in these locations. The filename for most preferences files will be something similar to com.*manufacturer's name.application name*.plist.

Over time, preferences files are read and written repeatedly, and can become corrupt. When you have a problem that's specific to one application, it's often because a preferences file is corrupt.

New in Mac OS X 10.4 is the Safe Launch feature. If an application crashes, a dialog may appear giving you the option of reopening the application. Because the application preferences might have been corrupted by the crash, or could have been the cause of the crash, on the next launch you will have the option of opening that application using a new, blank preferences file. This returns many or all settings to their defaults, so your application may behave differently when it's opened with the new preferences file. Mac OS X saves the old preferences by appending .saved to the file name, so you can always restore your old preferences manually if need be.

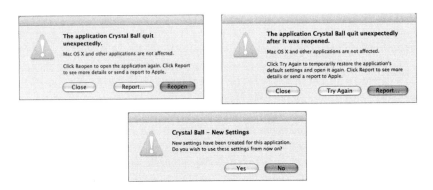

If the application successfully launches with the new preferences, the problem was probably caused by a corrupt preferences file. When you quit the application on that launch, you'll see a dialog asking if you want to keep the new settings. In most cases, you will want to keep the new settings.

Not all applications support Safe Launch. If the Safe Launch dialogs don't appear when an application crashes, you can manually force that application to create a new preferences file. In the Finder, navigate to /Library/Preferences and rename the application's preferences file for system-wide preferences, or navigate to ~/Library/Preferences to locate user-specific preferences. Then relaunch the application. A new preferences file will be created. Don't delete the old preferences file, because if you find that the preferences file was not the cause of the problem, you can restore the old preferences file.

If the issue does not appear to be related to preferences, there may be an issue with a cache file in your home folder. Delete the ~/Library/Caches folder, and delete the user cache from /Library/Caches. The user cache is the cache file in /Library/Caches that ends with the user's UID.

What You've Learned

▶   Mac OS X 10.4 includes the following application environments:

- •   Native Mac OS X

- •   Classic

- •   Java

- •   BSD/X11

NOTE ▶   For more information about the Classic environment, see Appendix C, "The Classic Environment."

▶   A process is a running program.

▶   Each process on Mac OS X runs in its own protected memory space.

▶   Classic runs in a single process called TruBlueEnvironment, but Classic applications do not use protected memory and can crash other Classic applications.

▶   Mac OS X includes functionality to assist users with difficulties seeing, hearing, and using the keyboard and mouse, enabled from Universal Access preferences. Enabling Universal Access functionality works for all applications in Mac OS X.

▶   There are many approaches and tools to help troubleshoot issues with applications on Mac OS X:

▶   System Profiler provides a list of all applications located in Applications.

▶   If an application does not respond to input from the keyboard or mouse, choose Apple > Force Quit or press Command-Option-Esc to open the Force Quit Applications window. Select the application to quit, and click Force Quit. You can also use the Dock or Activity Monitor to force quit an application.

▶   If a Mac OS X application is not running correctly, it might be due to a corrupted preference or cache file. Safe Launch makes it easier to identify and replace corrupt preferences files, but some applications may not support Safe Launch.

References

The following Knowledge Base documents (located at www.apple.com/ support) will provide you with further information regarding Mac OS X application environments.

Final Cut Pro

▶ 61477, "Final Cut Pro 3: Troubleshooting Installation Issues"

iApps (iMovie, iPhoto, iTunes)

▶ 42567, "You can't import photos from a Kodak Photo CD in iPhoto 1.0"

▶ 61018, "Troubleshooting songs that skip on iPod"

▶ 61771, "iPod does not appear in iTunes or on the desktop, an exclamation point or sad iPod icon appears onscreen"

▶ 75336, "iPhoto: Troubleshooting Camera Connections"

▶ 106137, "iMovie: FireWire 2.7 May Resolve Dropped Frames"

iSync

▶ 35013, "iSync 1.0: Troubleshooting Issues Synchronizing Palm OS Device"

▶ 61755, "iSync's log helps when troubleshooting issues"

▶ 107350, "Mac OS X 10.2.3 and Later: Some Window Buttons Lack Drop Shadow, Appear Countersunk"

Mail

▶ 25530, "How to tell Mac OS X Mail to forget remembered addresses"

▶ 61153, "Mac OS X Mail: How to Troubleshoot Undelivered Email"

▶ 106683, "Setting up Mail in Mac OS X"

Troubleshooting

▶ 25398, "Mac OS X: How to troubleshoot a software issue"

▶ 106677, "Troubleshooting the Classic environment in Mac OS X"

▶ 107918, "Mac OS X: Reading system memory usage in Activity Monitor"

URLs

Visit the following websites for more information:

- Mac OS X Applications: www.apple.com/macosx/applications
- Mac OS X Products: http://guide.apple.com
- The .Mac Learning Center: www.mac.com/1/learningcenter
- .Mac Support: www.apple.com/support/dotmac
- Java Web Start: http://developer.apple.com/java/javawebstart
- BSD: www.bsd.org
- Darwin kernel: www.opendarwin.org

Lesson Review

Use the following questions to review what you have learned:

1. What are the key application environments in Mac OS X? What are the differences among them?

2. What are three methods you can use to force quit an application in Mac OS X?

3. What quick fixes should you consider when troubleshooting Mac OS X application issues?

Answers

1. The key application environments in Mac OS X are Native, Java, Classic, and BSD. The differences among them are as follows:
   - Native — For applications that are designed specifically to take advantage of all the features of Mac OS X.
   - Java — Java is a cross-platform application environment, which allows developers to create applications that run on multiple operating systems.
   - Classic — The Classic application environment lets Mac OS X users run applications built for Mac OS 9 and earlier.
   - BSD — A UNIX-style environment that allows Mac OS X users to run command-line based tools and utilities.

2. To force quit an application, you can use the Activity Monitor utility to quit the process, Option-click the application icon in the Dock and choose Force Quit from the pop-up menu, or use the Force Quit Applications window. The Force Quit Applications Window can be opened by pressing Command-Option-Escape or by choosing Apple > Force Quit.

3. Try a different document; try a different user account; force quit; reinstall the application; remove application support files (for example, preferences files).

7

Time   This lesson takes approximately 1 hour to complete.

Goals   Identify reasons to use a command-line interface and ways
to access the command-line interface

Describe the syntax of commands entered at the
command line

Use the online manual to determine the syntax and sample
usage for a command

Run commands to view hidden files and folders and to
manipulate files and file attributes

Run commands to find files, manage processes, monitor
usage, and manage disks and volumes

Exchange data between the Finder and the command line

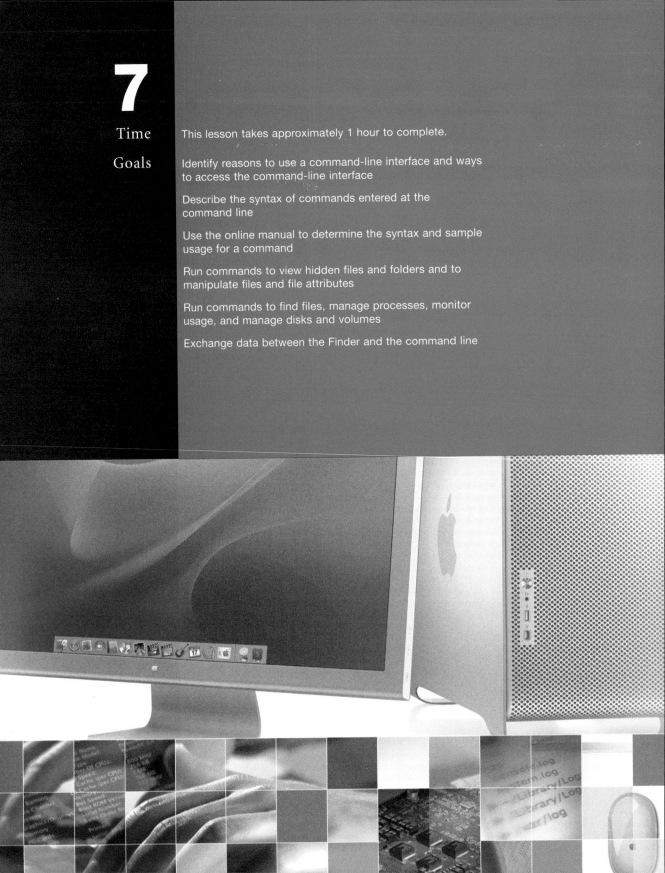

Lesson **7**
Command-Line Interface

Mac OS X is designed to give users all the power of an industry-standard UNIX-based operating system without having to know anything about BSD (Berkeley Software Distribution) tools. From an administrator and technical coordinator's perspective, however, you may find it convenient to use a command-line interface to accomplish certain administrative or troubleshooting tasks. Using the command-line interface is optional, but for the purposes of obtaining Apple Help Desk Essentials certification, it is necessary to understand the basics of when, where, and how to use these tools.

Sometimes referred to in UNIX environments as a *shell,* a command-line interface executes commands entered as text rather than from a menu selection or mouse click. The shell is the traditional interface to a UNIX system, and many features of Mac OS X can be accessed only as commands on the command line.

When you are shopping for a new car, one of the decisions you have to make is whether you want an automatic or manual transmission. Both types of transmission have advantages and disadvantages. Ultimately, your needs and preferences determine which you select.

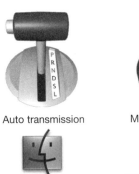
Auto transmission

Manual transmission

```
$ mkdir /Users/Shared/new_docs
$ mv hde*.txt /Users/Shared/new_docs
$ chown warren /Users/Shared/new_docs
```

Like selecting a transmission, the decision to use the graphical or the command-line interface depends upon your needs and preferences. Native Mac OS X applications, such as the Finder, simplify your computer experience, handling many tasks automatically. The command line allows you a greater degree of manual control and configuration of your computer. In Mac OS X, unlike a car, you don't have to choose—you have both interfaces to use whenever you need them.

> **TIP** ▶ As you become more comfortable with the command-line interface, you will use it more frequently for configuration and troubleshooting. However, when assisting others with troubleshooting, you should use the graphical utilities whenever possible; in these circumstances use the command-line only when absolutely necessary.

A Word of Caution

The command-line interface is an incredibly powerful tool, and that power comes with the potential for doing accidental damage to your files. In the Mac OS X graphical interface, if you make a mistake, you can usually choose Edit > Undo (Command-Z) to backtrack, and destructive actions usually are accompanied by dialogs requesting confirmation. There are no such safety nets with the command-line interface. If you enter the wrong command, you might delete documents or render the computer inoperable with no warning, and you will be able to undo the damage only by restoring your system from a backup or reinstalling Mac OS X.

The commands in this lesson's exercises are relatively harmless if entered as shown. But you should still be careful as you follow along with this lesson, and don't experiment unless you know exactly what you are doing.

Advantages of the Command Line

If you have never used the command-line interface, or have only used it briefly, you may not understand why you would want to use it. Like switching from using an automatic transmission to a manual one, you'll need some time to get used to it. Once you're comfortable with it, you will find that the command-line interface has some strong advantages.

Advanced Configuration or Features

The command line provides additional advanced commands to complement the graphical interface. And, in those cases where there is a graphical equivalent to a shell command, the shell command usually has additional options or features.

Running a Command as a Different User

The command line allows you to execute commands as a user other than your current login identity. For example, in the Finder, if you need to change permissions on a file that you do not own, you would need to log in as the owner of the file, change the permissions, and log out. With the command line, you can execute the command to change permissions using root access, without the need to log in as the root account.

Efficiency

Even when the same features are available in native Mac OS X applications and the command-line interface, the command-line interface can be more efficient, because you can combine commands. For example, if you want to use the Finder to change permissions for all files of a particular type, such as PDF files, you would have to manually select each of the files, open the Info window, and set the permissions. The same task in the shell can be done with one command:

*chmod o+rw *.pdf*

Remote Administration and Troubleshooting

You can run shell commands remotely without needing any additional software. In order to control the graphical interface remotely, you need to use special software such as Apple Remote Desktop or a VNC client application. However, any computer that has a terminal-style application or UNIX-style command-line interface can be used to send shell commands to a Mac OS X computer.

Using the Command-Line Interface

In a graphical interface, programs are controlled primarily by selecting and clicking menus and windows with buttons and text fields. As such, you can usually discover what a program is capable of doing just by examining the onscreen options. A command-line interface executes individual programs, called *commands* or tools, that you enter. A command consists of the name of the command followed by any options (often called *switches*) that you choose to provide, and any *arguments* for the command. Note that command names are case-sensitive. To execute a typed command, press the Return key.

The command prompt is the starting point for entering commands in a command-line interface. It can be daunting to stare at the command prompt if you're used to a graphical interface because there are no helpful onscreen hints suggesting what to do.

The command prompt indicates where you are—the name to the left of the colon (:) is the name of the computer. (If localhost is shown instead of the name of the computer, it is because a reverse DNS lookup could not be done on the computer's IP address.) The information to the right of the colon shows the working folder you are in. The tilde character (~) is an abbreviation representing your home folder.

Immediately following the working folder are the name of the currently logged-in user and a separator character (%, $, or #). If the separator character # is shown, it indicates that the current user is running commands as the System Administrator.

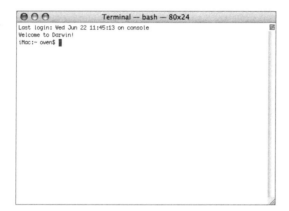

In this screen shot, the user named owen is logged in on a computer named iMac and is working in his home folder.

> **NOTE** ► The prompt is specific to each shell and is also user-configurable. What we show here is the default prompt you get with bash (*Bourne Again Shell*), the default shell.

NOTE ▶ Traditionally, UNIX users and UNIX commands use the word "directory" to describe the file system structure that can contain other file system items. This book follows the Mac OS X convention of using the word "folders" to describe these file system structures.

You can access the command line in Mac OS X in the following six ways:

▶ Terminal — For the remainder of this lesson, you will use Terminal (/Applications/Utilities) when you access the command line because it is the most convenient and secure method.

▶ Remote login using ssh (secure shell) or Telnet — You can log in to a remote Mac OS X computer from any computer by using ssh, provided that you use the user name and password of a user account on the remote Mac OS X computer. After you ssh into a remote Mac OS X computer, commands entered on your computer are executed on the remote computer as though you were using it locally.

There are two considerations for ssh login. The first is that Remote Login on Mac OS X is disabled by default. An administrator user can enable Remote Login in the Services pane of Sharing preferences. The second is that FileVault–enabled home folders must be mounted on that computer if you wish to access them across the network.

NOTE ▶ Terminal includes a Connect to Server command that simplifies connecting to a remote computer. In Terminal, choose File > Connect to Server. In the Connect to Server dialog, select the connection method, such as ssh, and the computer you are connecting to, enter the user name, and click Connect.

▶ Single-user mode — By pressing Command-S at startup until you see white text on a black background, you enter single-user mode. In single-user mode, you have access to the file system as the System Administrator without having to log in. You exit single-user mode by entering *exit*.

NOTE ▶ Single-user mode is a security risk because it gives the user System Administrator access to most of the files on the system. Setting an Open Firmware password on the computer will prevent a user from entering single-user mode. For more information, refer to Knowledge Base document 106482, "Setting up Open Firmware Password Protection in Mac OS X 10.1 or later."

▶ >console — If you enter >*console* as the user name with no password in the Mac OS X login window, the Mac OS X graphical interface disappears, and you are prompted to log in from a command-line interface prompt. At this point, you are using Mac OS X solely from a command-line interface. If you enter *exit* at the prompt, you return to the Mac OS X login window.

If you log in via >console, you will enter a user environment very much like Terminal. The only user process running is the BSD shell. If you need to use a processor-intensive BSD application, >console is the best way to run that application without other tasks taking up processor cycles.

NOTE ▶ Logging in with >console in effect enters a single BSD shell environment, with no graphical interface or other user processes active. As such, it should only be run when Fast User Switching is not enabled.

▶ Terminal from the Mac OS X Install DVD — This is a new feature in Mac OS X 10.4. Start up from the DVD, then choose Utilities > Terminal.

▶ X11 — The optional X11 application environment has an application similar to Terminal that can be used to execute BSD commands.

Unless otherwise noted, when this course mentions the command line, it refers to the interface and commands you will see in Terminal.

Entering Commands

Each BSD command is entered on a single line after the shell prompt and in the following format:

command option(s) (arguments)

For instance, the ls command lists the contents of the named folders. Adding an option to this command gives you a little more information in the listing. Entering *ls -lA ~/Documents* lists the contents of your Documents folder along with their permissions for files and subfolders. Regardless of where you are in the file system, ~ refers to your home folder.

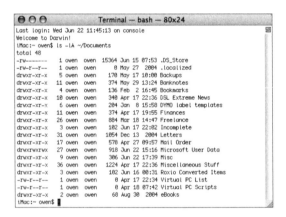

Many shell commands operate on or produce textual information. Shell commands that require input typically read their input from the *standard input device* (the keyboard), and commands that generate output typically write to the *standard output device* (the monitor).

Input/output redirection allows you to change the input device, the output device, or both for a given command. For example, you might want to redirect the output of an ls command to a file for inclusion in an email message. Such a command might look like this:

ls -lA ~/Documents > ~/Desktop/lstext.txt

The greater-than sign is used after the ls command (with its options and argument) to redirect output to a text file identified by path and filename. In this case, the list of items in the Documents folder would be saved to a text file named lstext in the current user's Desktop folder.

Accessing Online Help

All UNIX-based systems provide online help using the man (for manual) command. This command formats and displays pages describing the command, configuration file, or other item. The man pages for a command contain:

▶   The name

▶   A brief synopsis

▶   A description

▶   Examples of command syntax and usage (for most, but not all, commands)

The man command, followed by a command name, displays the manual pages for that command. For instance, on the command line, enter

man ls

This command displays information about the ls command, including its many parameters.

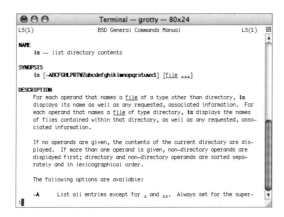

When you view a manual page, you are actually using a utility called more, so you can use commands to navigate the man page contents. If you press Return, you will move ahead one line. If you press the spacebar, you will move ahead one page. The up arrow and down arrow keys move up and down one line, respectively. If you are looking for a specific word on the man page, you can enter */word* and press Return, and your window will jump to the next instance of that word. Press Q to exit the man page and return to the command line.

You can also search the man pages for specific words using:

apropos keyword

where *keyword* is the specific word you're searching for. This command displays a list of commands whose man pages include this keyword. Using apropos is a good way to discover new commands.

> **NOTE** ▶ A newly installed system may not have had time to create the database used by the apropos command. You can force the update of the database by entering the following command:
>
> *sudo /etc/weekly*

The man pages are organized in numbered sections. If there is more information to display than fits on one screen, press the spacebar to page down. Sometimes you have to specify the section number to find the page you want. For example, open is the name of a command, but it is also the name of a Perl language construct, and a UNIX system call. To see the man page for the Perl language construct, you need to use

man 3 open

To find out what a section contains, enter

man section *intro*

For instance:

▶   Section 1 — General commands (tools and utilities)

▶ Section 2 — System calls and error numbers

▶ Section 3 — C libraries

There are some things to keep in mind when you use man pages as references. Not all commands have man pages, and sometimes the man pages have errors. Some man pages automatically redirect to other man pages with similar functionality. Also, because some man pages are derived from open-source documentation, they may be inaccurate, incomplete, or out-of-date.

Viewing man Pages Using Terminal

You can use a command-line interface to view the man pages for UNIX commands.

1 Open Terminal (/Applications/Utilities).

2 At the command prompt, enter

man ping

and press Return to obtain information on the UNIX command ping that corresponds to the Ping pane in Network Utility.

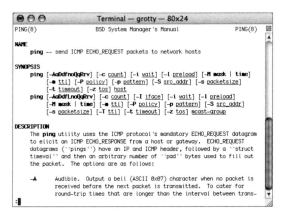

You can continue viewing the rest of the documentation by pressing the spacebar.

3   To quit viewing the documentation, press Q.

4   View the man page for traceroute, which corresponds to the Traceroute command used in Network Utility.

man traceroute

Using Edit Keys

Text entered at the command line must be exact, and some file systems require you to enter case-sensitive filenames. Fortunately, most shells, including those included by default with Terminal, provide several keyboard shortcuts that make entering and editing commands easier.

Tab Completion

Tab completion allows you to type just the first unique letters of a command or path. When you press the Tab key, the shell will complete the string. When you type a partial command and press the Tab key, but there are other commands or paths that start with the same letters, the shell will respond with a beep and wait for more input.

For example, suppose you want to list the contents of your Documents folder. You begin by typing

ls ~/D

At that point, you press the Tab key and the shell beeps because there are two folders that start with D: Desktop and Documents.

If you continue by typing *o* and then press the Tab key again, the shell completes the folder name to

ls ~/Documents/

because there is only one folder in your home folder that begins with "Do."

Using the Finder for Paths

A quick way to enter a very long path is to drag the folder from the Finder into the Terminal window. The path appears after the cursor on the command line, with the correct path to that folder.

Shells interpret spaces in filenames as command, switch, or argument separators. To get around this, you can either put the entire path in single or double quotes, or precede each individual space with a backslash (\). When a character is preceded by a backslash, it is called "escaping the character." This prevents the shell from doing anything special with the character. When a shell performs filename completion for you, it will escape spaces in filenames.

Reusing Prior Commands

The shell maintains a list of previously entered commands. The up arrow and down arrow traverse the history list of commands. To execute a command again, press Return when it is visible at the command prompt.

Editing Commands

Shells often provide a number of ways to speed the editing of commands. Use Control-A to move quickly to the beginning of a line. Control-E moves the cursor to the end of the line.

In addition to using the cursor keys to move the cursor forward and backward on the command line, Control-F moves forward one character and Control-B moves backward one character. To move forward and backward one word at a time, use Esc-F and Esc-B, respectively.

The cursor does not need to be at the end of the line when you press Return. The shell interprets all of the text entered on the current line regardless of the cursor's location when you press Return.

Miscellaneous Shortcuts

Use Control-L or the clear command to clear the screen.

Control-C terminates many commands in progress and will cause the shell to ignore any text currently being entered and return you to the command prompt.

The following table summarizes many of the command-line entry shortcuts and actions:

Shortcut	Action
Tab	Completes the word being typed
Drag folder to Terminal	Enters the path name
Up and down arrow keys	Accesses prior commands
Control-A	Moves the cursor to the beginning of the line
Control-E	Moves the cursor to the end of the line
Control-F	Moves forward one character
Control-B	Moves backward one character
Esc-F	Moves forward one word
Esc-B	Moves backward one word
Control-C	Terminates the command in progress
Control-L or "clear"	Clears the screen

File System Representations

Before you begin experimenting with some of the more useful command-line tools, make sure you understand how UNIX represents the file system. UNIX systems create a single hierarchy of folders and files (often described as an inverted tree) that includes all of the file systems available to the computer. The topmost folder is the root folder and is written as "/" (forward slash). There are no disks per se that are available to you via the command line. Instead, each disk is defined as a device in /dev, and each file system is mounted as a volume in /Volumes. Mounted volumes from connected devices appear as folders within the larger file system tree.

Consequently, locating files using the command line often involves specifying a path starting at the root folder and descending through the tree to the required file or folder. For example, the Finder might present a network drive on your desktop with the name Troubleshooting. In the command-line interface, this corresponds to the folder /Volumes/Troubleshooting.

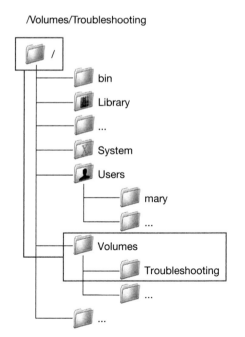

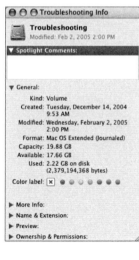

In Finder preferences, the General pane allows you to specify whether hard disks, removable media, and network volumes mounted with the Connect to Server command appear on your desktop. Volumes appearing on your desktop, however, are not really located in your Desktop folder. Therefore, they are not available to you on the command line with a path of the form *~/Desktop/volume*. Instead, those volumes are available in the command line in the /Volumes folder. If you are ever in doubt about the file system path to a folder or volume, you can drag it into a Terminal window. Terminal will enter its full UNIX path at the command line.

Volumes dynamically automounted from a server (such as network home folders) appear in the command line in the /Network/Servers folder.

Network volumes mounted from the Network icon in the Sidebar at the left of the Finder windows are available in the /Volumes folder.

Using Absolute and Relative Paths

To describe the location of a particular item, you can use either an absolute path or a relative path. An absolute path begins with / and indicates the path to the file starting at the root of the file system. A relative path indicates the path relative to where you are now. For instance, if you are logged in as chris and want to refer to the project folder inside the Documents folder for mary, you would need to include the file path starting at root:

/Users/mary/Documents/project

If, however, you were already in the home folder for mary, you could refer to the same folder with just Documents/project.

You can also use some shortcuts to refer to relative paths. For instance, home folders can also be referred to by the tilde (~) character. It can be used to specify paths starting at your home folder. So entering

~mary

refers to Mary's home folder. If you want to refer to the Library folder in your home folder, enter the shortcut

~/Library

If you want to refer to the current working folder, you can use a single period (dot). To refer to the parent folder of the working folder, you can use two periods (dot dot).

../project

Path names can be up to 1024 bytes long, starting from root.

Directories and Files Not Seen in the Finder

The Finder presents only a subset of the files that actually exist in any file system. Some files, such as the file system catalog and desktop database files, are marked as hidden. The Finder elects not to show some other files and folders, such as those that are used during system startup or are less likely to be of interest to general users.

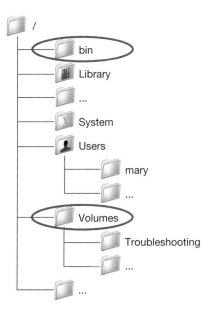

There are two types of hidden files and folders in Mac OS X: those with the invisible bit set, and those whose names start with a period (.).Using the command-line interface, you can list these hidden files. By entering the command *ls -la ~/*, for example, you can list all folders and files, including hidden files, located in your home folder.

NOTE ▶ Items that are hidden in Mac OS X are visible when using Mac OS 9. Be very careful never to delete a file or folder in Mac OS 9 unless you are absolutely certain it is not needed by Mac OS X.

Locating Files

Mac OS X introduces a number of predefined folders intended to contain files of particular types. Many applications depend on the name and location of these folders, and they should not be renamed or moved. Most applications in the Mac OS X graphical interface reside in /Applications, and operating system files reside in /System.

By convention, UNIX programs store their configuration information in the hidden folder /etc; most command-line tools are installed in the hidden folders /bin, /sbin, /usr/bin, or /usr/sbin. These four folders are the four locations that shells search to find programs whose names you enter on the command line. If you want to manually add a new program for the command line, you could place the file in one of these hidden folders, but a better solution would be to store it in a visible folder. Programs in locations other than the four default folders may be executed by specifying an absolute or relative path to the executable program.

The current folder is not part of the default search path on Mac OS X. This is important for Windows users, but it is a security risk to have a shell include the current folder in the search path, because it could allow unauthorized applications to execute.

Understanding Frequently Used Commands

Locating, creating, copying, and deleting files and folders are the main tasks that casual users will perform using the command line. The few commands described here allow you to complete such tasks many different ways. These commands are commonly used to administer and troubleshoot any UNIX-based system.

Although the names of commands may appear cryptic at first glance, you will find that most shell commands have been given names that attempt to be mnemonic. Oftentimes the command name is a common word without the vowels.

ls

The ls command, used to list one or more files, is probably the most frequently used command. As a consequence of its frequent use, the ls command supports many options. For example, using ls with the -l option displays the file type, size, date, and permission attributes along with the name of the requested files.

The use of many commands is simplified by the use of a current folder. All shells maintain a current folder for ease of specifying filenames used as arguments to commands. For example, entering

ls

with no files or folders specified will list the contents of the current folder. A file specification that doesn't begin with a forward slash (to identify the root) refers to a file or folder referenced from the current folder.

cd

The cd command changes the current directory (folder) to the directory you specify.

pwd

Use the pwd command to display or "print" the working directory (folder).

cp and mv

Use the cp and mv commands to copy and move, respectively, items in the command-line interface. To copy a file from your Public folder to your Documents folder, use the cp command. For example:

cp ~/Public/file_name ~/Documents/new_file_name

To move a file from the Shared folder to your Documents folder, enter

mv /Users/Shared/file_name ~/Documents/new_file_name

> **NOTE ▶** Mac OS X 10.4 changed the cp and mv commands so that they
> copy forked files. However, previous versions of the cp and mv commands
> ignored resource forks. If you are using a previous version, use ditto to move
> forked files or put your files into archives or packages before moving them.

rm

The rm command removes (deletes) the files that you name. You can list multiple files in a single command, use filename wildcards (discussed later in this lesson), or use a combination of both to remove many files with a single command. The command

rm -i ~/Documents/.rtf ~/Documents/*.txt*

removes all of the files whose name ends in ".rtf" or ".txt" that reside in your Documents folder. The -i option used in the example has rm ask whether or not you want to delete each file that you specify.

Another commonly used option of the rm command is -R. This option requests that rm recurse though all files and folders in the named folders deleting all of the files and folders that it encounters. The command

rm -iR ~/Documents/Projects

removes the Projects folder and all of its contents, including other folders, from your Documents folder. Since the -i option also appears, rm will prompt you to confirm the deletion of each file or folder that it finds.

> **NOTE ▶** Trash is not involved when you use these standard shell commands to remove files or folders. The files and folders that you remove cannot be recovered once the command has finished executing.

mkdir and rmdir

Use mkdir and rmdir, respectively, to make and remove empty folders.

Using File-Related Commands

Many command-line commands and troubleshooting tasks involve manipulating files and their attributes.

The more command allows you to view text files a page at a time. The touch command allows you to create an empty file with the specified name or, if a file with that name exists already, touch will update the modification date.

The cat command allows you to concatenate the contents of one or more files and display them on the standard output device. For example, typing *cat file1 > file2* causes the contents of file1 to be appended to the contents of file2.

It is sometimes important to know which application is the default for commands you execute in your current shell. There are some shell-specific command differences that might make a difference if you are performing advanced tasks. To determine the folder containing a particular command, use the which command.

To display a file's type, issue the file command followed by the name of the file or files whose type you wish to determine.

Finding Files Using Locate and Find

You can use both the locate and find commands to search the file system for files matching certain criteria.

The locate command uses a database describing the known files on your system. The locate database is built and updated automatically as long as your system is running at the appropriate time. By default on a Mac OS X system, the locate database is updated at 4:30 A.M. each Saturday. You can execute the script that updates the locate database using the command

sudo /etc/weekly

The locate command understands the wildcard characters used by the shell. In order to pass the wildcard character to the locate command, you must escape the character so that the shell doesn't process it. For example, the commands

locate ".rtf"*

or

locate *.rtf

will print a list of all files with names ending in ".rtf," but

*locate *.rtf*

results in an error.

The syntax for the find command is more complex than for the locate command, but the possible uses of find are much broader. The command

find ~ -name ".rtf"*

starts a search of the files in your home folder and lists all files with names ending in ".rtf."

Using Shell Filename Wildcards

Shell filename wildcards provide a convenient way to specify a group of files based on a pattern. The wildcards supported by UNIX shells are asterisk (*), question mark (?), and square brackets ([ ]).

The asterisk (*) wildcard matches any string of characters. For example, entering * matches all files, whereas entering *.rtf matches all files ending in ".rtf."

The question mark (?) wildcard matches any single character. As such, it's more precise than the asterisk. For example, typing *b?ok* matches "book" but not "brook."

The [ ] wildcard matches a single character in the list of characters appearing within the square brackets.

A few examples will build your understanding of wildcards. Consider a collection of five files with the names ReadMe.rtf, ReadMe.txt, read.rtf, read.txt, and It's All About Me.rtf. Among these files:

▶   *.rtf matches ReadMe.rtf, read.rtf, and It's All About Me.rtf

▶   ????.* matches read.rtf and read.txt

▶   [Rr]*.rtf matches ReadMe.rtf and read.rtf

▶   [A-Z]* matches ReadMe.rtf, ReadMe.txt, and It's All About Me.rtf

To test your understanding of wildcards, use the touch command to create files with these names and then try these expressions, as well as some of your own creation, as a file specifier for the ls command.

Executing Commands as Another User

There are two ways you can execute commands as another user. The sudo command lets you run a command as the System Administrator. In the default Mac OS X configuration, only users belonging to the admin group are permitted to act as the System Administrator in this way. Precede the command you want to execute with sudo, as in

sudo chown -R apple:staff ~apple/

and enter your password when prompted. In this way, you can run a command that must be executed as the System Administrator to complete successfully.

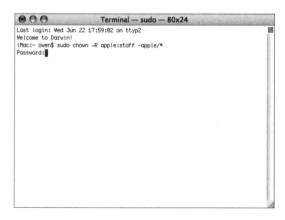

Two commands that might require sudo are chown (change owner) and chmod (change mode). For example, to change ownership of a file in your Documents folder to a user named "admin," enter

sudo chown admin ~/Documents/file_name

The chmod command changes the permissions on a particular file. To run chmod on a file that you do not own, you would need to use the sudo command and an admin password. The sudo command remembers the password for five minutes, so any further sudo commands entered during that time will not require you to reenter your password.

You can execute commands as another local user with the su (switch user) command. If you type su with a username argument, you will be prompted to authenticate as that user, and your login prompt will change to reflect your current user state. Entering

su apple

would switch you to the apple account, as long as it was not protected using FileVault.

Changing File Attributes

When you change the ownership or permissions of an item using a command-line interface, the changes are reflected in that item's Info window in the Finder. Likewise, when you change the permissions in the Info window, the changes can be seen when displaying the item in a command-line interface.

When displayed in a command-line interface, a file's permissions are represented by a ten-character descriptor. The first character indicates the type of file and is followed by three triplets of characters describing the read, write, and execute permissions (always in that order) for owner, group, and others, respectively. A hyphen serves as a placeholder if permission is not granted for a particular command.

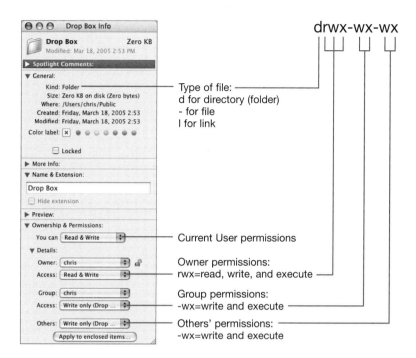

In this figure, the *d* in front of the permissions indicates that the file is a directory (folder). The permissions for the owner, *rwx*, correspond to Read & Write in the Info window for that folder.

The *x*, or execute, permission on a file identifies a program that can be run. For a folder, the execute permission determines whether or not the folder can be searched. To access a file in a folder, you must have search permission for each folder from the root down to and including the folder containing the file. Execute permissions are also set on applications and on shell scripts, which must be executed to work properly.

> **NOTE ▶** A shell script is a text file that contains UNIX commands to be executed together. Setting the execute bit indicates that this file is to function as an application (similar to an AppleScript file) as opposed to as a regular text file.

Continuing with the example in the figure, the permissions for both group and others is -*wx*. Since a hyphen appears in the place where the read permission would normally appear, neither group nor others can see the contents of the folder. However, they can write to the folder, so the folder acts as a drop box, into which items can be blindly copied.

Here are some examples of useful permissions you can set only from the command line:

▶ A user who has *x* but not *r* permission to a folder cannot list the folder's contents, but can access files in it if he or she knows the names of the files.

▶ If the "sticky bit" is set on a folder, along with *w*, anyone can write a file to it, but only the folder owner or a file's owner can remove a file.

The chown and chmod commands allow you to change the ownership and the permissions associated with one or more files. Use chown to change the owner or group assigned to a file. For example,

chown apple:staff /Users/Shared/ReadMe.rtf

assigns the user apple and the group staff to the file /Users/Shared/ReadMe.rtf. If you own a file, you can reassign the group for that file to another group as long as you are a member of the new group. You cannot, however, change the owner of a file unless you are the System Administrator.

The chmod command

chmod g+w,o-rw /Users/Shared/ReadMe.rtf

adds write permission for members of the group assigned to the file ReadMe.rtf and removes read and write permissions for other users.

The chmod command can also set the sticky bit on a file. A folder whose sticky bit is set becomes a folder with restricted permissions. A file in a sticky folder may only be removed or renamed by a user if the user has write permission for the folder and the user is the owner of the file, the owner of the folder, or the System Administrator. This allows you to create folders in common areas, such as /Users/Shared, that others can access but not delete.

Changing Ownership of a File

In this exercise, you will use a command-line interface to change ownership of a file.

1   Log in as Chris Johnson.

2   Open Terminal (/Applications/Utilities).

The Terminal window will appear, with the chris home folder as the working directory. You can tell it is the active user's home folder because of the tilde (~).

3   Use the touch command to create a file called CMDTest.txt in ~/Documents:

touch ./Documents/CMDTest.txt

4   At the prompt, use the cd command to navigate to ~/Documents:

cd ~/Documents

5   Display a long list of the items in that folder:

ls -l

6   Because Chris Johnson is not an administrator user, Chris's account cannot perform some administrative tasks from the command line. Switch to apple using the su command.

su apple

7   Enter the password when prompted.

You will see a warning message at the command line, because you are now the Apple Admin user, and your present working folder is someone else's home folder. You can ignore the error for now.

Notice how the prompt changes to indicate that you are now running commands as apple. You must authenticate as an administrator user to run sudo.

8 Use the chown command to change the owner of the CMDTest.txt file to root.

sudo chown root CMDTest.txt

You can change who owns the file and the group that has access to it by specifying *owner:group* after the chown command, where *owner* is the user to which you are changing ownership and *group* is the name of the group to which you are giving permissions.

9 When prompted, enter Apple Admin's password.

10 Display a long list of the items, and verify that the CMDTest.txt file is owned by root.

ls -l

The command fails because Apple Admin does not have permission to view or list Chris's Documents folder. There are several layers of protection to prevent unauthorized access. Try the command again using sudo.

sudo ls -l

Most of the folder contents, such as secret.rtf, are owned by chris. However, because you performed the chown command, CMDTest.txt is owned by root.

11 Note the permissions on the CMDTest.txt file: -rw-r--r--

Changing the Permissions of a File

In this exercise, you will use the chmod command to change the permissions of a file and try to open it, and then use the chmod command to change the permissions again so that you can open the file.

1 While still in Terminal, use the following command to change the permissions on CMDTest.txt so that group and everyone have no permissions:

sudo chmod go-r CMDTest.txt

2   If prompted, enter the password for the Apple Admin account.

3   Display a long-format list of the items, and verify that the owner has read and write permissions, and group and everyone have none:

ls -l

4   In TextEdit, choose File > Open to open CMDTest.txt.

An Open Failed error message should appear. This is because Chris no longer has read permissions for the file.

5   Using the chmod command in Terminal, add read and write permissions to group, and read permissions to others:

sudo chmod g+rw,o+r CMDTest.txt

6   Verify the change:

sudo ls -l

7   Verify that you can now open CMDTest.txt with TextEdit.

8   Exit your apple user session in Terminal. Enter

exit

and press Return.

You should always exit user sessions when you no longer need the access provided by that user account. Also, if you exit Terminal with switched user sessions active, you will get an error message when you try to quit.

10   Quit Terminal.

11   Quit TextEdit.

Logging In Remotely

The ssh command lets you log in to a remote computer and execute commands as though you were at that computer. The ssh command makes its remote connections using SSH, which stands for secure shell. All communication between your computer and the remote computer is encrypted during your SSH session. The -l option allows you to provide a login name to the remote system, although the same can be accomplished by using *username@hostname*. Otherwise, your current short name will be used as the login name for the remote computer.

To let another user access your computer remotely, you must select the Remote Login checkbox in the Services pane of Sharing preferences. Once enabled, a user can connect to your machine using ssh provided they know a user name and password that is defined on your machine.

Note that remote connections are not possible with FileVault–protected accounts, because encrypted home folders require a local login before they are accessible in the file system.

When logged in remotely, the commands you enter in that session are sent over the network by SSH and are executed on the remote machine. This has two primary consequences:

► You can start a remote application and it will continue running even if you disconnect from your remote login session. You should explicitly stop your remote applications, so that you do not waste system resources on the remote computer.

► Your encrypted SSH tunnel to the remote computer is established with your authentication. You should always use the exit command at the end of your remote login sessions to close the SSH tunnel and avoid a potential security hole.

Using Apple Remote Desktop to Send Commands

In addition to using SSH to execute commands on a remote computer, you can also use Apple Remote Desktop (ARD) to run shell commands or scripts on a remote computer.

NOTE ▶ While the ARD client is included with Mac OS X 10.4, the full administration application for ARD is available separately in either a 10-client or unlimited-client edition. For more information, visit www.apple.com/remotedesktop.

The Execute UNIX Commands feature in ARD 2.1 allows sending a UNIX command or script to a Mac OS X client computer, provided that computer's access privileges are properly configured in the Services pane of Sharing preferences. After the command completes, Apple Remote Desktop displays a window listing the results of the command.

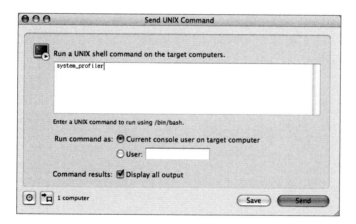

The advantage of using ARD to send shell commands is that ARD allows you to execute shell commands on multiple computers, where SSH only connects to a single computer at a time. A downside to using ARD is that it is not interactive like SSH. You send a command and get the results in a new window.

NOTE ▶ Turning on ARD or SSH access can potentially present a security hole, as both allow remote users access to the computer. If you do enable either, be very strict with sharing the ARD or admin account passwords. Users with either password can enable both SSH and ARD access and gain complete control of the computer and monitor.

Using Mac OS X–Specific Commands

Mac OS X systems have some important commands that you won't find on other UNIX platforms. They are stored in /usr/bin.

The pbcopy and pbpaste commands (located in the folder /usr/bin) are used to move text to and from the "pasteboard," which is called the clipboard in Mac OS X. For example,

ls -lS ~/Documents | pbcopy

places a listing on the clipboard of all files in your Documents directory sorted by file size, which you could then paste into a TextEdit document or Mail message.

Property-list (plist) files are used to store preference settings such as system settings and application preferences. The plutil command can be used to check the syntax of plist files, or convert a plist file from one format to another. For example,

plutil /Library/Preferences/.plist*

verifies the format of the plist files in /Library/Preferences.

The softwareupdate command allows you to view the list of available updates and install updates that you specify.

GetFileInfo and SetFile are installed as part of the Developer Tools package in /Developer/Tools. These tools allow you manipulate HFS files with resource forks, and get and set file attributes (such as type and creator) associated with HFS files.

The open command allows you to use the command line to open a file as if you had double-clicked it in the Finder.

The asr command allows you to perform tasks using Apple Software Restore.

The system_profiler command provides command-line access to the same information as the System Profiler application.

The hdiutil command allows you to perform hard drive configuration at the command line.

The ditto command is a copy command that works with flat files and files with resource forks. To copy a file and its resource forks, enter the following command:

ditto -rsrcFork source_file destination_file

> **NOTE ▶** The standard command-line utilities in the versions of Mac OS X prior to 10.4 did not include support for resource forks.

GetFileInfo and SetFile commands are installed into the folder /Developer/Tools as part of the Developer Tools package. They allow you to manipulate HFS files with resource forks, and to get and set file attributes (such as type and creator) associated with HFS files.

Managing Processes from the Command Line

Instead of using the Activity Monitor, you can determine the currently running processes from the command line using the ps or top commands.

Use top to view a regularly updated view of system utilization, including memory usage, page faults, and the set of currently executing processes.

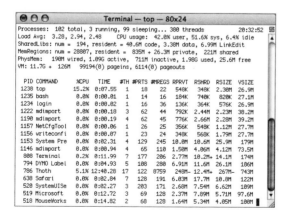

In the leftmost column of top's tabular output, you will find the process identifier (PID) associated with that process. You can also use the ps command to determine the PID of a process. The PID is used to send a message to a particular process. For example, the command

ps -auxww | grep TextEdit

prints the PID and other information for the TextEdit process.

You can send signals from the CLI to running processes requesting actions such as rereading a configuration file, logging additional information, or quitting. For example, with the kill command, you can send a signal to a process with a specified PID. The command

kill -TERM PID

asks the process with the given PID to terminate.

To force quit a process from the command line, use the kill signal as follows:

kill -KILL PID

The killall command allows you to signal processes using the name of the process rather than the PID. The command

killall -KILL TextEdit

force quits all processes that belong to you with the name TextEdit.

Monitoring System Usage

Many shell commands exist to help you monitor the system. The last command shows you which users have logged in most recently or when a specified user last logged in to your system.

The id command allows you to determine which groups a particular user has access to or to determine the short name for a user, given their UID.

Mac OS X systems maintain many log files. Viewing log files on your system or on another system using ssh can help you troubleshoot any number of problems. The command

tail -n 10 /Library/Logs/Software\ Update.log

displays the 10 most recently installed software updates. The command

tail -f /var/log/system.log

displays the current contents of the system log, then continues to print new lines as they are added to the file.

Managing Disks and Volumes

You can get all of the functionality available in Disk Utility with two commands accessible from the command-line interface. The first is hdiutil, which handles disk image management. The second is diskutil, which handles the rest of the Disk Utility functionality. You can read man pages to learn how to use the different features, or you can enter either command at the command line to read text describing the different options you can use.

You can use the command-line utilities df and du to determine free space and space utilization on a volume. The utility tar can create archives, but note that tar does not preserve resource forks.

Using the Command Line with the Graphical Environment

In Mac OS X, the command line and the graphical interface work hand-in-hand. You can easily transfer data from one environment to the other and move between the two environments.

You can select a group of files in the Finder and drag them to a Terminal window to add their paths to a command.

The pbcopy and pbpaste commands allow you to copy and paste, respectively, data to and from the clipboard.

The open command allows you to open files and URLs as if you had double-clicked them in the Finder. For example,

open ~/Documents/ReadMe.rtf

launches TextEdit (or your preferred application for dealing with RTF files) and opens the specified ReadMe.rtf file. The command

open http://www.apple.com

launches your preferred web browser (set in Internet preferences) and opens the Apple home page.

Advanced Commands

Use the grep command to search the contents of the listed text file or files. In the example,

grep domain /etc/resolv.conf

the file resolv.conf is searched for the word "domain," and the lines containing that word are displayed.

The process status command, ps, displays information about the processes running on your computer, or on the remote computer if you are logged in remotely. The optional arguments to ps used in the command

ps -auxww

tell ps to list information about all processes on your computer in wide format.

The ps command displays the Process ID or PID of a process. Once you know the PID, you can use the kill command to terminate the process.

Often, the output of one command can be used as input for another command. The UNIX pipe character (|) is used for this purpose. The command

ps -auxww | grep Finder

executes both the ps and grep commands. The output of the ps command is sent to the grep command as input that searches for the word "Finder" and displays any lines containing that word.

Mac OS X 10.4 also includes three new commands related to Spotlight.

The mdls command lists all of the metadata associated with any document. The mdfind command performs a fast Spotlight search and offers several flexible search options. The mdutil command provides a number of functions to manage Spotlight indexes.

Command-Line Cautions

The command line offers a very powerful tool for administering and troubleshooting a Mac OS X system. Using the command line, however, calls for great attention to detail and involves fewer safety nets than interacting with the system using the graphical interface.

Things to watch for when using the command line include the following:

▶ Shells don't provide an undo feature, and you can't retrieve deleted files from the Trash.

▶ The numeral 0 (zero) and the uppercase letter O, and the numeral 1 (one) and the lowercase letter l often look the same but rarely mean the same thing to a shell.

▶ Spaces in filenames need to be escaped from the shell.

▶ The man pages come in numbered sections. Sometimes you have to specify the command and also the name section number to display the page you want.

▶ Occasionally you might find a man page that is out-of-date.

What You've Learned

The command-line interface provides an additional method for configuring and troubleshooting a computer running Mac OS X. You shouldn't think of it as a replacement for the graphical interface, but rather as a complementary interface that allows you to do some things more efficiently.

▶ The command line gives you another way to execute commands in Mac OS X.

▶ Interfaces to the command line include console, ssh, single-user mode, and Terminal.

▶ The man pages provide online help.

▶ You can navigate around the file system and move, copy, and rename files from the command line.

▶ You can make changes to file ownership and permissions at a more granular level using a command-line interface.

▶ You can use locate and find to find files.

▶ The last command helps you keep track of user logins.

▶ The id command helps you keep track of user and group IDs.

▶ The tail command helps you view recent activity in a log file.

▶ The command-line interface gives you another way to force quit applications and processes.

References

The following Knowledge Base documents (located at www.apple.com/support) will provide you with further information regarding using the command-line interface.

Open Firmware Password

▶ 106482, "Setting up Open Firmware Password Protection in Mac OS X 10.1 or later"

Terminal

▶ 25591, "Mac OS X 10.3: Terminal Commands That Require Authentication Unlock Other Applications"

▶ 61357, "Mac OS X: About Entering Commands in Terminal"

▶ 106712, "Troubleshooting permissions issues in Mac OS X"

URLs

Visit the following website for more information.

▶ Apple Remote Desktop: www.apple.com/remotedesktop

Lesson Review

Use the following questions to review what you have learned:

1. What are some of the ways to access the command-line interface in Mac OS X?

2. What is sudo?

3. Name some commands that require sudo if you are logged into Mac OS X as an administrator user.

Answers

1. You can access the command line by logging in as >console, remotely logging in using ssh, putting Mac OS X into single-user mode, or using Terminal. Additionally, you can access the command line by booting from the Mac OS X Install DVD or from within the X11 application.

2. The sudo command lets you run a command as if you were logged in as a different user.

    Most commonly, sudo is used to run commands as the System Administrator.

3. The chown and chmod commands require that you used sudo to execute them if you are operating on files or folders that you do not own or have permission to modify.

8

Time
This lesson takes approximately 1 hour, 30 minutes to complete.

Goals
Describe basic networking concepts and terms

Use Network preferences to configure Mac OS X to receive an IP address from a DHCP server, communicate with other computers on the same network, and access network services

Use Network Diagnostics, Network Utility, and Network preferences to troubleshoot networking issues

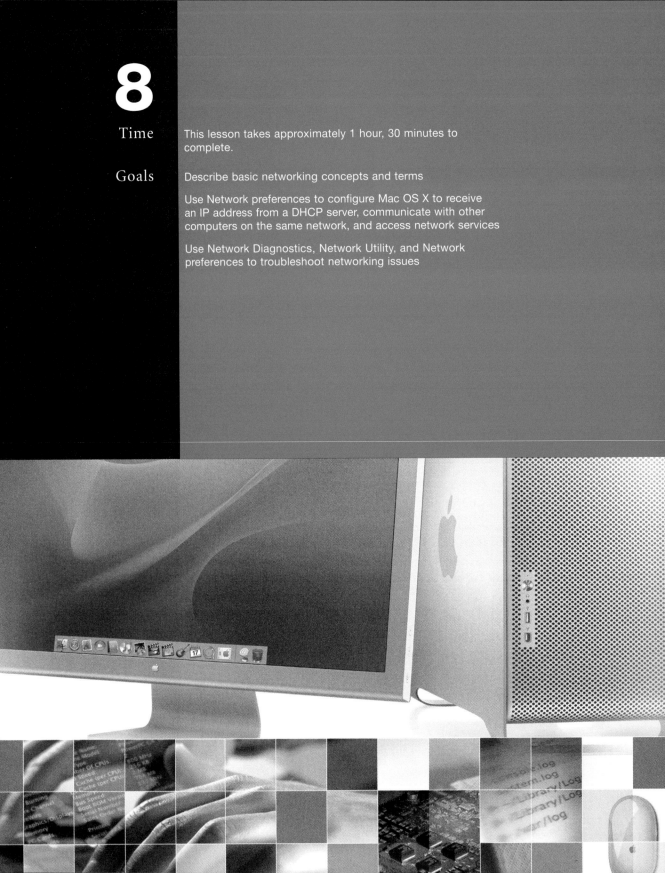

Networking Configuration and Troubleshooting

One of the strengths of Mac OS X is its integration with network and Internet services. Network data storage, such as iDisks (one of the benefits of an optional .Mac subscription), can be mounted and accessed just as if it was a local disk drive. iCal and Address Book are able to seamlessly store and retrieve calendar and contact data over a network, allowing data to be synchronized between multiple computers. With just one click, users can purchase a song online and have it downloaded and added to their iTunes Music Library. However, the key to accessing those services is the correct configuration of network hardware and software.

While Mac OS X simplifies network configuration, there are still times when you will need to create a specific network configuration or troubleshoot a network issue. In this lesson you will learn basic networking concepts and how to set up and troubleshoot Mac OS X network configurations.

Understanding Networking Concepts

Before you troubleshoot networking problems, you need to understand the basic concepts of how computers communicate, whether across the room or around the world.

If every computer in the world could be connected to one single Ethernet network, your computer would be able to send data directly to every other computer. However, computers are actually linked to a collection of connected networks. The largest IP networks are made up of smaller networks. Large networks, which span a large logical area, are called *wide area networks,* or WANs. As networks become smaller and more specific to an audience, they are called *local area networks,* or LANs. Finally, LANs can be divided into physical or logical *subnetworks* or *subnets*. Although the distinction between LAN and WAN is arbitrary, you can think of a LAN as the devices in your network you can touch without leaving the building, and a WAN as all the network devices beyond the building's walls.

Internet Protocol (IP) Address

In order to communicate with computers across the various networks, each interface is assigned an Internet Protocol (IP) address. The IP address is not permanently fixed to an interface. Instead, the IP address assigned to an interface is based on the network to which the computer is connected.

A network uses an IP address for its unique identification. The IP address in a TCP/IP packet encodes the information necessary to deliver the packet to the network through to the subnet of the recipient. An IPv4 address is a 32-bit number that is divided into four 8-bit parts called octets. These octets can have a value from 0 to 255. An example IP address is 10.1.45.186.

Subnet Masks

In addition to the IP address, a computer also needs a subnet mask to help it identify the address range for the local network. Like the IP address, the subnet mask is a 32-bit number made up of four 8-bit octets. The local IP address range is determined by applying the subnet mask to the computer's IP address.

The bits that are turned on in the subnet mask specify which bits of the IP address define the local address range. For example, a subnet mask of 255.255.255.0 applied to an address of 10.1.2.3 means the local address range is 10.1.2.0 to 10.1.2.255.

Whenever a computer needs to send out a packet of data, it applies the subnet mask to the destination IP address to determine if the packet is to be sent to a computer on the local network. If the address is within the local IP address range, then the data is packaged and sent across the local network to the destination computer.

Media Access Control (MAC) Address

A computer uses a network interface to connect to a network. Network interfaces are hardware devices that support various protocols for network communication. The most common type of network interface is Ethernet. By design, every Ethernet interface has a unique identifier called a Media Access Control (MAC) address, also referred to as an Ethernet address. These addresses are used in the MAC layer of the network to uniquely identify network ports. One or more IP addresses may be associated with a single MAC address, but MAC addresses are unique to each Ethernet interface. A MAC address is made up of a series of octets, much like an IP address, although different MAC addresses may have a different number of octets, and MAC addresses commonly incorporate alphabet characters in addition to numbers.

Several other technologies use MAC addresses to uniquely identify devices, although not all of them use IP networking. For example, each Bluetooth device has a MAC address with six octets. You can see the MAC address for any device in System Profiler.

When your computer sends data to another device on the local Ethernet network, the IP data, including the destination and origination IP addresses, are grouped into Ethernet packets. The Ethernet packets are then sent across the network using the MAC address. The destination device then extracts the IP data from the Ethernet packets and handles it appropriately.

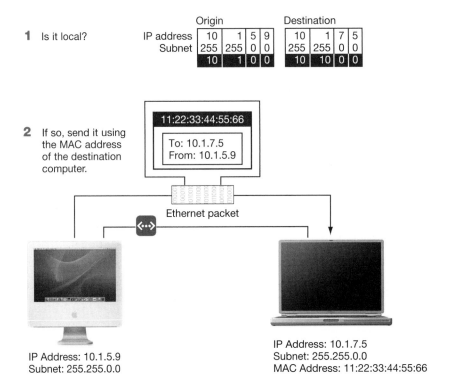

1   Is it local?

Origin

IP address
Subnet

10	1	5	9
255	255	0	0
10	1	0	0

Destination

10	1	7	5
255	255	0	0
10	10	0	0

2   If so, send it using
the MAC address
of the destination
computer.

11:22:33:44:55:66

To: 10.1.7.5
From: 10.1.5.9

Ethernet packet

IP Address: 10.1.5.9
Subnet: 255.255.0.0

IP Address: 10.1.7.5
Subnet: 255.255.0.0
MAC Address: 11:22:33:44:55:66

Sending Packets Over a WAN

A WAN is different than a LAN. In most cases, a WAN describes a connection
that crosses network regions that you do not control. For example, you might
be connecting to a remote web server in the simplest example, or you might
have a WAN link between offices in two cities, or you might create a secure
VPN connection across the Internet.

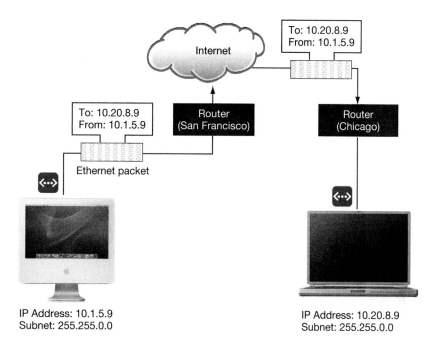

In the illustration above, you can see that packet transfer across a WAN is heavily managed. Our iMac G5 (at the left) applies the subnet mask to the destination address, and determines that the data is intended for a computer beyond our local network, so it sends the packet to its local San Francisco router. The router receives the network traffic and uses a routing table to determine where it should go.

The San Francisco router is responsible for extracting the IP data and forwarding it, either directly to the destination computer if it is on a network connected to the router, or onto another router to be passed along to another network. It finds a routing table entry for the remote destination, and it connects to the Chicago router using the MAC address and sends the packet. The Chicago router checks the IP address for the packet, finds it in its routing table matched up with a MAC address on its local network, and delivers it to the PowerBook's network interface.

NOTE ▶ This network diagram uses simple non-routable addresses for the purposes of this example. These addresses would not be used on most networks.

Domain Name System

To make it easier for people to remember addresses, an IP address can have an associated name called a host name, such as www.pretendco.com or info.pretendco.com. The host name is associated with a domain name, such as pretendco.com.

Because IP networking is based on the IP addresses, you need a method to translate the host name into its corresponding IP address. The entire system of host name and domain name mapping is called the Domain Name System (DNS). Dedicated hosts that provide DNS services are called DNS servers. Whenever your computer needs to look up an IP address that corresponds to a domain name, it consults the local DNS server.

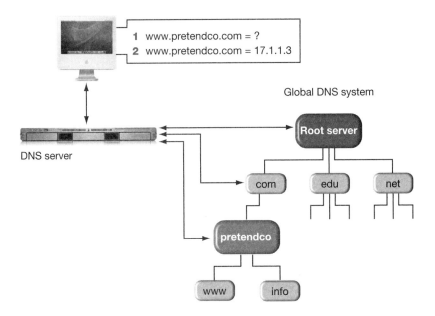

The problem is that the Internet is extremely large and constantly changing. New computers are added, servers are turned off, companies change names, and so forth. It would be impossible for your local DNS server to keep track of every possible domain name.

Fortunately, it doesn't have to. Instead of needing to know every domain name and address combination, the DNS server looks up the address through a tiered server scheme. Your DNS server queries a series of DNS servers to find the IP for the given domain name. Once it has identified the IP address, it temporarily stores the address in a local cache so that the next time the server receives a request to look up the address, the server can quickly return it without having to look it up again.

This is similar to when you need to call someone but do not know their phone number. If you need to call Chris Johnson at PretendCo, you would first call information to get PretendCo's main phone number. You would then call that number to get Chris's phone number. After you have Chris's phone number, you would store it in an address book to allow you to quickly recall it, instead of having to call PretendCo again to get it.

Network Ports and Protocols

A *port* (sometimes called a *network interface*) is an interface to similar devices within a LAN, or it serves as an interface to outside networks. Ethernet cards, modems, and AirPort cards are types of ports. Virtual ports, such as VPN, don't match directly to a physical interface. If you activate a port in Network preferences, you can configure the protocols available on that port.

A *protocol* is a special set of rules that relate to communication between systems. In Network preferences, you can configure two protocols: TCP/IP and AppleTalk. TCP/IP protocol supports FTP, Server Message Blocks (SMB), and Apple Filing Protocol (AFP) network connections; AppleTalk is used for AFP discovery and printer connections on the network. Some ports only support certain protocols. For instance, the AppleTalk protocol is not supported over PPP modem connections.

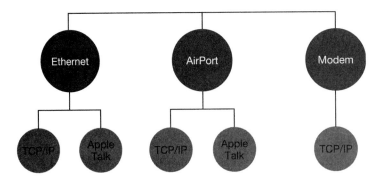

NOTE ▶ The above diagram is not a comprehensive illustration of all ports and protocols available on a Macintosh computer.

NOTE ▶ Beginning with Mac OS X 10.4, AFP is not supported over AppleTalk. AFP discovery over AppleTalk still is supported, but AFP uses IP to actually complete the connection.

Using Network Configuration Applications

As complex as networking may seem, Mac OS X greatly simplifies network configuration. Almost all configuration is performed using just three applications:

▶ Network Setup Assistant — Configures Mac OS X for the most common methods of connecting to the Internet. You can open Network Setup Assistant by clicking the "Assist me" button in Network preferences. During the initial Mac OS X setup, networking is configured in the Setup Assistant if you do not have an active Ethernet port available. If that port is available, Ethernet is automatically enabled and configured using Dynamic Host Configuration Protocol (discussed later in this lesson).

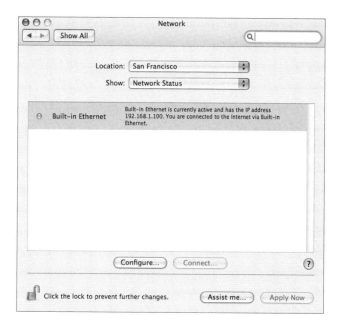

▶ Network preferences — Configures the network settings beyond the basic configuration provided by the Network Setup Assistant.

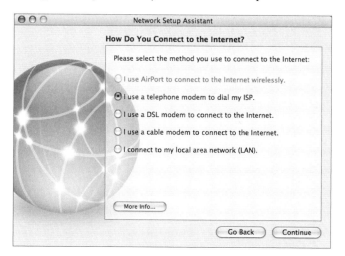

▶ Internet Connect application — Establishes connections to remote networks. Most frequently it is used to establish an Internet connection with
   an Internet service provider (ISP) via Point-to-Point Protocol (PPP) or
   Point-to-Point Protocol over Ethernet (PPPoE), but it is also used to
   establish VPN connections and provide authentication for 802.1x-enabled
   networks.

   You can also import and export Internet Connect configurations. This
   allows network administrators to create and distribute network-specific
   configurations that users can import and use.

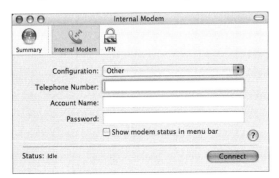

Understanding Network Ports

You need to understand three important concepts about network ports. A port
must be *active* and *configured* to be used for networking, and each port has a
priority that is either automatically or manually assigned.

An active port is one that has been enabled in Network preferences, and then
connected to its network type: AirPort connects to a local wireless network;
Ethernet requires a network cable with a responder of some sort; the modem
requires a dial tone. The configuration might be as simple as selecting a base
station or setting a TCP/IP address, but it is an essential part of the port
definition.

If you have two or more active ports, the computer needs to know which port
should be used to send nonlocal network data. For example, if you have a
computer connected to both an Ethernet and an AirPort network, and you

attempt to access an address not found on either network, the operating system needs to know which network contains the router that should be used to access the WAN. Choose Network Port Configurations from the Show pop-up menu to set port priority.

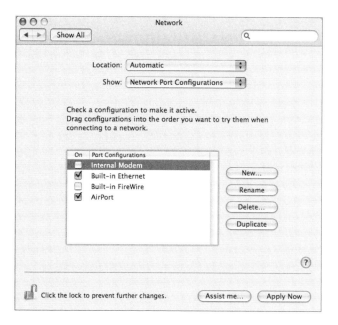

When the computer needs to send network packets, it sends through the active port with the highest priority. The higher the port in the list, the higher its priority. In the Network Port Configurations pane above, both the Built-in Ethernet and AirPort port configurations are enabled. If both ports are active and connected to networks, any packets would be sent to the router on the Ethernet network, because the port configuration Built-in Ethernet has the highest priority.

Mac OS X is designed to change its highest priority network port automatically to maintain valid network connections. If your Ethernet cable is unplugged or fails, or if your computer loses Internet connectivity due to a server problem, Mac OS X would automatically attempt to make AirPort the primary network port. If Internet services are restored on the Ethernet interface, Ethernet will become active again, and automatically receive its former priority.

NOTE ▶ If you have two or more active ports, the DNS servers associated with the port with the highest priority are used for domain name conversion. If you are having problems locating servers on a network connected to a lower priority port, those services might not be accessible by the DNS servers on the highest priority port. For example, in the preceding screenshot, if both the Ethernet and AirPort ports are active, DNS lookups will occur using the DNS servers listed with the Ethernet port. If the AirPort network is a private network, your computer will not be able to perform a domain name lookup for services on that network, even though your computer is directly connected to it.

Enabled ports are listed in the Show pop-up menu in Network preferences. Choosing a port from the Show pop-up menu allows you to configure the port.

Which Network configuration panes are available depends upon which port is chosen in the Show pop-up menu. The order of the panes corresponds with the most likely use for that type of port. When an Ethernet port is chosen, five panes are available: TCP/IP, PPPoE, AppleTalk, Proxies, and Ethernet. When AirPort is chosen, the five panes are AirPort, TCP/IP, PPPoE, AppleTalk, and Proxies. With modems, the available panes are PPP, TCP/IP, Proxies, and Modem.

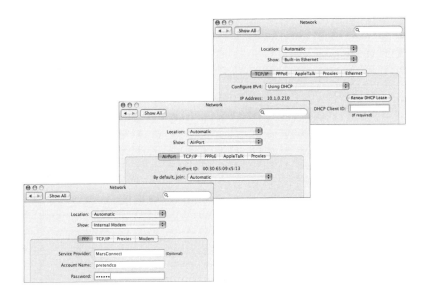

Using TCP/IP

In the Configure IPv4 pop-up menu in the TCP/IP pane, you can configure how the computer obtains IP address information. IPv4 is short for Internet Protocol Version 4. It is currently the most widely used protocol.

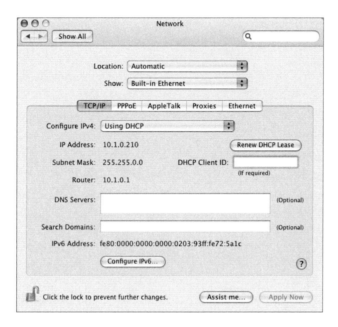

Setting the IP Address

The methods for obtaining and setting the IP address vary depending upon the network port. The Ethernet and AirPort ports provide four configuration methods: Manually, Using DHCP with manual IP address, Using DHCP, and Using BootP.

A fifth option, Off, disables IP addressing on the port. The Built-in Modem configuration menu includes the Manually configuration method, but it also includes Using PPP and AOL Dialup.

IPv6 Support

In addition to supporting IPv4, Mac OS X natively supports Internet Protocol Version 6 (IPv6), the next-generation protocol for the Internet.

IPv6 is a new protocol designed by the Internet Engineering Task Force (IETF) to replace the aging IPv4 protocol. The two protocols will coexist until IPv6 eventually replaces IPv4.

IPv6 resolves some of the limitations of IPv4, such as address size. The address size increases from 32 bits (current IPv4 standard) to 128 bits. Also, IPv6 improves the process of routing and network autoconfiguration.

By default, IPv6 is configured automatically in Mac OS X. However, if you need to configure IPv6 manually, click the TCP/IP tab in Network preferences, click Configure IPv6, choose Manually from the Configure IPv6 pop-up menu, and enter the IPv6 address, router address, and prefix length that your system administrator supplied.

Using Static IP Addresses

Choosing Manually from the Configure IPv4 pop-up menu means that you are assigning this computer a static IP address. You will also need to enter the subnet mask, router, and DNS information in the appropriate fields.

One way to provide a device with an IP address is to manually configure it. In Mac OS X, for example, you use Network preferences to enter a static IP address. But manually configuring static IP addresses can be inconvenient for short-term or dynamic networks, because you need to physically enter an assigned address on each computer.

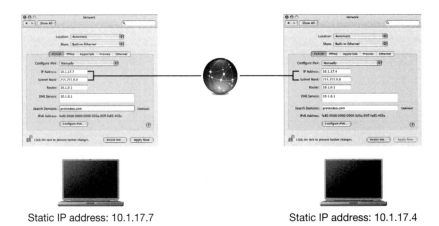

Static IP address: 10.1.17.7   Static IP address: 10.1.17.4

Setting a New Location with a Static IP Address

This exercise demonstrates how you configure a location that uses a static IP address. If you have a working network connection already, following these steps will disrupt your connection, so you may prefer to simply read along.

1   In Network preferences, note the name of your current location, then choose Location > New Location.

    A configuration sheet appears, asking you to name your new location.

2   Enter the name *Static* and click OK.

3   Choose Show > Network Port Configurations, then disable all network ports other than Built-in Ethernet.

4   Click Apply Now.

5   Choose Show > Built-in Ethernet.

6   Choose Configure IPv4 > Manually.

7   Enter the necessary information into the following fields:

    ▶ IP Address

    ▶ Subnet Mask

    ▶ Router

    ▶ DNS Servers

    ▶ Search Domains

8   Click Apply Now, then choose Show > Network Status.

    Mac OS X attempts to connect to the network using the settings entered in the previous step. If any of them are incorrect, Built-in Ethernet will not have a green light in the Network Status pane.

9   From the Location menu, choose your original setting noted in step 1 and then click Apply Now to restore your network connection.

Setting Up Dynamic IP Addresses

Assigning networking configuration information, such as the IP, router, and DNS address, for every computer can be tedious and time-consuming, especially for mobile hosts. For this reason, a protocol was created to simplify the configuration of hosts; it is called Dynamic Host Configuration Protocol (DHCP). DHCP allows the dynamic assignment of host configuration information to hosts as they come on the network. Instead of manually entering a static IP address, a computer can be assigned a dynamic IP address either by a DHCP server or by self-assigning a link-local address if no DHCP server can be found on the network.

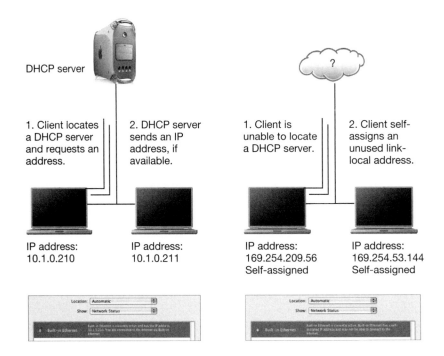

Using DHCP

Choosing Configure IPv4 > Using DHCP requests network configuration information from a DHCP server. This server assigns unique addresses to each Mac from a range of available addresses. In addition to the IP address, the router (gateway) address, the DNS server addresses, and the subnet mask can be configured by the DHCP server. The administrator decides how much information is supplied by the DHCP server. The setting "Using DHCP with manual IP address" allows you to receive configuration information such as router and DNS servers, while using a specific IP address that you assign manually.

Dynamic IP Address Assigned by DHCP Server

A server, such as a computer running Mac OS X Server, can provide DHCP services. Any computer or device configured to get a dynamic IP address will query the network for DHCP servers when it is connected. If present, the DHCP server responds, and after some additional communication, assigns the client computer an IP address, along with any other configuration information defined by the server administrator.

Self-Assigned Link-Local Address

DHCP servers work well, but sometimes you need to connect devices together on a network when no DHCP server is available. For example, you and a friend might have AirPort-equipped PowerBooks and just want to exchange some files. When you don't have a DHCP server on your network, devices and Mac OS X computers on your network can use self-assigned addressing to configure their own IP addresses.

In Network preferences, open the Network Status pane by choosing Show > Network Status. Network Status indicates when a computer is using a self-assigned address instead of receiving an address from a DHCP server. Self-assigned addresses begin with 169.254 and are known as link-local addresses.

> **NOTE** ▶ Link-local addresses are only assigned on active ports. A location in Network preferences will not request a DHCP address from a server or set a link-local address unless it is the active location.

DHCP Client ID

Some DHCP servers, such as those used by cable modem ISPs, require the computer to provide a client ID, an alphanumeric identifier for the computer. This identification is set in the DHCP Client ID field. A DHCP client ID can also be seen on the DHCP server, which makes it useful in managed environments to identify DHCP clients.

DHCP Lease

When you are assigned an address by a DHCP server, you are allowed a set amount of time to use that address, called a lease. During that time, the DHCP server will associate your Ethernet ID with an IP address so that your computer has a unique address. To reduce network traffic and server load, your computer will automatically request extensions to the lease, but only when the lease expires. If the lease expires, the DHCP server is free to assign that address to another computer. Clicking the Renew DHCP Lease button is a manual method to restart your lease time, or reconnect to a DHCP server that was temporarily unavailable.

> **NOTE ▸** A Mac OS X 10.4 computer receiving an address from a DHCP server retains that address until the lease expires. If a DHCP server is not available when you attempt to renew the lease, a link-local address will be used.

> **TIP ▸** Although DHCP does not guarantee what IP address your machine will have, you can access your machine on the local network using the local hostname, which will remain constant and always ends in .local. You set the local hostname in the Services pane of Sharing preferences.

Configuring BootP

If you choose Configure IPv4 > Using BootP, Mac OS X will obtain an IP address from a Bootstrap Protocol (BootP) server, similar to receiving an address from a DHCP server. However, unlike when using DHCP, a computer set to use BootP will receive the same address each time it requests one. BootP is rarely used, except for some managed networks.

PPP and AOL Dialup

When configuring TCP/IP for a modem port, the DHCP and BootP choices are
not available in the Configure IPv4 pop-up menu. Instead, the PPP and AOL
Dialup options are provided to use dynamic IP addresses provided by an ISP.

> **TIP** ▶ Always double-check TCP/IP changes by sampling a range of
> services. For example, after you make changes, check to see if you can use
> a web browser to access an external web page, then see if you can access a
> file server. (Accessing file servers is covered in Lesson 9, "Accessing Network
> Services.")

Using PPPoE

If you are using an Ethernet connection to a Digital Subscriber Line (DSL)
modem, PPPoE may be required by your ISP. With an Ethernet port chosen in
the Show pop-up menu, configure the account name and password in the PPPoE
pane. You can configure additional PPPoE options by clicking the PPPoE Options
button. You can also choose to display the PPPoE status in the menu bar.

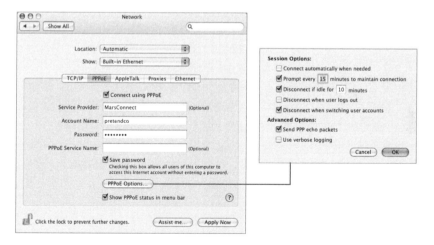

Just as with PPP, you can also use Internet Connect to establish the connection
to the ISP as well as enter the account information.

NOTE ► When PPPoE is configured on the Ethernet port, AppleTalk is disabled.

Using AppleTalk

The default network protocol in Mac OS X is TCP/IP. AppleTalk is disabled by default, but may be enabled to support AppleTalk printers on an AppleTalk network. While AppleTalk was used extensively in Mac OS 9 and earlier, TCP/IP is preferred in Mac OS X because it is nonproprietary and works well with other platforms. However, TCP/IP and AppleTalk are not exclusive and can be active at the same time.

NOTE ► AppleTalk can be enabled on only one port at a time. If you enable AppleTalk on a second port, AppleTalk will be automatically disabled on the first port.

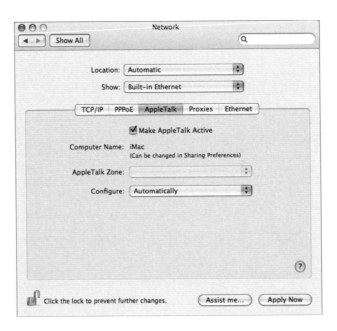

You can configure the AppleTalk protocol for an Ethernet or AirPort network port in the AppleTalk pane. The AppleTalk computer name is listed and you can select the AppleTalk zone if one is available. You can also configure the AppleTalk node ID and network ID manually, using the Configure pop-up menu. You can also enable AppleTalk by browsing for an AppleTalk printer in Printer Setup Utility.

> **NOTE ▶** If AppleTalk is enabled on AirPort instead of Built-in Ethernet, you won't be able to locate any AppleTalk printers on the Ethernet network. If you are having problems locating a network printer, check to see if AppleTalk is enabled on the highest-priority network port. You can also use the AppleTalk pane in Network Utility to test AppleTalk connectivity.

> **NOTE ▶** While Mac OS X 10.4 supports AppleTalk for discovering Apple Filing Protocol (AFP) servers, TCP/IP must be enabled for the connection to occur. Mounting AFP servers over AppleTalk is no longer supported. If you discover an AFP server via AppleTalk and double-click it, Mac OS X will automatically make the connection via TCP/IP. AFP servers are discussed in Lesson 9, "Accessing Network Services."

Using Proxies

All network port configurations have a Proxies pane. In this pane, you can configure Mac OS X to use any proxy servers that might be in use on the network interface. A proxy server is a host computer that acts as an intermediary between a computer user and the Internet. In this way, an enterprise can ensure security by limiting access to specific domains and can provide administrative control and caching services. Proxy servers are popular because the caching services can significantly reduce Internet traffic, especially for high-traffic sites and sites with large graphic files.

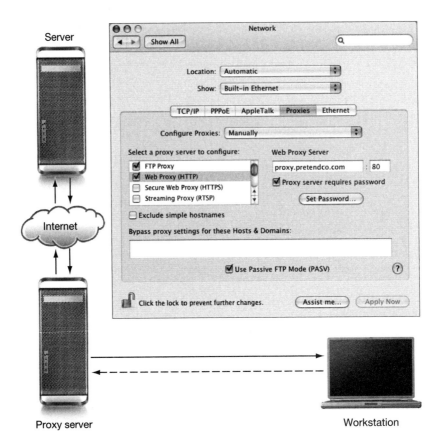

In a proxy configuration, requests for information—such as web pages or lists of files—are sent to the proxy server. The proxy server checks the request against a database of restricted servers and, if approved, forwards that request to the server that has the information you are requesting. When the request is answered, the proxy server receives the information, checks it against a database of restricted content, caches the content for later use, and passes the information to the requesting workstation. Subsequent requests for the same information are answered with the cached content on the proxy server.

Proxies can be configured for file transfers using FTP, Gopher, the SOCKS Firewall protocol (which checks information while hiding the IP address of the client), the Real Time Streaming Protocol (RTSP) media streaming protocol (such as QuickTime streaming servers), Secure Web, or HyperText Transfer Protocol (HTTP).

In the Proxies pane of Network preferences, you select the checkboxes for the type of proxy servers to use. Once enabled, you specify the address of the proxy server. You can also specify a user name and password to use if a proxy server requires one for security reasons.

In the Proxies pane, you can configure FTP to use passive mode, which allows the client computer to make the data connection rather than the FTP server. You can also configure domains that you want to access directly, bypassing the proxy servers.

Using Ethernet

In most cases, Mac OS X correctly configures the Ethernet port to match the network configuration. However, in some cases, you may be required to manually override these settings. When Manually (Advanced) is chosen from the Configure pop-up menu in the Ethernet pane of Network preferences, you can specify the speed, duplex, and packet size used when communicating via the Ethernet port.

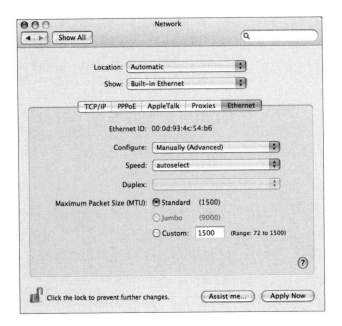

You may need to set a custom packet size when your broadband ISP adds packet overhead. Many DSL and cable modem ISPs add a few header bytes to packets, which can add a significant amount of packet traffic. If you are using the standard 1500-byte packet size, and your ISP adds six to eight bytes, the extra data must be sent in another packet. You may see performance improve if you reduce your packet size, because you will be sending fewer overflow packets.

NOTE ▶ You should only change these settings if instructed to do so by your network administrator, or if you are certain that you can undo any changes. Incorrect settings can prevent your computer from communicating properly, and can interfere with network devices or other computers on the network.

Using AirPort

AirPort has been a feature of Mac OS X since its introduction. AirPort is Apple's implementation of the industry standard 802.11b protocol, which provides 11 Mbit/s of bandwidth. AirPort Extreme is Apple's implementation of the 802.11g protocol, allowing more bandwidth (up to 54 Mbit/s) and advanced features such as bridging for extended range. AirPort and AirPort Extreme are cross-compatible, and can be used simultaneously, although AirPort Extreme (802.11g) devices making AirPort (802.11b) connections will communicate at the slower rate.

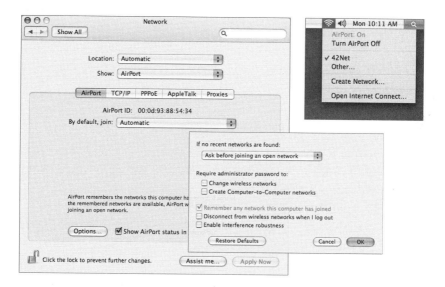

Because AirPort is a wireless implementation of Ethernet, an AirPort wireless port supports all of the same protocols as a wired Ethernet port. The AirPort pane is used to specify which AirPort network the computer should join, or if the computer is to create a new AirPort network. You can also set AirPort to automatically attempt a connection to any networks within range.

You can use a number of AirPort utilities when troubleshooting your AirPort connection. Mac OS X includes the AirPort Admin Utility for configuring your base station, as well as Internet Connect for checking the signal level from a base station. Additionally, the AirPort Extreme Base Station ships with the AirPort Management Utility, which is used to manage a number of AirPort devices, and the AirPort Client Monitor, which gives you performance statistics and connection status for your AirPort interface. For more information about AirPort troubleshooting and support, visit www.apple.com/support/airport.

AirPort uses industry-standard components and drivers, and is compatible with third-party base stations and most wireless access points, although third-party base stations are usually configured with software from the vendor. If you find that you cannot connect to a third-party device, you can use Network Diagnostics to test connectivity, but you might not be able to completely troubleshoot the third-party device.

Using a Modem

With a modem port chosen in Network preferences, you use the PPP pane to enter the phone numbers and PPP login information for your dialup connection. This information is normally included with the configuration information from your ISP. You can configure several modem ports, each with unique dialup and IP address configurations.

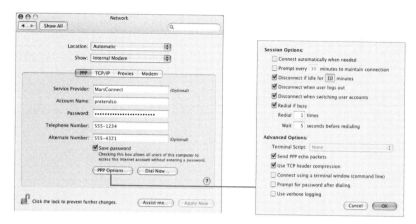

Click the PPP Options button to open a configuration sheet with many advanced options. You can configure PPP to connect automatically when starting a TCP/IP application, such as a web browser or mail application. You can also connect using a command-line interface.

You might not want to select the "Connect automatically when needed" checkbox. There are many daemons and background services running in BSD that may trigger an automatic connection, whether you want one or not. PPP connections can always be established manually by choosing Connect from the Modem menu extra or by clicking Connect in the Internet Connect utility.

In the Modem pane, you choose the type of modem your computer uses and set the preferences for it. The Modem pop-up menu contains a long list of Apple and third-party modems; to use the modem provided in most Macintosh computers, choose one of the Apple Internal 56K Modem varieties. You can opt to show the modem status in the menu bar.

> **NOTE ▶** If AOL software is installed, the options in the PPP and Modem panes are inactive, because connection settings and modem configuration are handled through AOL's software.

Configuring Virtual Ports

Not all ports listed in Network preferences are associated with a hardware interface. Some listed ports may be virtual ports, which take network data and reroute it through another physical port. Internet Connect can create two virtual ports: Virtual Private Networks and 802.1X.

Virtual Private Networks (VPNs)

Mac OS X supports VPN technology, which lets IP traffic travel securely over a public TCP/IP network using tunneling to encrypt data between the client system and host network.

Mac OS X supports two VPN protocols over an existing Internet connection: Point-to-Point Tunneling Protocol (PPTP) and Layer Two Tunneling Protocol (L2TP) over IP Security (IPSec).

The PPTP protocol supports client-to-gateway and network-to-network connections. L2TP over IPSec supports network-to-network connections only and offers strong authentication using IPSec, Microsoft Challenge-Handshake Authentication Protocol (CHAP), or third-party solutions such as SecurID.

To configure your computer to connect to a VPN, follow these steps:

1   Obtain the VPN configuration and connection settings from your system administrator.

2   Configure VPN connection settings in Internet Connect (/Applications).

3   Configure the TCP/IP and Proxies VPN settings in the VPN pane of Network preferences.

To connect to a VPN server that implements the L2TP and PPTP standards, such as the VPN server that comes with Mac OS X Server, use Internet Connect. If the VPN server you want to connect to does not implement the L2TP and PPTP standards, you'll need to configure the appropriate TCP/IP settings in Network preferences and use special VPN client software to connect to the network.

VPN connections terminate if they are not kept active. For example, VPN is disconnected when switching between users using fast user switching.

802.1X

The Institute of Electrical and Electronics Engineers (IEEE) 802.1X standard is intended to enhance network security by requiring a user to authenticate before accessing the network. Currently, 802.1X is primarily used with wireless networks; however, it can also be implemented on a wired network. To configure in Internet Connect, begin by choosing File > New 802.1X Connection.

When a user attempts to access a network through an access point, such as an AirPort Base Station or an Ethernet switch that has 802.1X enabled, the user must provide identity information that the access point forwards to an authentication server. If the authentication server is able to validate the user, the access point allows normal access to the network.

Your network administrator provides a user name and password that you enter in the 802.1X pane in Internet Connect. If required, you can create multiple configurations, each with unique user information, allowing the computer to connect to different networks.

Creating and Choosing Locations

A *location* is a set of active network ports and configurations for the protocols on those ports. It is meant primarily as an organizational tool to manage connectivity.

From the Location submenu in the Apple menu, you can directly choose a location, and the network settings you have configured for that location will be activated. You can also use this submenu as an easy way to open Network preferences, where you can change configuration settings for the current location, and manage all of your configured Locations. The Automatic location is the default configuration that was created when the computer was originally set up.

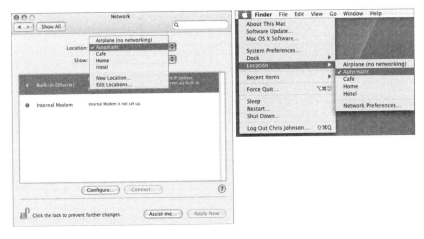

Any ports that are configured in a location are active when the location is chosen. For example, you could configure built-in Ethernet, a modem port, and AirPort in a "Traveling" location. If you choose the Traveling location when you're in a hotel room with no AirPort or Ethernet available, and you plug a phone cord into your modem, Mac OS X will use the modem port for its connections. If you travel where there is an AirPort network, Mac OS X will attempt to use AirPort first. If all ports are connected, Mac OS X determines the default path for network traffic based on the priority specified in the Network Port Configurations pane.

TIP ▶ When traveling, to eliminate electrical interference from your AirPort card, you should set up a "No Network" location that you can use on aircraft or in environments where electrical interference may be troublesome. Many devices now use the 2.4 GHz band to communicate, including some telephone handsets and foreign military communications. When in doubt, disable unneeded devices.

NOTE ▶ New in Mac OS X 10.4, AirPort no longer uses specific networks per location. AirPort now allows you to set the default option to join networks by selecting Automatic or Preferred Networks. Automatic is global across locations and remembers the networks this computer has joined. Preferred networks allows you to rank your wireless networks and will connect to the first available network on the list. See the AirPort pane of Network preferences for more information.

From the Location pop-up menu in Network preferences, you can choose a preconfigured location with network settings already in place. You can also use the Location menu to create new locations or edit existing ones. To create a new location, choose New Location from the Location pop-up menu, name the location, and click OK. The new location is listed in the Location pop-up menu. Changes made in Network preferences apply only to the location currently chosen in that menu.

TIP ▶ The Automatic network location is set up to work in most networking environments. Remember that Mac OS X can automatically switch ports, and will automatically prioritize its network connections to retain a valid connection. For this reason, when possible, users should rely on the Automatic location instead of creating a new network location for every place that the computer is used.

All network settings, including locations, are system-wide, meaning that any user can choose any location. However, while any user can choose among different locations, you need to authenticate as an administrator to make changes to the locations or to the network settings stored in a location. You authenticate by clicking the lock in the lower-left corner of Network preferences.

> **TIP** Whenever you are troubleshooting network settings, you should make a duplicate of the current network location before you modify any settings. This provides you with a backup of the settings that you can restore as needed.

Troubleshooting Network Issues

Troubleshooting network issues can be difficult because many times the problem is not local to your computer. You can break down network issues into three categories: those local to the computer, those with the network itself, and those with a network server being used.

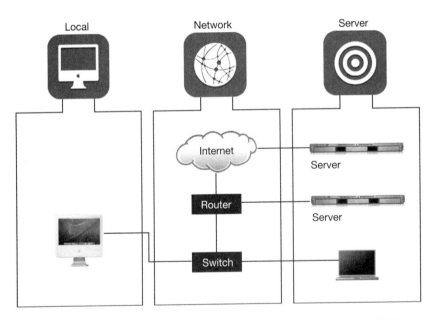

When troubleshooting, it's best to first consider local potential points of failure, then move outward because local issues are more likely to be under your control than issues with the WAN.

Local Issues

Check to make sure the settings in Network preferences are set correctly. The Network Status pane provides an overview of the enabled and active port configurations, allowing you to quickly determine which one is having problems.

Network Issues

You should be familiar with the physical topology of your network. Any computer, cable, switch, or router can be a point of failure. When troubleshooting a network, try to isolate the problem by eliminating points of failure. If a computer can reach other computers through switches and hubs, that connection indicates that the physical network is functioning properly. If not, try to work backwards and see if you can reach computers on the same subnet. If not, check your Ethernet cable, and then your Ethernet card to make sure they're functioning properly.

Server Issues

If you have determined that the problem is not local to the computer nor caused by the network, the problem is probably with the server that the user is attempting to use. The server might not be configured correctly or might be down completely.

Through good troubleshooting techniques, you should be able to isolate the cause of the problem. If it is with the network or the server, you might not be able to fix the network or server problem, but you should eliminate local factors before escalating.

Using Network Diagnostics

New in Mac OS X 10.4 is the Network Diagnostics utility that guides you through troubleshooting common networking issues. Some networking applications, such as Safari and Mail, will automatically open Network Diagnostics when they encounter a networking issue. You can open it manually by clicking the "Assist me" button at the bottom of Network preferences, then clicking Diagnostics. You can also open Network Diagnostics in the Finder (/System/Library/CoreServices).

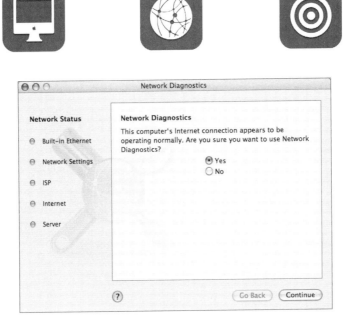

Network Diagnostics automatically runs tests to determine where the problem might be occurring. The results of the tests are displayed as colored indicators on the left side of the window. These indicators will help you determine if the problem is with the local configuration, the network, or possibly a server.

The right side of the screen presents simple questions to diagnose network issues. Based on your answers, it performs additional tests and suggests steps that can be taken to try to resolve the problem. For example, if a user has never connected to the Internet before, it will suggest opening Network Setup Assistant to guide the user through setting up the network. If the computer is connected to a DSL or cable modem, Network Diagnostics might suggest restarting the modem.

Monitoring Network Status

The state of network connections is not static. As connections become active, such as when a PowerBook with AirPort moves within range of a base station, or inactive, such as when an Ethernet cable is unplugged, Mac OS X reconfigures and reprioritizes the network settings to reflect the changes.

You can get a quick overview of the network connection status of your computer by opening Network preferences, which defaults to the Network Status pane. Network Status displays a list of all the currently available port configurations if they are enabled (such as Ethernet, PPTP, VPN, and AirPort). Colored indicators show the activity status of each available port configuration:

▶ Green — The port configuration is active and has been assigned an IP address, either manually or by a DHCP server.

▶ Yellow — The port configuration is active but may not be able to connect to the Internet.

▶ Red — The port configuration is not active.

In addition to colors, the Network Status pane displays a message next to each configuration in the list describing the port configuration's status.

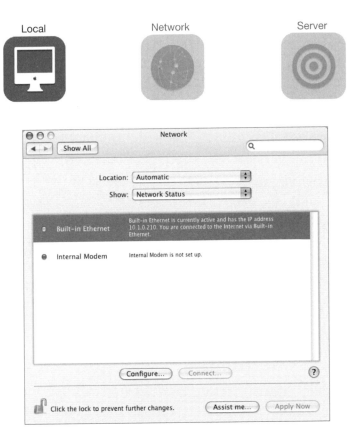

Starting in Mac OS X 10.3.4, Network Status only displays AirPort and Ethernet ports that are both active and enabled. If an enabled AirPort or Ethernet port becomes inactive, such as when an Ethernet cable is unplugged, the message displayed in Network Status announces the problem. After the message displays for a few seconds, the now-inactive port configuration disappears from Network Status. This feature is handy when you're trying to troubleshoot network problems. A quick look at the Network Status pane shows you which ports are active and configured correctly so that you can focus your diagnostic time.

To configure a port, you can select a port and click the Configure button, or choose the port from the Show menu. Choose Show > Network Port Configurations to enable or disable a port configuration.

If a VPN or Modem port is not connected, select the port and click Connect to launch Internet Connect so that you can connect to a network. For example, if you have configured your modem settings in Network preferences but are not connected, select the modem entry and click the Connect button in the Network Status pane. When Internet Connect launches, click the modem's Connect button to connect to your ISP.

Using the Network Status Pane to Monitor Connectivity

To make the most of this lesson, you should have access to a Mac OS X 10.4 computer on a network. Ideally, the network provides Internet access, not just local file and printer sharing services. The exercises in this lesson explain how to set up such a computer, but it's not imperative that you actually do so. You should be able to follow along by reading the step-by-step instructions and examining the screen shots.

The Network Status pane in Network preferences provides a quick overview of the status of each of the enabled network interfaces in order of priority.

1   Open Network preferences.

2   Choose Show > Network Status.

The Network Status pane lists each of the enabled network interfaces and the status of each one.

Assuming you are properly connected to an Ethernet network, the indicator next to Built-in Ethernet should be green, indicating that the interface is active and has an IP address assigned to it.

3   Unplug the Ethernet connector from your computer.

Notice that the indicator in the Network Status pane has changed to red, and the status text states that the cable is not plugged in. After a few seconds the now-inactive port disappears from the list.

If your Ethernet cable is plugged in to an inactive port, for example on a switch that is broken or unplugged, you will see similar behavior.

4   Plug the Ethernet connector back into your computer.

Notice that the indicator in the Network Status pane returns to green.

Using Network Utility

If you have trouble accessing the network, it is important to double-check that all the information you entered earlier in the Network pane is correct. Verify that you have a valid IP address and subnet mask and that the DNS entry is correct. An IP address that starts with 169.254 is self-assigned by Bonjour, which may not be what you wanted.

Network Utility (/Applications/Utilities) is a very valuable tool for testing network connectivity. You can use it to view network information and test network connectivity using commands such as Ping, Lookup, and Traceroute. The Info pane of Network Utility shows a quick interface overview. The left side has details about the interface itself, such as its MAC address, the assigned IP address, and its link speed. The right side shows packet transmission statistics.

Local

 Network

 Server

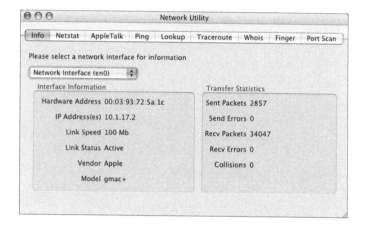

NOTE ▸ Some servers are configured to ignore particular types of network packets, and some may not identify themselves. Also, routers may not pass certain types of packets. If you think a server or router is configured in this way, contact your network administrator or the owner of the server.

If you notice a high number of send, receive, or collision errors, try resetting your network interface or the devices connected to it. For example, if you are using a DSL or cable modem, turn it off, wait a few seconds, and then turn it back on.

NOTE ▶ Networking is enabled when booted from the Mac OS X Install DVD. By choosing Network Utility or Terminal from the Utilities menu, you can use the disc to troubleshoot network problems that may be a result of how your system is configured.

The rest of this lesson will consider the troubleshooting commands Ping, Lookup, Traceroute, and Port Scan. Network Utility has four other tools that are not necessarily concerned with troubleshooting:

▶ Netstat — An advanced command that system administrators use to monitor the network activity of their machines and the network.

▶ AppleTalk — Provides details and statistics for local and network AppleTalk configurations.

▶ Whois — Used to find out the registrant of a particular domain name.

▶ Finger — Used to get information about users on UNIX-based machines.

Ping

Ping, one of the tools in Network Utility, sends signals (packets) to a network interface to see if the computer responds, or echoes. If all the signals time out, the computer might be disconnected from the network, set to ignore ping packets, or unreachable from your computer.

Ping is often used to isolate a networking issue. Try pinging the server using its IP address. If that works, you've established that the server is up and your computer is able to reach it via the network. Use ping with the server's domain name to find out if DNS is working correctly. The following output shows using Ping in this manner:

```
Ping has started ...
PING 10.1.0.1 (10.1.0.1): 56 data bytes
64 bytes from 10.1.0.1: icmp_seq=0 ttl=64 time=0.410 ms
64 bytes from 10.1.0.1: icmp_seq=1 ttl=64 time=0.323 ms
64 bytes from 10.1.0.1: icmp_seq=2 ttl=64 time=0.363 ms
Ping has started ...
PING mainserver.pretendco.com (10.1.0.1): 56 data bytes
64 bytes from 10.1.0.1: icmp_seq=0 ttl=64 time=0.637 ms
64 bytes from 10.1.0.1: icmp_seq=1 ttl=64 time=0.314 ms
64 bytes from 10.1.0.1: icmp_seq=2 ttl=64 time=0.366 ms
```

If you are unable to ping the server, try pinging another computer that is nearby on the network to isolate if the problem is with your local network or router settings. If this works, check to make sure your Router entry in Network preferences is set correctly. See if another computer is able to ping the server.

Keep in mind that ping tests very basic network connectivity. Even if you can ping a server, its services may be blocked by a firewall, or the service may be turned off or misconfigured on the server.

Determining System Accessibility on an IP Network

This exercise walks you through the steps required to determine whether a machine is reachable on a given IP network. It assumes that your computer is properly configured for Internet access.

1   Open Network Utility.

2   Click Ping.

3   In the "Please enter the network address to ping" field, enter *www.apple.com*.

4   Select Send only and set it to 2 pings.

5   Click Ping.

    You should see information regarding the packets returned by Apple's server.

6   Scroll to the end of the results list.

7   Record the min/avg/max round-trip latency times that give you an indication as to how long it took for the server to respond, in milliseconds.

8   In the "Please enter the network address to ping" field, enter *www.apple.com.au* which is Apple's Australian server.

9   Click Ping.

    If you are physically closer to Apple's main server in the United States, it shouldn't surprise you that the latency times are higher for Apple's Australian server.

Looking Up Internet Addresses

A frequent problem is that a particular server could not be found. This could be caused by DNS problems: either the computer is configured with invalid DNS addresses, or the DNS server is not functioning correctly.

Local

Network

Server

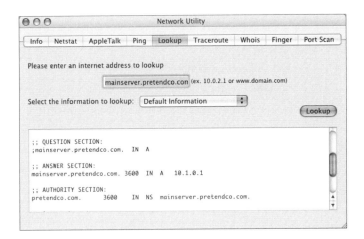

You can use the Lookup pane in Network Utility to help determine if you are accessing a valid DNS server or to determine the IP address for a given domain name. You can query the DNS server using Network Utility to convert a numerical IP address to a domain name or to convert a domain name into a numerical IP address, but the results may not always be accurate, because Lookup depends upon the server's configuration. If the server configuration is wrong, Lookup will return incorrect information. You can also specify which information to look up, such as the mail records in the DNS server and so on. A sample of Lookup output is as follows:

```
Lookup has started ...
; <<>> DiG 9.2.2 <<>> mainserver.pretendco.com
;; global options: printcmd
;; Got answer:
;; ->>HEADER<<- opcode: QUERY, status: NOERROR, id: 50843
;; flags: qr aa rd ra; QUERY: 1, ANSWER: 1, AUTHORITY: 1, ADDITIONAL: 0
;; QUESTION SECTION:
```

```
;mainserver.pretendco.com.INA
;; ANSWER SECTION:
mainserver.pretendco.com. 3600INA10.1.0.1
;; AUTHORITY SECTION:
pretendco.com.3600INNSmainserver.pretendco.com.
;; Query time: 4 msec
;; SERVER: 10.1.0.1#53(10.1.0.1)
;; WHEN: Thu Mar 31 15:05:56 2005
;; MSG SIZE rcvd: 72
```

Using Lookup to Verify DNS Is Set Properly

Here you will use the Lookup tool in Network Utility to compare known IP addresses to their domain names.

1   In Network Utility, click the Lookup button.

2   Enter Apple's domain:

www.apple.com

3   Click Lookup.

You should see the IP address for Apple in the lower window.

DNS also keeps track of mail records and aliases. You can get this information by choosing the different types of options from the "Select the information to lookup" pop-up menu.

Tracing Routes

The Traceroute command in Network Utility traces the route through an IP network from your computer to the destination computer and shows the hop count, or the number of trips a packet took from one router or network device to another, needed to make the journey. This information is useful in determining where network delays are occurring.

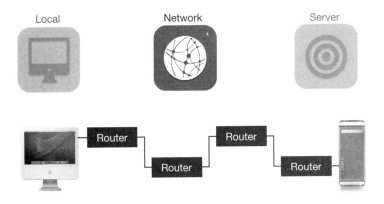

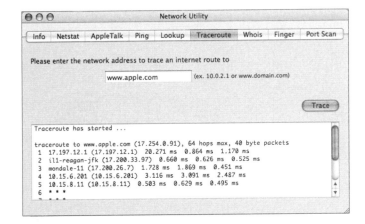

The output should look like this:

traceroute to www.apple.com (17.254.0.91), 64 hops max, 40 byte packets

1 17.197.12.1 (17.197.12.1) 20.271 ms 0.864 ms 1.170 ms

2 il1-reagan-jfk (17.200.33.97) 0.660 ms 0.626 ms 0.525 ms

3 mondale-11 (17.200.26.7) 1.728 ms 1.869 ms 0.451 ms

Each line represents a network hop on the way to the destination. The numbers at the beginning of the line indicate the order in which the hops were traversed. The time in milliseconds indicates the time it took for the network device to respond.

NOTE ▶ Not all routers display the comprehensive network route demonstrated here, as this is optional information for the router to return to a client requesting a traceroute. It is common to see certain portions of the trace turn up with no data, because some administrators configure their routers not to pass this data back to the client.

Scanning Ports

Port Scan displays a list of open IP ports on a targeted computer. Port Scan is mainly used for security reasons. However, it can also be useful in troubleshooting. For example, if you are trying to connect to a web server without success, you can scan the open ports on the web server and ensure that the machine is running, and more importantly, that port 80, the HTTP port, is open. You can also do this with the FTP ports when trying to connect to an FTP server, or the NFS port, and so on.

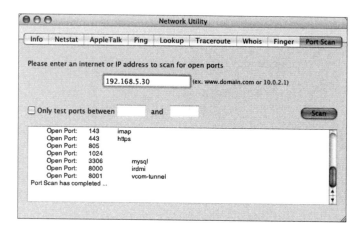

The output of Port Scan should look something like this:

```
Port Scanning host: 192.168.5.30
Open Port: 21 ftp
Open Port: 139 netbios-ssn
Open Port: 427 svrloc
Open Port: 515 printer, spooler
Open Port: 548 afpovertcp
Open Port: 660
```

If Port Scan recognizes the use of the port, it will tell you what the port is being used for. The example above shows that port 21 is being used for FTP.

NOTE ▶ Port Scan may look like a port attack to a system administrator. Do not use it to probe other computers without first notifying the system administrator. Otherwise, you may find yourself the recipient of a visit from your company security department or a flustered system administrator, even though you were only using the command for troubleshooting purposes.

Determining the Open Ports on a System Connected to the Network

In this exercise, you will use Port Scan to determine the open ports on a computer. You will need two Macintosh computers on the same local network.

1 On one computer, open Sharing preferences.

2 Click Services.

3 Note which services, if any, are already turned on.

4 Turn on all services.

5 Note the computer's local subnet address at the top of the window.

6 On the other computer, open Network Utility.

7 Click the Port Scan button.

8   In the IP address field, enter the other computer's local subnet address noted in step 5.

9   Click Scan.

This scan may take a few minutes.

10 Review the ports that are open.

Port 21 is the FTP port, so if you want to test whether a machine is running an FTP server, you can run Port Scan on it and test whether port 21 is open or not. HTTP uses port 80, and HTTPS uses port 443.

NOTE ▶ You cannot scan the open ports on the system that you are using. You have to use Netstat to identify the open ports on your current system.

11 Quit Network Utility.

12 On the other computer, turn off all services that weren't originally on in Sharing preferences.

13 Quit System Preferences.

Common Networking Issues

Even though the number of dialup modem users is decreasing, they still make up a large percentage of home users and mobile users. When assisting those users, verify that the dialup account is still active. Because many ISPs provide a trial account, users frequently mistakenly try to use an expired account.

If you are using a modem, double-check the PPP settings in Network preferences. The account password may be incorrect or the phone number may no longer be valid. If using a DSL or cable modem, try restarting the modem. Sometimes a cable or DSL modem will become unresponsive and the simplest method for resetting it is to turn the modem off, wait a few seconds, and then turn it on. This may also fix a known problem where some cable modems only recognize the first MAC address that is connected to their network port.

NOTE ▶ If you have a cable modem directly connected to your Macintosh, then add an AirPort Base Station to your home network, you would disconnect the Ethernet cable from your computer and attach it to the WAN port on the AirPort Base Station. In that situation, the cable modem may not recognize the AirPort Base Station (which has a different MAC address than your Macintosh). In this case, power cycle the cable modem, then connect it via Ethernet to the WAN port of your AirPort Base Station, configure the AirPort Base Station to authenticate with your cable ISP, and set your Macintosh to use the wireless connection.

NOTE ▶ If your DSL or cable modem connection lights indicate a valid ISP connection, but the modem is not supplying an address to your computer, try shutting off the modem and disconnecting its power for several minutes. This clears its list of local MAC addresses and forces it to reconnect to your computer as well as to the ISP.

If there is a router between the DSL or cable modem and the computer, make sure the router has all of the correct ISP settings. A common problem with broadband connections is for a user to change the password for their ISP account and update their mail application, but forget to update the router settings. Because the password is only used while establishing a connection, the user might not immediately experience any problems. A router in this context is any device, such as an AirPort Extreme Base Station, which retains the ISP user name and password.

TIP ▶ When troubleshooting connection issues with DSL and cable modems, and a router is connected, try validating the ISP connection with a computer connected directly to the modem. This helps eliminates any issues that could be caused by a misconfigured router. Some ISPs will not provide assistance if there is a router connected.

If you are having difficulty accessing a network service such as FTP, it might be blocked by Mac OS X's built-in firewall. If the firewall is turned on in Sharing preferences, turn it off and see if you are able to access the service in question. You will learn more about turning on and configuring the personal firewall in Lesson 10, "Providing Network Services."

What You've Learned

▶ You need to understand the basics of IP networking to be able to configure and troubleshoot IP networks.

▶ In Mac OS X, simple networking configuration is done with the Network Setup Assistant. Additional configuration is done in Network preferences.

▶ AppleTalk is no longer enabled by default. AppleTalk also has changed in Mac OS X 10.4, in that it is now used only for printers and not for AFP file services.

▶ A proxy server can significantly reduce your Internet traffic for commonly-used sites or for sites with large graphic files.

▶ To effectively troubleshoot your IP network, you need to be familiar with the network topology.

▶ Mac OS X provides you with a set of network tools that can help you in troubleshooting. These tools (Ping, Lookup, Traceroute, and Port Scan) are in Network Utility (/Applications/Utilities).

▶ You can use Network Utility or Terminal from the Mac OS X Install DVD to troubleshoot local, network, and server problems.

References

The following Knowledge Base documents (located at www.apple.com/support) will provide you with further information regarding network configuration in Mac OS X.

Cable Modem/DSL/LAN

▶ 106747, "Mac OS X: Troubleshooting a PPPoE Internet Connection"

▶ 106749, "Mac OS X: Troubleshooting a cable modem, DSL, or LAN Internet connection"

Dial-Up/PPP

▶ 106748, "Mac OS X: Troubleshooting a dial-up/PPP Internet connection"

Internet and Networking

▶ 25270, "Mac OS X: Do Not Use Leading Zeros in IP Address"

▶ 106260, "Your computer's name does not appear on the network"

▶ 106439, "'Well Known' TCP and UDP Ports Used By Apple Software Products"

▶ 106796, "Mac OS X: Connect to the Internet, troubleshoot your Internet connection, and set up a small network"

▶ 106797, "Mac OS X: Slow Startup, Pauses at 'Initializing network' or 'Configuring network time'"

Network Utility

▶ 61426, "Mac OS X: About Network Utility"

Modem

▶ 24803, "Troubleshooting Phone Line Issues That Affect Modem Connections"

▶ 106446, "Mac OS X: Apple System Profiler Modem Information Incorrect or Missing"

▶ 106447, "Mac OS X: How to Gather Modem Troubleshooting Information"

Lesson Review

Use the following questions to review what you have learned:

1. Where do you configure network settings in Mac OS X?

2. What is the difference between static and dynamic IP addressing?

3. List four tools in Network Utility that are used for troubleshooting.

4. How does Ping work?

5. What does Traceroute do and how is it useful?

6. How can you use Port Scan for troubleshooting?

Answers

1. Basic network configuration can be done using the Network Setup
    Assistant. Additional or advanced configuration is done in Network pref-
    erences. Configuration and connection to remote networks through PPP,
    PPPoE, and VPN is done with Internet Connect.

2. Static IP addresses are those that are manually set in Network preferences.
    The computer always uses the same address. Dynamic addresses are those
    that are either assigned by a DHCP server, or when a DHCP server is
    unavailable, created by the computer. Unlike static addresses, a dynamic
    address is not permanent and will change.

3. Ping, Lookup, Traceroute, and Port Scan aid in troubleshooting.

4. Ping sends signals to another computer on the Internet to see if that com-
    puter echoes.

5. Traceroute traces the route through the Internet from your computer to
    the destination computer and shows the number of hops needed to make
    the journey. This is useful in determining where any network delays are
    occurring.

6. You can use Port Scan to determine if certain ports that should be open
    are in fact open.

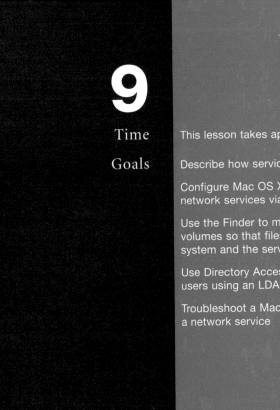

9

Time

Goals

This lesson takes approximately 1 hour to complete.

Describe how service discovery is implemented in Mac OS X

Configure Mac OS X using Directory Access to access network services via AppleTalk, SMB, SLP, and Bonjour

Use the Finder to mount remote AFP, SMB, FTP, and WebDAV volumes so that files can be transferred between the local system and the server volume

Use Directory Access to configure Mac OS X to authenticate users using an LDAP or Active Directory server

Troubleshoot a Mac OS X computer that is not able to access a network service

Lesson 9
Accessing Network Services

In Lesson 8, "Networking Configuration and Troubleshooting," you learned how to configure a Mac OS X computer for network access, connect to a network, and troubleshoot networking issues.

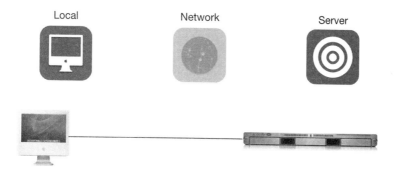

Once your connection to the network is established, you are ready to access network services. This lesson addresses what's needed to access and troubleshoot connections to any network service, with specific attention to:

▶ General services such as web and mail — Available to anyone with an Internet account

▶ File services — Typically found within an organization

▶ Directory services — Also typically found within an organization

To access a service on another computer on your network, you must find the service, make the connection, and prove your identity. In the past, finding out where to connect was often haphazard and inefficient. Users had to get information from their system administrator or from other users, store it somewhere, and then remember where they stored the information when they wanted to connect. Today, computer software does most of that work for you, especially in Mac OS X. Most of the time, you can browse a list of available servers.

Connecting to a service is also easy in Mac OS X. In most cases, you make a selection from a list and click. In a few cases, you might have to enter a computer name or address.

Most network services require that you prove you are who you say you are, or *authenticate*, typically by providing a password. Mac OS X helps you manage your passwords so that you don't have to enter them over and over again, and also uses modern security methods to protect computers against unauthorized access.

Understanding Basic Requirements for Accessing Network Services

There are two basic requirements for accessing any network service:

▶ Correct client-side software for accessing the network service

▶ Correct configuration settings for your client-side software

Understanding that there is a direct relationship between the client side and the server side of any network service will help troubleshoot accessing that service. Just as a service is basically an application running on a network server, your client needs similar software that understands how to access that service. In some cases, such as accessing mail, the client software is an application. In other cases, such as file servers, the client software is integrated into the operating system.

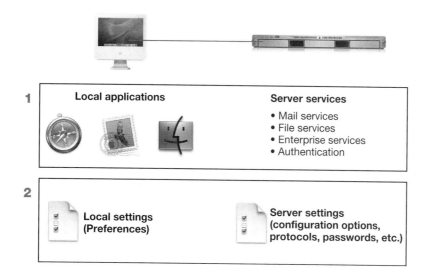

A network or server administrator might have spent days, weeks, or months properly architecting, configuring, and administering the network service, such as choosing the correct options and protocols that the service will use. This process has a counterpart on the client where a user or administrator needs to make sure the client software is also configured properly. Having a simple mismatch of settings, such as which mail protocol is used or which server address to access, can easily prevent users from accessing a network service.

Accessing Internet Services

Mac OS X includes support for accessing a wide variety of Internet services, including web, email, online chatting, and streaming media servers.

Each of these services requires a client application to access the service. While Mac OS X includes client applications for these services, you are not restricted to using them. You may prefer to use an alternative application developed by a third party. Sometimes, while troubleshooting, using a third-party application is a great way to determine if a problem is specific to a single application.

Using Safari for Web Browsing

Because there is almost no configuration required to access websites, most web-related issues are caused by a network configuration error, an incorrect website address, or a website code that isn't compatible with the browser being used. If you can't access a website, try accessing a different website, and then try accessing the problem website from a different computer. This will help determine if the problem is network-related.

> **NOTE ▶** Typically, you won't need to specially configure a web browser. However, you might need to configure a browser when using proxy servers or enabling support for cookies, Java, JavaScript, or other web plug-ins.

Web communication is done through the HTTP protocol. To interpret and display the results of the HTTP data, Mac OS X includes a web browser called Safari. While HTTP is a standard, not all websites and browsers follow the standard in the exact same way. Some popular browsers include features that are not part of the standard, and some websites will try to take advantage of those features. Unfortunately, this causes problems for people using other browsers. If you encounter a site where some web pages are partially displayed, or some buttons don't function, try a different web browser, such as Internet Explorer, Firefox, or OmniWeb.

> **NOTE ▶** If you encounter a website that does not display correctly with Safari, choose Safari > Report Bugs to Apple. If you have access to another browser, you can try using it to see if the problem is browser-specific.

Chatting with iChat AV

In addition to textual chatting, the version of iChat AV included with Mac OS X 10.4 allows you to participate in video conferences with up to three other users and in audio conferences with a maximum of nine other users. (Earlier versions of iChat also supported conferences, but with fewer users.) In most cases, iChat AV uses AOL Instant Messaging (AIM) to locate and communicate with other users. An organization may decide, however, to set up a chat server within their firewall using Mac OS X Server 10.4. This allows much more secure communications, because most chat messages are sent as clear text on the network and can be read by others.

Setting up a chat server is beyond the scope of this course, but there are other Apple certification-track courses that address that topic. Visit www.apple.com/training for details.

Troubleshooting with Network Diagnostics

New in Mac OS X 10.4, Network Diagnostics is designed to check your network setup and ensure that your network connection is working properly. Network Diagnostics includes the following features to help you troubleshoot network issues:

▶ It is used by Safari, Mail, iChat, and QuickTime Player. If those applications encounter a network problem, you will automatically have the option to open Network Diagnostics.

▶ It provides a network status overview.

▶ It allows you to choose which active network interface to troubleshoot.

▶ It detects network changes interactively.

Network Diagnostics can be launched manually by clicking "Assist me" in Network preferences, or by opening the application in /System/Library/CoreServices.

NOTE ▶ While Network Diagnostics can isolate a network problem, it does not address "configuration" problems, such as an incorrect setting in an application's preferences.

Troubleshooting Email with Mail Connection Doctor

As with web browsing, support for mail is not built into the operating system. Instead, Mac OS X includes the Mail application to allow you to access mail servers. This allows users the flexibility of selecting an alternative mail client application, if they choose.

The most common problem when accessing a mail server is misconfigured Mail application settings. While Mail includes an assistant to guide the user through account setup, the user typically must have all of the access settings for the server, including the server's address, the user's account name and password, and the authentication type. Mail is usually autoconfigured when .Mac accounts are added.

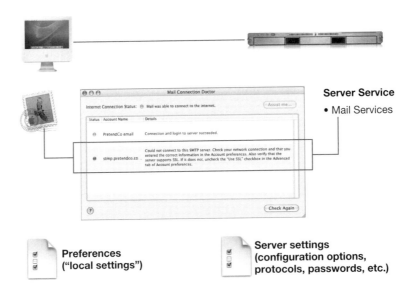

If you encounter a problem while attempting to establish a connection to either the incoming or outgoing mail servers, choose Window > Connection Doctor to get help diagnosing the problem. The status of your Internet connection appears near the top of the Mail Connection Doctor window. If Mail Connection Doctor detects an Internet access problem, you can click the "Assist me" button to open Network Diagnostics. (For more information, see

"Troubleshooting Network Issues" in Lesson 8, "Networking Configuration and Troubleshooting.") If Mail Connection Doctor is unable to access either the incoming or outgoing mail servers, you can double-click the server entry in the list to open the settings for that account.

> **NOTE** ▶ Earlier versions of Mail were unable to access mail accounts on some Microsoft Exchange servers, because Mail did not support NTLM authentication, and some Exchange servers only allowed NTLM authentication. The version of Mail included with Mac OS X 10.4 supports NTLM to access mail on NTLM-enabled servers.

Accessing File Services

One of the strengths of Mac OS X is its ability to easily access networked file services provided by a variety of different operating systems. In addition to accessing Mac OS X Server computers, Mac OS X is able to access files stored on Windows and UNIX file servers and allow applications to work with the files on the servers as easily as working with files stored on local volumes. This allows Mac OS X computers to be integrated into mixed-computer networks.

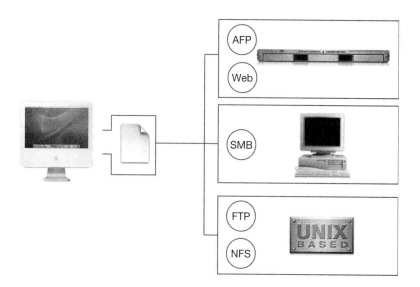

Using Connect to Server

The Finder is the primary application used to access files, including those stored on file servers. To connect to these servers, begin by choosing Go > Connect to Server (Command-K).

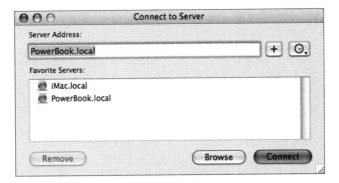

When you choose Connect to Server, the Finder prompts you for an address. You can use an IP address, DNS name, or local hostname for the server to which you want to connect. The prefix to the address tells Mac OS X which file sharing protocol to use. When you connect to a shared volume in this manner, the volume is mounted in /Volumes and appears on the desktop and in the Finder with other network and local volumes.

In addition to manually mounting a network volume, you can configure your user preferences to automatically mount a shared volume. Once the shared volume is mounted on the desktop, open Accounts preferences, select the user account, and click Login Items. The Login Items pane lists items that will open automatically when the user logs in (the list may be empty). Drag the icon for the shared volume from the Finder desktop into the list, and verify that the volume name is listed. The next time that user logs in, the volume will be mounted. (The user may be asked to authenticate if the password was not saved to the user's keychain when the volume was originally mounted.)

To unmount a shared volume, either drag it to the Trash (which changes to an Eject icon) or choose File > Eject (Command-E). Either action effectively breaks the connection with the shared resource.

If you are connected to a network volume and the server or network goes down, the volume will remain listed in the Finder. If you attempt to access an unreachable server, the spinning cursor will appear as the Finder attempts to reconnect to the server. If it is unsuccessful, it will remove (unmount) the volume.

Using Connect to Server, you can connect to the following types of servers:

- ► Apple Filing Protocol (AFP)
- ► Server Message Block (SMB)
- ► WebDAV
- ► Network File System (NFS)
- ► File Transfer Protocol (FTP)

The following sections explain how to connect to the various types of servers. Since few readers have access to a computer with all types of servers, you are not expected to actually perform these step-by-step instructions. Simply read along to understand the procedures.

Apple Filing Protocol (AFP)

The file sharing protocol most commonly used in Mac OS X is Apple Filing Protocol (AFP). This protocol allows you to mount volumes from computers running Mac OS 9 or earlier, as well as computers running Mac OS X.

These steps demonstrate the process of using Connect to Server to mount an AFP volume.

1   Choose Go > Connect to Server (Command-K).

    The Connect to Server window appears.

2   In the Server Address field, enter

    afp://

    followed by the server's IP address, DNS name, or local hostname, option- ally followed by a trailing slash.

NOTE ▶ Connect to Server assumes that you want an AFP volume if you do not specify a protocol.

3   Click Connect.

4   When prompted, specify that you want to connect as a registered user, then enter a user name and password for an account on the server.

NOTE ▶ If the account doesn't have a password, you won't be prompted for one.

5   Click Connect.

A list of shared volumes to which you have access appears.

6   Select the volumes you wish to mount (Shift-click to select more than one), then click OK.

The shared volumes appear in the Sidebar at the left of the Finder window.

NOTE ▶ Previous versions of Mac OS X supported AFP connections using AppleTalk networking, but Mac OS X 10.4 does not.

7   Select the mounted volume(s) and begin dragging them to the Trash.

As you begin to drag the volumes to the Trash, the Trash icon changes to the Eject icon. You can also eject volumes by selecting them and choosing File > Eject (Command-E) or by clicking the eject button next to the volume name in the Sidebar.

Server Message Block (SMB)

Another common file sharing protocol is Server Message Block (SMB). Computers running Microsoft Windows use this protocol to share files. Use it on Mac OS X to access files shared by computers running Windows.

These steps demonstrate the process of using Connect to Server to mount an SMB volume.

1 Choose Go > Connect to Server (Command-K).

The Connect to Server window appears.

2 In the Server Address field, enter

smb://

followed by the server's IP address, DNS name, or local hostname, optionally followed by a trailing slash.

> **NOTE ▶** When browsing for SMB servers in the Connect to Server brows-
> ing window on a network where DNS provides reverse lookups, the
> domain name will be displayed instead of the computer name. For details,
> refer to Knowledge Base document 107085, "Mac OS X 10.2: Expected,
> User-Defined Windows (SMB) Computer Name Does Not Appear in
> Connect to Server Dialog."

3 Click Connect.

The SMB Mount dialog appears.

A Connecting to Server status dialog also appears.

4 In the SMB dialog, from the "Select a share" pop-up menu, choose the
desired item.

Shared items are sometimes called *share points,* because you don't necessarily have to share an entire volume. You can choose to share only a particular folder on a volume, if you wish.

5 Click OK.

The SMB/CIFS (Common Internet File System) Filesystem Authentication
dialog appears.

6 Enter the workgroup/domain, user name, and password for an account on
the server.

The administrator of the Windows computer can provide you with the
name of the workgroup. The default name is WORKGROUP.

NOTE ▶ SMB won't let you log into an account without entering a password. For accounts with no password, the user can enter anything.

7   Click OK.

The shared volume appears in the Sidebar at the left of the Finder window.

NOTE ▶ New in Mac OS X 10.4 is the ability to authenticate to Windows servers using NT LAN Manager version 2 (NTLMv2). NTLMv2 provides the most secure way of authenticating for Windows computers and is the default authentication method on Windows Server 2003. Support for NTLMv2 from Mac OS X 10.4 means that Mac clients can connect to Windows servers without requiring a Windows administrator to enable a less secure authentication method for Mac clients.

WebDAV

WebDAV is an extension of the Hypertext Transfer Protocol (HTTP), typically used for editing web content. (This is the same protocol you use when you access pages on the web with a browser.) With WebDAV, however, you mount the website as a volume, and you can add and modify files as well as read them.

These steps demonstrate the process of using Connect to Server to mount a WebDAV volume.

1   Choose Go > Connect to Server (Command-K).

The Connect to Server window appears.

2   In the Server Address field, enter

http://

followed by the server's IP address, DNS name, or local hostname, optionally followed by a trailing slash.

3   Click Connect.

4   If a WebDAV File System Security Notice appears, click Continue.

5 If prompted, enter a user name and password for an account on the server, then click OK.

The shared volume appears in the Sidebar at the left of the Finder window.

NOTE ▶ New in Mac OS X 10.4 is the ability to connect to WebDAV servers using the secure HTTPS protocol. To connect to a secure WebDAV server, specify the address using the prefix https, such as: https://secureserver. pretendco.com. You can use Get Info to see if a volume is mounted via HTTPS by looking at the server URL under the General disclosure triangle.

Network File System (NFS)

NFS is the file sharing protocol used by most UNIX systems. NFS servers are not considered as secure as other file servers, such as AFP, because NFS authorizes access based on the computer's IP address, rather than prompting a user for a name and password. Because it is easy for a user to change a computer's IP address, it is extremely easy for a computer to pose as an authorized computer to gain access to the NFS server.

These steps demonstrate the process of using Connect to Server to mount an NFS volume.

1 Choose Go > Connect to Server (Command-K).

The Connect to Server window appears.

2 In the Server Address field, enter

nfs://

followed by the server's IP address, DNS name, or local hostname, optionally followed by a trailing slash.

3 Click Connect.

The shared volume appears in the Sidebar at the left of the Finder window.

File Transfer Protocol (FTP)

FTP is important primarily because it is widely used on the Internet for trans-ferring files. Most UNIX-like operating systems provide FTP services, and FTP clients are available for nearly every computer operating system; Mac OS X is no exception in either regard.

These steps demonstrate the process of using Connect to Server to mount an FTP volume.

1   Choose Go > Connect to Server (Command-K).

    The Connect to Server window appears.

2   In the Server Address field, enter

    ftp://

    followed by the server's IP address, DNS name, or local hostname, option-ally followed by a trailing slash.

3   Click Connect.

4   When prompted, enter a user name and password for an account on the server.

    NOTE ▶ FTP won't let you log in to an account without entering a pass-word. For accounts with no password, the user can enter anything. FTP transmits all data, including the user name and password, in the clear, and is not a secure method of exchange.

5   Click OK.

    The shared volume appears in the Sidebar at the left of the Finder window.

    NOTE ▶ In Mac OS X, you can download files after mounting an FTP volume using Connect to Server, but you cannot upload files over FTP using the Finder. Uploading files to an FTP server can be accomplished only with an FTP client such as Fetch (www.fetchsoftworks.com) or Transmit (www.panic.com).

Dealing with File Sharing Protocol Issues

Usually, the protocol you need to use is dictated by the server to which you are connecting. Even though you may not have a choice, you should be aware of issues that can arise when using the different protocols.

▶ Files with resource forks — As explained in Lesson 4, "File Systems," Mac OS X files can have a resource fork in addition to the traditional data fork. Just as non–Apple file systems such as UFS and FAT don't support files with resource forks, file sharing protocols other than AFP do not either. To compensate, Mac OS X will send the resource fork out as a separate file with a prefix of period and underscore (for example, ._TestFile.pdf), just as it does when writing to non-Apple file systems. Because Mac OS X handles the conversion between resource forks and ._ files automatically, you will not see the files in the Finder. However, users on other operating systems such as Windows will see two separate files.

▶ Windows servers — To provide file sharing for Macintosh clients, some administrators have configured Services for Macintosh (SFM) on their Windows NT servers to provide AFP access. Unfortunately, SFM does not provide full AFP 3.1 support. In addition to the problems managing resource forks, SFM is also limited to 65,000 files on a volume. Whenever possible, use a server that fully supports AFP 3.1, such as Mac OS X Server. For Windows servers, you can use third-party AFP servers such as Group Logic's ExtremeZ-IP (www.grouplogic.com).

Discovering File Services

Mac OS X automatically can find computers and other devices that offer services on the network. An application requests the names of available servers, which the operating system returns. The application, in turn, displays the list in a user-browsable format. This feature is known as *service discovery*.

One application that uses service discovery information is the Finder, which displays a list of computers you can connect to when you click Network in the Sidebar of a Finder window. You connect to a discovered resource by clicking

Connect under the volume icon (in column view) or double-clicking the volume icon. You will be prompted to authenticate with a user name and password of an account on the file sharing server.

While service discovery can be used by a variety of applications, such as Printer Setup Utility and iChat, this lesson will focus on using the Finder to discover file servers. Printer discovery will be covered later in Lesson 12, "Printing."

A network can be broken up into logical sections called zones. Usually zones are created to group-related networked resources, such as all of the servers and printers for the marketing department. Each zone is presented as a separate folder when you select the Network icon from the Sidebar in the Finder.

Understanding Dynamic Service Discovery

Dynamic service discovery protocols reflect the current state of the network, because they update whenever new services appear or disappear on the network. The protocols usually work without needing a dedicated server.

Mac OS X includes support for four dynamic service discovery protocols:

▶   Bonjour (previously called Rendezvous) is Apple's implementation of an emerging industry standard called Zeroconf. Bonjour provides service discovery functionality for IP-based networks using standard IP protocols. Bonjour is always enabled in Mac OS X 10.4.

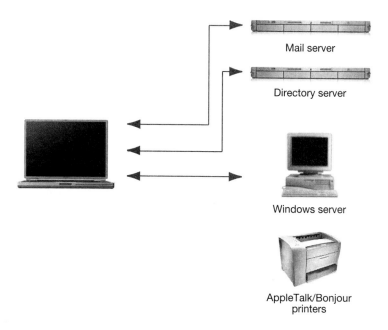

Mail server

Directory server

Windows server

AppleTalk/Bonjour
printers

▶ AppleTalk is the legacy Mac OS protocol for file and print services. Mac OS X 10.4 uses AppleTalk to discover file and print services, but no longer supports using AFP over AppleTalk to send or receive files.

▶ Service Location Protocol (SLP) was used for service discovery in earlier versions of Mac OS X. It has been superseded by Bonjour but is still supported.

▶ SMB, the file sharing protocol for Microsoft Windows computers, is a service discovery protocol for file and print services. It can be used as a hybrid system, with dynamic discovery on the local network and a server-based lookup for clients on nearby networks.

NOTE ▶ Because of its architecture, SMB clients can take several minutes to appear on the network.

Configuring Service Discovery

Service discovery in Mac OS X is provided by Open Directory. Directory Access (/Applications/Utilities) determines which directory services Open Directory uses and how it connects to specific directory domains. The Services pane of the Directory Access application enables you to select and configure the services that Mac OS X uses to obtain information, including the service discovery protocols.

To make changes to the service discovery protocols, you must first click the lock icon in the lower left and then authenticate by typing the name and password of an administrator. Then you can select the checkbox next to the protocol you want to enable or disable. Some services (Active Directory, BSD Flat File and NIS, LDAPv3, NetInfo, and SMB/CIFS) are configurable. You can tell a service is configurable if the Configure button becomes active when you select that service. You'll learn how to configure these services later in this lesson. When you have finished selecting and configuring service protocols, click Apply.

If you know that you don't need a particular protocol, you can disable it in Directory Access (Bonjour can't be disabled). If you disable a protocol, Open Directory does not use it for service discovery on the computer. However, other network services may still use the protocol. For example, if you disable the AppleTalk protocol in Directory Access, Printer Setup Utility can still use AppleTalk to browse for printers whether or not you've enabled AppleTalk in Network preferences.

Authenticating in Directory Access

Before you can make any changes in Directory Access, you must authenticate as an administrator user.

1   Open Directory Access (/Applications/Utilities).

2   Click Services.

    If you have not yet authenticated as an administrator user, the list of services is dimmed.

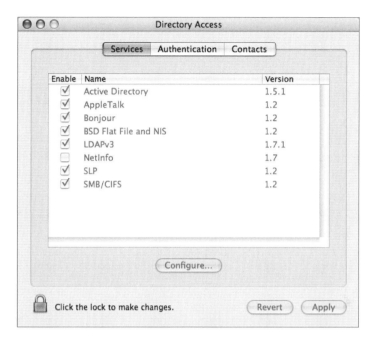

3   Click the lock icon in the lower-left corner. You will be prompted for a
user name and password.

4   Use your administrator user name and password and click OK.

The list entries are no longer dimmed, indicating that you are authenticated as an administrator capable of configuring the services.

Viewing Configuration Options

You can configure a variety of directory service options with Directory Access.
However, some of these directory service options are not configurable and can
only be enabled or disabled.

1   In the Services pane of the Directory Access window, select Bonjour.

Note that the Configure button is dimmed. This is because Bonjour has
no configuration options.

2   Select NetInfo.

Note that the Configure button is active for this service because it has configuration options.

3   Click Configure.

A configuration sheet appears.

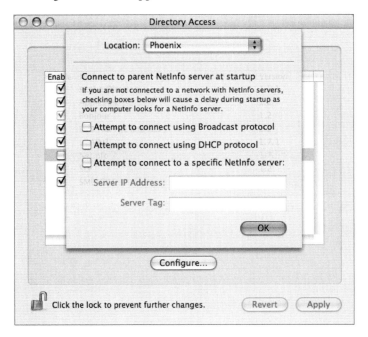

NOTE ▶ Depending upon your system configuration, your NetInfo settings may differ from the screen pictured.

4   Read the text on the configuration pane, then click OK.

5   Disable the NetInfo service.

6   Click SMB/CIFS.

Note that the Configure button is active.

7   Click Configure.

A configuration sheet appears. This allows you to enter the workgroup name and WINS server for SMB discovery.

You can configure your computer to use a specific WINS server for SMB service discovery. WINS is a Microsoft NetBIOS name server. WINS servers maintain a name-to-address mapping for networks of Windows computers, which reduces traffic on the network. If no WINS server is available to the client, names are looked up on a network through broadcasts.

8   Click Cancel unless you want to configure your computer to use SMB.

Troubleshooting Network Services

When troubleshooting network service problems, try the following strategies:

▶   If you are unable to locate other services, such as printers or file servers, on the network:

1.   Verify that Network preferences are correctly configured.

2.   Make sure that you have a working network connection.

3.   Use the network troubleshooting techniques covered in Lesson 8, "Networking Configuration and Troubleshooting," to verify that you have network connectivity from the computer to the server.

▶   Examine the log files located in /Library/Logs/DirectoryService. The two log files, DirectoryService.error.log and DirectoryService.server.log, will list which plug-ins loaded successfully and which ones failed.

▶   If you are able to browse AFP file services, but cannot connect, make sure TCP/IP is enabled on the primary network interface. AppleTalk is not supported for AFP networking in Mac OS X 10.4.

▶   If you are unable to browse for a Windows server, remember that you can only browse SMB servers that are on the same subnet. To connect to SMB servers outside the subnet, you need to provide the address of the server. Also, if an SMB server just started, it can take 10 minutes or more for it to be located on the network.

MORE INFO ▶ Refer to Microsoft's Knowledge Base document 188001, "Description of the Microsoft Computer Browser Service" (http://support.microsoft.com).

▶ When using the Finder's Connect to Server command to browse for SMB servers on a network where DNS provides reverse-lookups, the domain name will be displayed instead of the computer name.

MORE INFO ▶ Refer to Knowledge Base document 107085, "Mac OS X 10.2: Expected, User-Defined Windows (SMB) Computer Name Does Not Appear in Connect to Server Dialog."

▶ When Connect to Server cannot connect to a server, a dialog may appear with an error code and no explanation (viewing logs with Console may provide more helpful information). Common error codes include:

–36 Error in URL

–43 Error in URL, probably the volume name

–47 Already connected to this server as the same user

–5000 Access denied

–5019 Volume does not exist

–5023 Bad password

MORE INFO ▶ Refer to Knowledge Base document 9804, "Mac OS System Error Codes: –299 to –5553."

Managing Multiple User Accounts

Many processes on Mac OS X require user account information. Applications often ask for your identity and for a means of authenticating that identity. The Finder needs to translate user and group IDs to user and group names when displaying file information. The identification information and the authentication information (or methods) must be stored in a way that makes it easy for applications to access.

In a networked environment, a user will regularly access different servers, including servers for mail and file sharing. For each of these servers, the user will also need to provide a user name and password to gain access. In a corporate environment, a user can quickly become overwhelmed with having to track a different user name and password for each server. It is much simpler for the user if the account information is also stored in a way that it could be shared with servers.

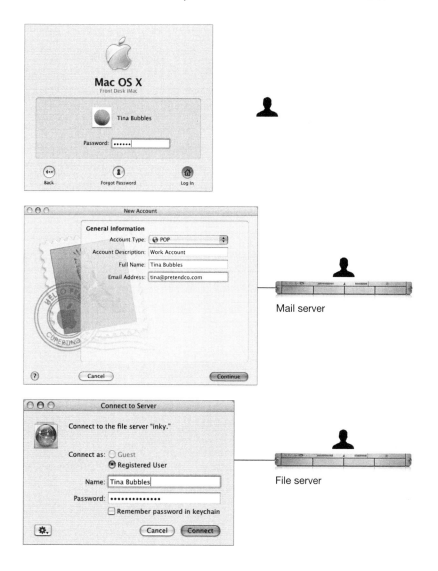

Mail server

File server

Instead of each application or service storing its own copy of user account information, Mac OS X uses directory services to allow different processes to access a common set of user account information. Directory services is a database service that keeps track of the resources that are available to the users of that database. In addition to providing service discovery, Open Directory also provides directory services for Mac OS X.

Using Local User Accounts

Each Mac OS X computer has a database that contains records for the local user accounts, such as the main administrator account. When a process such as the login window needs to access account information, it calls Open Directory, which is responsible for retrieving the data from the local directory service database. Because the different applications all use Open Directory, they all have access to the same user account information.

> **NOTE ▶** Only user account information that is needed by multiple processes is stored using Open Directory. User data that is specific to an application, such as preferences, is still managed by the application.

You do not need to do any configuration for local directory services. Open Directory is preconfigured to store local directory information using the NetInfo protocol. If you use Directory Access to turn off NetInfo, you are only turning off access to networked NetInfo directories; NetInfo will still be used for local directory service data.

Using Network User Accounts

Because processes such as loginwindow don't access the directory service database directly, a database doesn't have to be stored on the local computer. With the proper configuration, Open Directory can retrieve user records from a network database in addition to those in the local database.

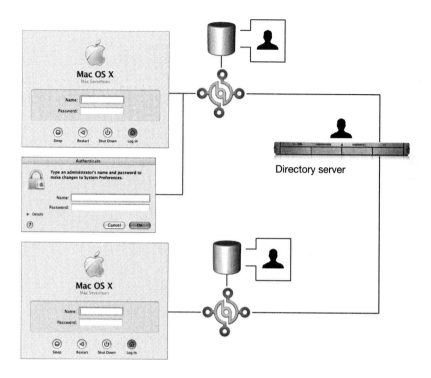

The advantage of network user accounts is that a user in your network can log in to any computer on the network using the same user name and password and, if used in conjunction with network home folders, the user environment will look the same on each computer. A user is no longer tied to a single computer, but can log in from any computer that has access to the networked database.

There are some things to keep in mind when using networked user accounts. Networked user accounts used to require constant access to the directory server where the user account information was stored. To help manage accounts on computers that are not always connected to the network, such as portable computers, Mac OS X Server allows you to create mobile user accounts. A mobile user account is a Mac OS X Server user account that resides in a shared domain but is copied to the local computer. This allows a user of a portable computer to log in using a network account even when the computer is not connected to a network.

There are a number of ways to implement a networked directory service, but the industry has mostly settled on Lightweight Directory Access Protocol (LDAP). Closely related to LDAP is Microsoft's Active Directory. Active Directory is based on LDAP, with some additional extensions that are specific to Microsoft clients.

Setting up a networked directory service is a job for the server administrator (and it is covered in the Mac OS X Server course). You will learn how to set up Mac OS X to connect to the directory services that you are most likely to encounter.

Sharing User Accounts with Directory Services

Another advantage of storing user accounts on a directory server is that multiple servers can access the directory server's user accounts for authentication. Just as a directory server allows a user to access the same user account on different computers, sharing the user account with different servers allows the user to access different services using the same user name and password.

Multiple user accounts become an issue when a number of systems use their own private user information to authenticate users. When you check your mail, the mail server doesn't know what user name and password you used to log in. The login window checks your user name and password against its local users list. The mail server has its own user list for authentication. The login name and password for one service isn't necessarily related to the login name and password for another service.

One way to approach this problem is to make one list of users available to all of these different systems. If the login window, the email server, and the AFP server all look to the same list of users, they can all accept the same user name and password. If your password is changed on that master list, all of those services will recognize the change at once and use your new password.

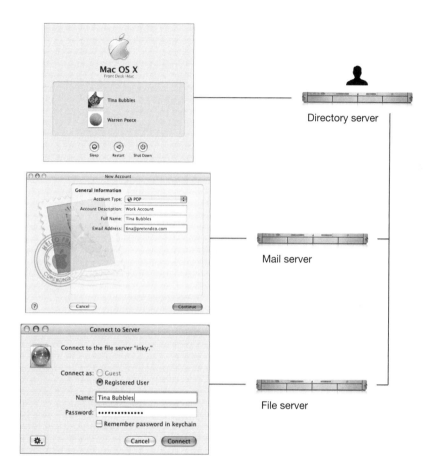

Using Static Directory Discovery

A directory server can provide more than just user account information. It can also provide a list of available services.

Earlier you learned that Mac OS X uses dynamic service discovery to scan the network and locate available services. Mac OS X can also query a directory server for a list of services that the server knows about. This is called static service discovery because the server has to be explicitly queried to show any

changes to it. Each time a service is added to the network, the administrator
has to manually edit the static list of services.

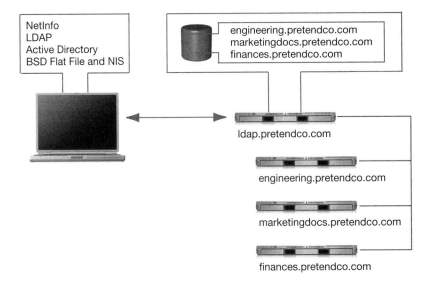

Configuring Network Directory Services

In addition to configuring discovery service protocols, the Directory Access
utility is also used to configure directory service options. You select which
directory service methods to use and the configuration options for each service. Although Mac OS X includes support for several different networked
directory services, this lesson will focus on how to configure the two most
common types of directory services: LDAP and Active Directory.

Configuring LDAP in Mac OS X

As mentioned earlier, LDAP is the industry-standard method for communicating directory information over a network. Unfortunately, there is much varia-
tion in the organization of that information. The configuration options range
from very easy to very difficult.

Automatically Configuring with DHCP

DHCP gives system administrators a standardized way to distribute LDAP information to client computers when they request an IP address. In fact, if your site is using Mac OS X Server to provide DHCP services, the default setting is to distribute LDAP binding information to DHCP clients. For this reason, it is possible to find and use a directory server on a newly installed computer without any additional configuration.

Manually Configuring for Specific Directory Servers

If your site doesn't use DHCP to distribute LDAP information, you'll have to add some information so that the client can find and use the directory information. The information you'll need to get from your administrator includes:

▶ The address of the LDAP server

▶ The type of server you are connecting to: Open Directory (for Mac OS X Server), RFC 2307 (for many UNIX servers), or Active Directory

   Normally, for Active Directory servers you'll want to use the Active Directory plug-in, as explained later in this lesson.

▶ The search base of the LDAP server

   The search base is a string of text that will be different for every site. It should look something like dc=pretendco, dc=com.

Manually Configuring for Custom Directory Server

This is an advanced configuration, which will not be covered in this book. It allows a very flexible but complex configuration that would enable you to work with a customized LDAP server. This configuration is covered by the Apple Certified System Administrator classes.

Finally, after you have configured Mac OS X to use your LDAP server, you need to tell Mac OS X to use this LDAP server for all authentication attempts. You do this by choosing Search > Custom path in the Authentication pane of Directory Access and adding the LDAP server to the Directory Node list.

Note that Directory Access configurations are independent of network locations. Selecting a different network location does not change LDAP settings.

> **NOTE** ▶ If you misconfigure directory services on Mac OS X, your computer can become unresponsive. To fix this, start your computer in single-user mode and reset the directory service settings by deleting the configuration files in /Library/Preferences/DirectoryService.

Configuring Active Directory in Mac OS X

In addition to LDAP, Mac OS X can use Active Directory for authentication information. There are three pieces of information you will need to obtain from your system administrator:

▶ Active Directory Forest address

▶ Active Directory Domain address

▶ Computer ID

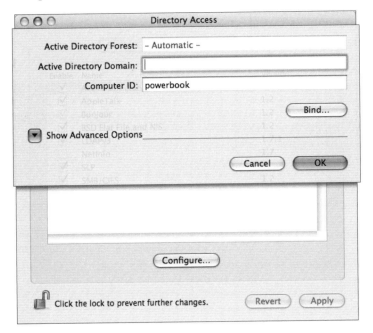

Additionally, you can configure advanced options such as mobile account settings, network home directory protocols, and Active Directory attribute mappings.

After you have configured Active Directory, you will again need to configure the authentication search path to include Active Directory.

Authenticating Your Identity

While you use your computer, a number of applications will need to know who you are. *Authentication* is the name of the process that lets you prove your identity to the computer system.

You regularly use authentication, even when you are not using your computer. When you call someone using a phone, the person you call responds by answering the phone. You, in turn, let the person know who's calling, and, hopefully, the person you called recognizes your name and voice, thereby authenticating you.

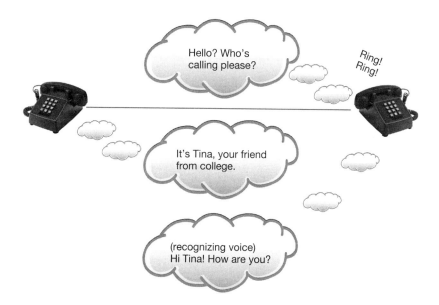

You've already seen several examples of authentication in Mac OS X: login window, Mail, and the Connect to Server window in the Finder. Each of these applications needs to know your identity so that you can access some resource. In the case of the login window, your identity is needed to verify that you have an account: either on the computer you are logging in to, or on a server if your computer is configured for network user accounts. If you have an account, you are then given access to the Finder and all of your files.

Often, it is some other computer on the network that needs to know who you are. The mail server may need to know your identity in order to know which mailbox holds your messages. The AFP server needs to know your identity to know which volumes you can mount and which files you can access.

> **NOTE ▶** Authentication is not the same as authorization. *Authentication* is simply identification of a person. *Authorization* is what services or data you are allowed to access based on who you are authenticated as. In the case of the phone call, you were authenticated when the person recognized your name and voice. Whether or not the person continues to talk to you is authorization.

Typically one thinks of authentication as entering a user name and password. While that is usually the first step, authentication also includes how a service verifies the information. There are several authentication methods. Which ones are available depends upon the client application and service protocols being used.

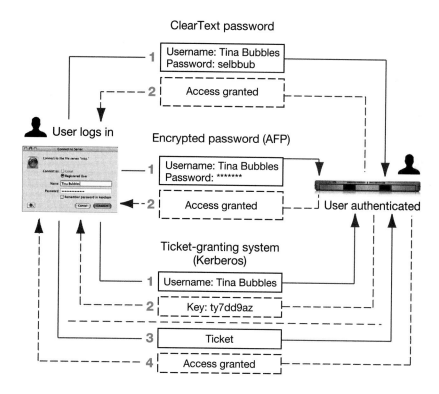

NOTE ▶ Mac OS X supports third-party User Authentication Mechanism (UAM) plug-ins to control access to file servers. To use a UAM, place the UAM plug-in in /Library/Filesystems/AppleShare/Authentication.

Mac OS X supports natively written UAMs from Microsoft. The Microsoft UAM allows you to use long and encrypted passwords when logging in to a Windows server running AFP services. While running Classic applications, you can continue to use the UAMs written for Mac OS 9.

Authenticating Using Basic/ClearText

The simplest form of authentication is Basic, also known as ClearText because the client application sends the user name and password in an unencrypted form to the server. Basic authentication is not secure because anyone on the network can monitor network traffic and spot the passwords. Basic authentication should only be used on a private, secure network.

Authenticating Using an Encrypted Password

This is similar to ClearText authentication, except the application sends the password in an encrypted form. This is more secure than basic authentication, but still not completely secure, as someone monitoring the network traffic can eventually decrypt the password.

A more secure method is for the server to send the client computer a random number or string. The client computer encrypts the string using the password and sends the result back to the server. Meanwhile, the server also encrypts the same string with its copy of the user's password. When the server receives the encrypted string from the client, the server compares the client's encrypted string with the string it created. If the two strings match, the user is authenticated.

This is more secure because the user password is never sent across the network. Also, because the initial string that the server sends can change, someone monitoring the traffic can't later recreate the response.

Authenticating Using Tickets

You can see how user names and passwords quickly proliferate. Imagine if you needed to access a dozen different servers—you might have a dozen different passwords. Even if you had the same name and password on every one of them, when you change your password, you would have to change it twelve times if you wanted to keep all of your passwords the same.

Keychain in Mac OS X is one way to address this issue. Keychain keeps your many passwords in a secure file format. Depending on your site, Keychain may be your only way to address the multiple password issue, because the other solutions rely on changes in the configuration of servers on the network that you may not control.

Another way to deal with the problem of multiple login accounts is through the use of tickets. Rather than proving your identity to network services by presenting a user name and password, you prove your identity by presenting a piece of data (the ticket). The service verifies your ticket, and if the ticket is valid, you are granted access. The name of the system that implements this ticket architecture is *Kerberos*.

A directory service solves the multiple account problem by coordinating all of its associated servers to use a single list of users. Kerberos simplifies this by keeping the list of users on one computer only. The ticket mechanism ensures that the rest of the services don't need your name and password; they only need a valid ticket.

With Kerberos, you negotiate with one system on the network, called a Key Distribution Center (KDC). When the KDC is satisfied that you have authenticated (typically by entering the correct user name and password), it gives you the ticket required to access other servers on the network. In Mac OS X, this is integrated with the login window, so the initial login results in the user obtaining a ticket that can be used for the duration of the login session.

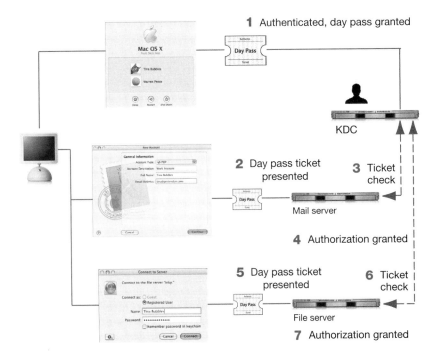

1 Authenticated, day pass granted

KDC

2 Day pass ticket presented

3 Ticket check

Mail server

4 Authorization granted

5 Day pass ticket presented

6 Ticket check

File server

7 Authorization granted

A ticket is a piece of data. Tickets are encoded in such a way that each one is unique. Each service can inspect the ticket and verify that the ticket is valid. To prove your identity to a server, you send your ticket instead of sending a name and password. Because the user's password is never sent across the network, it can't be stolen by someone monitoring the network.

A ticket is not something an end user normally works with directly. If the system is set up and working correctly, a user's system will acquire tickets and present them when required to access a server, all in the background. A Kerberos system, when properly configured, is not only very secure but it is also very user-friendly, because the user only has to authenticate once and Kerberos handles the authentication in the background for all servers accessed.

Kerberos was developed at MIT, and is widely accepted as one of the most secure ways to perform authentication. However, using tickets is a fundamental change from the more familiar method of requiring a user name and password.

It requires modification of both the client software and the server software so that they present and accept tickets, respectively. A service that has been modified to work with Kerberos ticket authentication is said to be *Kerberized*. If you experience trouble authenticating, it is possible that your site either doesn't implement a Kerberos ticket infrastructure, or that only a few of the most important servers are Kerberized.

Working with Kerberos Tickets

If your site is using Mac OS X Server for the directory server, your clients will automatically be using Kerberos when you configure Mac OS X to connect to an Open Directory server, as explained earlier in this lesson.

Kerberos can work with other types of servers, such as UNIX or Linux servers, running the standard MIT Kerberos. Such configurations are complex, and often are customized for each individual site. Details of these configurations are beyond the scope of this book.

In either case, if your site is configured for Kerberos, your users may use the Kerberos applications on Mac OS X. In a perfect Kerberos configuration, Kerberos is integrated with the login window, and the Kerberos login is not exposed to the user.

The Kerberos tickets are visible in the Kerberos application (/System/Library/CoreServices). Here are five tasks that you can perform with the Kerberos application:

▶ View the tickets

With Kerberos, the client presents a ticket to the network services. If the client never received a ticket, it will not be able to connect to Kerberized services. You can use the Kerberos application to view the tickets received from the client. If the window is blank, then there might be a problem with the KDC, which should have provided the ticket to the client.

▶ Get the tickets

If you notice that you don't have any Kerberos tickets, you can force login to the KDC and attempt to get a ticket.

▶ Destroy the tickets

If you use the Kerberos application to destroy your Kerberos tickets, accessing Kerberized services will require you to reenter your name and password to get a new ticket from the KDC.

▶ Change the password

After selecting a ticket or principal, you can change the password used to get tickets.

▶ Renew the tickets

Kerberos tickets are only good for a specified period of time (usually 8 to 10 hours); renewing a ticket resets its expiration time.

TIP ▶ Because Kerberos tickets remain active for many hours, anyone accessing your computer during that time would have access to the Kerberized services available to you. Take steps to restrict physical access to your computer while you have a valid ticket.

Troubleshooting Authentication

Troubleshooting authentication can be particularly tricky.

You can view the ticket using the Kerberos application (/System/Library/
CoreServices) to check whether the ticket has expired. Also, be sure the clocks
on your computers are synchronized within five minutes. (Using a network
time server is a good idea.)

The error and server logs may contain useful information. Error messages in
/Library/Logs/DirectoryService.error.log can help identify which plug-in is
having problems.

To locate the source of an authentication problem, try logging in locally on the
server, or from other clients.

What You've Learned

This lesson introduced finding and connecting to different network services,
including how directory services are used for service discovery, account management, and authentication.

▶   Mac OS X includes support for a variety of Internet services, including
    mail, web, instant messaging, and networked scheduling. Each of these
    services requires an application that the user must configure in order to
    locate and access the appropriate server.

▶   Support for networked file services is built into the operating system,
    allowing users to access networked file servers as easily as accessing local
    hard drives. Mac OS X includes support for several network file system
    protocols, including AFP, SMB, NFS, WebDAV, and FTP.

▶   You use service discovery protocols to find out what network services are
    available. Key service discovery protocols are Bonjour, SMB, AppleTalk,
    and SLP. You use Directory Access to configure service discovery protocols.

▶ User account information is provided to applications through Open Directory, the implementation of directory services on Mac OS X. Directory services also allow multiple computers, including different servers, to share user account information. Information about networked services can also be provided by directory services.

▶ Authentication is the process of identifying a user. Each server can require a different user password, but if you use a directory service or Kerberos, users don't have to use different passwords for each network service.

References

The following Knowledge Base documents (located at www.apple.com/support) will provide you with further information regarding service discovery in Mac OS X.

Mac OS X

▶ 9804, "Mac OS System Error Codes: −299 to −5553."

▶ 107804, "About network browsing and connected servers in Mac OS X 10.3"

AppleTalk

▶ 106298, "Mac OS X: Using AppleTalk With PPPoE"

▶ 106613, "Mac OS X: 'No AppleTalk printers are available' Message"

Bonjour

▶ 107346, "Mac OS X 10.2: Rendezvous Name Fails to Save"

▶ 106472, "Mac OS X: FTP, Internet Sharing, Rendezvous, SSH, and Telnet Require the BSD Subsystem"

▶ 106964, "Mac OS X 10.2: About Your Computer's Rendezvous Name"

▶ 107174, "Mac OS X 10.2: About Multicast DNS"

Windows (SMB)

▶ 107085, "Mac OS X 10.2: Expected, User-Defined Windows (SMB) Computer Name Does Not Appear in Connect to Server Dialog"

▶ 107117, "Mac OS X 10.2: Windows File Sharing (SMB) Computers Beyond Your Subnet Do Not Appear in Connect to Server Dialog"

▶ 19652, "Networking with a Windows PC"

▶ 61646, "Mac OS X 10.1: About Improving SMB File Transfer Speed with cp or CpMac"

▶ 106471, "Mac OS X 10.1 or later: How to Connect to Windows File Sharing (SMB)"

▶ 107943, "Using network homes with the Active Directory plug-in for Mac OS X 10.3.3 or later"

URLs

Visit the following websites for more information:

▶ Microsoft Knowledge Base article 188001, "Description of the Microsoft Computer Browser Service"

http://support.microsoft.com

▶ Windows NT Services for Macintosh:
http://www.microsoft.com/resources/documentation/windowsnt/4/server/proddocs/en-us/network/xns15.mspx

Books

Read the following books for more information:

▶ LDAP overview: Carter, Gerald, *LDAP System Administration,* Sebastopol, CA: O'Reilly and Associates, March 2003.

▶ Kerberos overview: Garman, Jason, *Kerberos: The Definitive Guide,* Sebastopol, CA: O'Reilly and Associates, August 2003.

Lesson Review

Use the following questions to review what you have learned:

1. What is meant by the term *service discovery?*

2. What are some applications that use service discovery information?

3. What are four protocols Mac OS X can use for service discovery? How do you enable or disable them?

4. What is the impact of disabling a service discovery protocol? Does it mean the computer cannot use that protocol at all?

5. Which files should you check for service directory errors?

6. Can the computer discover SMB servers beyond the local subnet?

7. What protocol would you use to share files with computers running Microsoft Windows?

Answers

1. It is the ability of a computer to find out about computers and other devices that offer services on the network.

2. One is the Finder, which displays a list of computers you can connect to when you select Connect to Server. Another is Printer Setup Utility, which displays a list of available printers in the Printer List window.

3. They are AppleTalk, Bonjour, SLP, and SMB. Use Directory Access to enable or disable the protocols the computer uses for services discovery.

4. If you disable a service discovery protocol, Open Directory does not use it for service discovery on the computer. However, other network services may still use the protocol.

5. You should check DirectoryService.error.log and DirectoryService.server.log.

6. No, SMB browsing in Mac OS X is limited to discovering workgroups and shared computers on the subnet.

7. You would use Server Message Block (SMB).

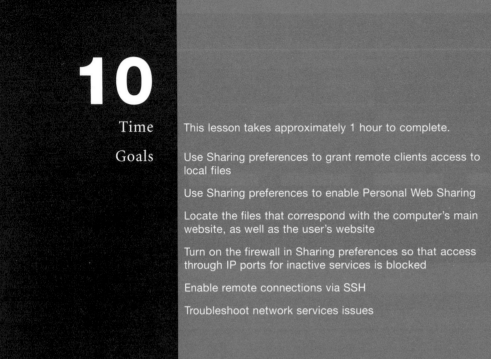

10

Time This lesson takes approximately 1 hour to complete.

Goals Use Sharing preferences to grant remote clients access to local files

Use Sharing preferences to enable Personal Web Sharing

Locate the files that correspond with the computer's main website, as well as the user's website

Turn on the firewall in Sharing preferences so that access through IP ports for inactive services is blocked

Enable remote connections via SSH

Troubleshoot network services issues

Lesson 10
Providing Network Services

In the previous two lessons, you've seen how you can configure networking and access network services in Mac OS X. To complete the network picture, this lesson discusses providing services to other clients on the network. For example, you can share a file or folder with a group of people you're working with, or host a website on your computer.

You make items on your computer available to other users by enabling network services. A network service is a protocol, or set of rules, for communication. Examples of protocols for network services include Apple Filing Protocol (AFP), File Transfer Protocol (FTP), and Secure Shell (SSH). When you activate a network service, your computer responds to requests that use that protocol.

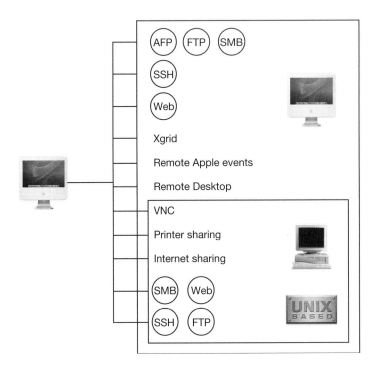

With Mac OS X, you can provide several network services. You can choose a
network service based on the items you're sharing and the types of computers
and users to which you want to provide access. While every service shared is
available to other Mac users on the network, many services are also available to
Windows and UNIX users. This lesson explores services to be shared and the
network clients that can access these services. We also discuss the built-in firewall in Mac OS X and how it can be used to safeguard your computer while
providing network services to others.

To make the most of this lesson, you should have access to at least two Mac OS X
10.4 computers on the same network. Ideally, they should be physically close
so you can make changes on one computer and see the effect on the other. The
computer that is sharing services is called the server. The computer that is

accessing the services on the server is called the client. This section explains how to set up these computers, but it's not imperative that you actually do so. You should be able to follow along by reading the step-by-step instructions and examining the screen shots.

Sharing Files

When you enable one of the file sharing services in Sharing preferences, anyone who knows the user name and password of a local account can log in over the network and access files and folders on your computer. Exactly which files and folders they can access is determined by the file sharing service used and the existing permissions. File permissions visible in the Info window (or Terminal) not only protect your files and folders from unauthorized access by local users, they also restrict access by remote users.

For example, if you've enabled Personal File Sharing in Sharing preferences (explained in the next section), remote Mac clients can talk to your server using Apple Filing Protocol. Using AFP, standard users can mount the home folders of other users, but they have full access only to the files and folders in their own home folders. Administrators can mount their own home folder or the entire volume because they may need to make changes outside their own home folders, such as installing new applications or deleting preferences files. However, that doesn't mean administrators can access all the folders in all users' home folders. The default permissions allow access to only the Public and Sites folders, whether you're authenticated as a standard user or as an administrator.

> **NOTE** ► Mac OS X Server can configure arbitrary share points, but Mac OS X is more limited. When you create a user account, Mac OS X automatically configures folder permissions in the home folder to allow only certain types of access.

Log in as a standard user

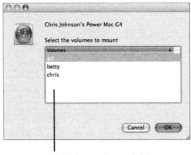

List of user home folders

Log in as an Admin user

Admin user's home folder
and all mounted volumes

The Public and Drop Box folders are useful for sharing files with other users. The permissions for the Public and Sites folders in each user's home folder allow Read Only access to Group and Others. This allows users to view and open the folder contents, but not to change the contents. Within each Public folder is a Drop Box folder with the permissions for Group and Others set to Write Only. This allows users to copy files into the Drop Box, but not to view the files in the folder.

NOTE ▸ Items on the root level of your home folder are visible to those who connect to your computer—even if those users don't have permission to open them. If you have documents or folders with sensitive names, store them in ~/Documents.

Sharing Files with Mac Clients Using AFP

In this exercise, you will enable Personal File Sharing on your server to allow users to connect to your computer from other Macintosh computers using the AFP protocol.

1   Open Sharing preferences.

2   Click Services.

3   Select Personal File Sharing, then click Start, or turn on Personal File Sharing by selecting its checkbox.

It may take a moment for Personal File Sharing to start. When it does, the Start button changes to Stop, and the top of the window explains how other computers on your local subnet can access your computer. At the bottom of the window are similar instructions that are also applicable to local users, but intended primarily for users outside your local subnet. For these instructions to work properly, it may be necessary to enable port forwarding on your router, and that's beyond the scope of this book.

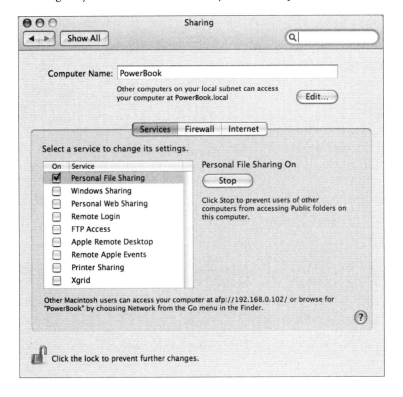

4   Note the address given to your computer at the bottom of the window.

It should be afp:// followed by the IP address, DNS name, or local hostname of your server, such as

afp://192.168.0.102/

Connecting to AFP Services

In this exercise, you use your Mac OS X client to connect to a server over AFP using a variety of methods.

1   Choose Go > Connect to Server (Command-K).

The Connect to Server window appears.

2   In the Server Address field, enter

afp://

followed by the IP address, DNS name, or local hostname of the server, optionally followed by a forward slash (in this example, you should enter *afp://192.168.0.102/*).

3   Click Connect.

An authentication dialog appears.

4   Specify that you want to connect as a registered user, then enter a user name and password for any standard or administrator account on the server.

NOTE ▶ If you're authenticating using an account that is not password-protected, leave the Password field blank.

5   Click Connect.

A list of mountable share points will appear.

If you connected as a user with a standard account on the server, or you connected as a guest, you'll see share points for each user with a home folder on the server. If you mount the share point of the account used to authenticate in step 4, you'll see the contents of that user's home folder. If you authenticate as yourself, then mount another user's share point, you'll see the contents of their Public folder.

NOTE ▶ FileVault-encrypted home folders do not appear in the list of mountable share points unless you connect as the owner.

If you connected as an administrator, the volumes listed are your own home folder plus each mounted file system (hard drive, CD-ROM, disk image, and so on) on the server. Although an administrator can navigate to any user's home folder, access to that folder is restricted based on file and folder permissions.

6   Select the volumes you wish to mount (Shift-click to select more than one), then click OK.

The shared volumes appear in the Sidebar at the left of the Finder window.

7   Eject any volumes mounted in step 6 by clicking the Eject icon next to the volume icon in the Sidebar.

8   If your server has a DNS name, choose Go > Connect to Server again, but this time specify the server's DNS name instead of its IP address.

For example:

afp://powerbook

You should be able to connect, log in, and mount volumes as you did before.

You can use either uppercase or lowercase letters in the server name, but *afp* must be lowercase.

9   Eject any mounted share points by dragging their icons to the Trash.

10 Choose Go > Connect to Server again, but this time specify the server's local hostname instead of its IP address.

For example:

afp://powerbook.local

You should be able to connect, log in, and mount volumes as you did before.

11 Eject any mounted share points by selecting them and choosing File > Eject (Command-E).

12 Click the Network icon in the Sidebar in the Finder.

You should see the server listed as a network service.

13 Select the server and click Connect.

You should be able to connect, log in, and mount volumes as you did before.

14 Eject any mounted share points using any of the methods previously employed.

> **NOTE ▶** Mac OS X 10.4 supports AFP sharing using TCP/IP only. Mac OS 9 users won't be able to access Mac OS X 10.4 computers using AFP unless they are configured for TCP/IP networking. The handoff is seamless to the end user: If users discover Mac OS X 10.4 file servers via AppleTalk, AFP will use TCP/IP for the connection without notification, and no special configuration is required for the handoff.

Sharing Files with Windows Clients Using SMB

SMB/CIFS is a versatile protocol. It is used primarily in Windows for file sharing and printing, and is commonly provided in UNIX distributions in the form of the open source Samba server. To allow Windows and UNIX users (including Linux) to connect to your Mac OS X computer and print to shared printers, enable the Windows Sharing service in the Sharing pane of System preferences. Of course, Mac OS X users can also connect using SMB, too. However, if you need to share files with only Mac OS clients, use AFP instead since SMB is somewhat less secure.

In this exercise, you will enable Windows Sharing on your server to allow users to connect to your computer using the SMB protocol. We will not discuss the printing capabilities of Windows Sharing.

1 Open Sharing preferences.

2 Click Services.

3   Select Windows Sharing, then click Start, or turn on Windows Sharing by selecting its checkbox.

It may take a moment for Windows Sharing to start. When it does, the Start button changes to Stop, and the top of the window explains how other computers on your local subnet can access your computer. At the bottom of the window are similar instructions that are also applicable to local users, but intended primarily for users outside your local subnet. For these instructions to work properly, it may be necessary to enable port forwarding on your router, and that's beyond the scope of this book.

NOTE ▶ SMB servers (whether running on Windows or Mac OS X) can take 10 minutes or more to broadcast their availability for sharing. For more information on SMB, refer to Microsoft's Knowledge Base article 188001, "Description of the Microsoft Computer Browser Service" (http://support.microsoft.com).

4   Click Enable Accounts.

A configuration sheet appears listing all local accounts on your computer.

Turning on AFP automatically enables AFP access to all local accounts, but SMB works a little differently in Mac OS X 10.4; you must specifically enable the accounts you wish to share. That's because when sharing files using SMB, Mac OS X 10.4 stores account passwords in a less secure manner than that used by AFP or an encrypted protocol like SSH. This dual-password method does not change file permissions or user access in any way, other than requiring you to specifically enable accounts for Windows Sharing.

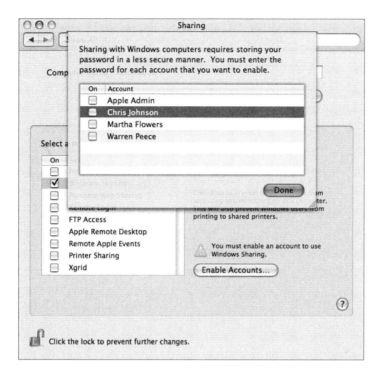

5 Click the checkbox for the account you wish to use with Windows Sharing.

You will immediately be prompted to authenticate to enable Windows Sharing for the selected account only.

6 Enter the selected account's password and click OK.

7 Repeat steps 5 and 6 for any other accounts whose home folders you wish to share using SMB, or click Done to close the configuration sheet.

8 Read the information below the list of services to see how other SMB users can access your computer and which accounts are enabled for Windows Sharing.

Note the address given to your computer at the bottom of the window. It should be the IP address, DNS name, or local hostname of your server, followed by a short name, such as

\\192.168.0.102\chris

NOTE ▶ Windows Sharing is not as secure as Personal File Sharing. If you do not need to use Windows Sharing, do not turn it on. If you need to use it only temporarily, turn it off when not in use, but first turn off all the enabled accounts; otherwise, the passwords are still stored insecurely.

Connecting to SMB Services

The example SMB address at the bottom of the Sharing preferences window always shows the short name of the current user, whether or not that account has been enabled for Windows Sharing. To connect properly via SMB, you must substitute the short name of an enabled account.

Windows users connect using a back slash (*192.168.0.102\chris*). Macintosh users connect using a forward slash (*smb://192.168.0.102/chris*). Furthermore, because Mac OS X uses the SMB/CIFS (Samba) standard for Windows Sharing, Mac clients can also use *cifs://192.168.0.102/chris*.

Mac OS X users need not enter a user name in the Connect to Server dialog. For example, if a Mac user enters the following in the Connect to Server dialog

smb://192.168.0.102/

he or she can then authenticate using the user name and password of the home folder to which he or she wants to connect.

Sharing Files Using FTP

Enabling FTP Access in the Services pane of Sharing preferences allows users to exchange files with your server using FTP client applications that are available for practically every operating system.

When you enable FTP Access, note the address given to your computer at the bottom of the window. It should be ftp:// followed by the IP address, DNS name, or local hostname of your server, optionally followed by a forward slash, such as

ftp://192.168.0.102/

Remote clients need to know the user name and password of a local account to connect via FTP. Some operating systems allow you to set up anonymous FTP access, so that users who do not have accounts on your computer can log in, but this is inherently not secure. If you want to provide anonymous FTP access, the feature is available on Mac OS X Server, but it is not part of the default FTP setup on Mac OS X.

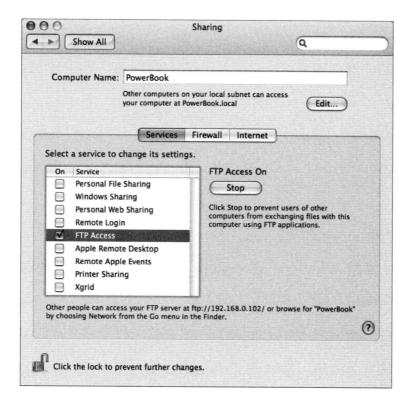

When a Macintosh client logs in to an FTP server using the Finder, his or her home folder is accessible, but regardless of the actual permissions for items, the user has Read Only access. If you want access to all files and folders on the server with their proper permissions respected, you must log in using a third-party FTP client. Keep in mind that regardless of how you log in using FTP, items that are normally hidden by the Finder are visible, and information exchanged between the client and the server is not encrypted.

Providing Web Services

When you perform a default installation of Mac OS X, the industry-standard Apache Web server software is installed. This powerful software allows you to host websites on your Mac, serving HTML pages to remote users across the Internet or to local users on an intranet.

By default, Mac OS X creates a single main website for the computer and separate websites for each user with a home folder on that computer. These aren't full-blown sites like you find when you surf the Web; they are placeholders for sites that you can create.

If you choose to create your own sites, which is completely optional, you need to understand how to create HTML documents, which is beyond the scope of this lesson. However, you can find many books on the subject, as well as third-party programs that make the process simple enough for nonprofessionals. To allow users to view web pages on your Mac OS X computer, enable Personal Web Sharing in the Services pane of Sharing preferences.

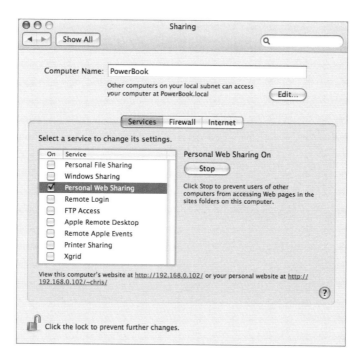

Using the Mac OS X Main Website

Your computer's main web page is located in /Library/WebServer/Documents, and the default "home page" is index.html.en, assuming you selected English as your language during the installation of Mac OS X. (The two-character extension identifies the document's language.) When accessing the Mac OS X main website, it is not necessary to include the two-character language extension; the page will display in the system default language.

> **NOTE ▶** This description of file locations assumes the default Apache configuration that installs with Mac OS X. It is possible to reconfigure Apache by editing configuration files, but that topic is beyond the scope of this lesson.

You can modify or replace the files in /Library/WebServer/Documents with the actual content you want to present, and you can delete all of the HTML pages for languages you do not plan to support.

To access the main web page of your computer, open a web browser such as Safari, and in the address field, enter the URL followed by the IP address, DNS name, or local hostname of your computer, such as

http://192.168.0.102

Creating Mac OS X User Websites

Whenever a new user account is created, Mac OS X creates a ~/Sites folder containing a file called index.html and an images folder.

If you want to create and display a personal web page, you can replace this file and folder with whatever you need.

To access your personal web page on your computer, open a web browser such as Safari, and in the address field, enter the URL followed by the IP address, DNS name, or local hostname of your computer, followed by a slash (/), a tilde (~), and your short name, such as

http://192.168.0.102/~chris

Enabling Personal Web Sharing

To allow users to view web pages on your Mac OS X computer, enable Personal Web Sharing. When you do so, Sharing preferences displays the URLs for your main web page and for user web pages. Users should enter these URLs into the address field of their web browsers to connect to this computer.

Follow these steps to enable Personal Web Sharing on your computer:

1 Open Sharing preferences.

2 Click Services.

3   Select Personal Web Sharing, then click Start, or turn on Personal Web
Sharing by selecting its checkbox.

It may take a moment for Personal Web Sharing to start. When it does, the
Start button changes to Stop, and the top of the window explains how
other computers on your local subnet can access your computer. At the
bottom of the window are similar instructions that are also applicable to
local users, but intended primarily for users outside your local subnet. For
these instructions to work properly, it may be necessary to enable port forwarding on your router, and that's beyond the scope of this book.

4   Note the clickable web addresses given to your server at the bottom of the
window.

The first URL is for the Mac's website and should be http:// followed by
the IP address of your server, followed by a slash, such as

http://192.168.0.102/

The second URL is the same as the first, with a tilde (~) and your short
name appended. This is the URL for your personal website, such as

http:// 192.168.0.102/~chris/

Verifying Personal Web Sharing

In this exercise, you will view the web pages on your server.

1   Click the first link at the bottom of the Sharing preferences window to
view the computer's website. Safari will automatically open and display the
default web page.

2   In addition to clicking the link to view the server's main website, in the
browser's address field, enter *http://* followed by your server's IP address,
DNS name, or local hostname, then press Return.

For example:

http://192.168.0.102

http://powerbook

http://powerbook.local

You should see a web page in a window titled "Test Page for Apache Installation."

3   Try using the other address formats.

All of them should work.

4   To view a user's personal website, in the browser's address field, enter *http://* followed by your server's IP address, DNS name, or local hostname, followed by a slash, a tilde, and the user's short name, then press Return.

For example:

http://192.168.0.102/~chris/

http://powerbook/~chris/

http://powerbook.local/~chris/

You should see a web page in a window titled "Mac OS X Personal Web Sharing."

5   Try using the other address formats.

All of them should display the same page.

Modifying the Home Page Files

Editing and creating HTML is beyond the scope of this book, but the basic concept is presented here to show the results of simple changes to the default web pages.

To edit the main and user web pages, follow these steps:

1   In the Finder on your server, open TextEdit (/Applications).

An empty window appears.

2   Choose TextEdit > Preferences.

The Preferences window appears.

3   Click the "Open and Save" button.

4   Select the "Ignore rich text commands in HTML files" checkbox.

This setting allows you to edit HTML files as text.

5   Close the Preferences window.

6   Close the blank document.

7   In the Finder, navigate to /Library/WebServer/Documents.

A useful shortcut to navigate to deeply-nested folders is the Go to Folder command. Press Command-Shift-G, then enter the path directly. Tab-completion works in the Go to Folder dialog, so you could navigate to /Library/WebServer/Documents with the following steps:

a   In the Finder, press Command-Shift-G to open the Go to Folder dialog.

b   Enter /Li and press Tab to auto-fill "/Library/"

c   Enter webs and press Tab to auto-fill "WebServer/"

d   Enter do and press Tab to auto-fill "Documents/"

e   Press Return to open the folder.

8   Open the index.html.en file by dragging and dropping the file onto the TextEdit icon.

9   Change the line that reads

<title>Test Page for Apache Installation</title>

to read

<title>Test Page for Reader</title>

10 Save and close the document.

11 Navigate to /Users/apple/Sites/ in the Finder.

12 Open the file index.html by dragging and dropping the file onto the TextEdit icon.

13 Change the line that reads

`<BODY BGCOLOR=#FFFFFF>`

to read

<BODY BGCOLOR=#FFFF00>

14 Save the file.

15 Quit TextEdit.

Testing the Modified Home Page Files
To verify the changes you made, follow these steps:

1 Open Safari on the client.

2 In the Address field, enter the web address of your server's main website, for example:

http://powerbook.local

The title at the top of the page should now reflect the change you just made.

NOTE ▶ It might be necessary to refresh the contents of your browser's cache. In Safari, choose View > Reload Page (Command-R).

3 Enter the web address of your computer's personal website for the user Apple Admin, and verify that the page's color has changed.

Providing Other Network Services
In addition to sharing files and providing web services, Mac OS X includes network services that provide other functionality. Remote Login allows users to use Secure Shell (SSH) to log in to your computer from another Macintosh computer, or even another platform. Remote Apple Events allow applications on other computers to execute Apple events on your computer.

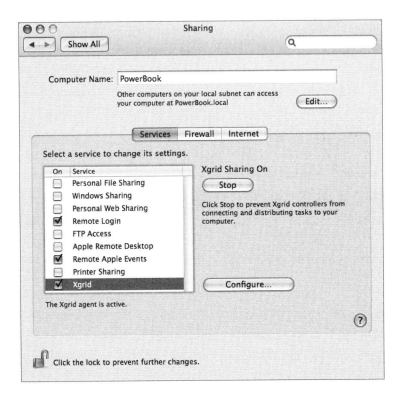

Consider the security implications before you enable Remote Login or Remote Apple Events. Anyone who logs in to your computer via SSH can run applications remotely, and secure FTP is automatically enabled when you enable Remote Login. Enabling Remote Apple Events allows users to create an application on another computer that sends Apple events that control applications running on your computer. Remote Login or Remote Apple Events potentially give control of your computer to other users on your network.

Xgrid is a new feature in Mac OS X 10.4 that allows computers on a network to work together in a grid to process a job. Administrators of Mac OS X Server can group locally networked computers into grids. Xgrid participation is available for any computer using Mac OS X 10.2.8 or later. If you want to make your computer available for use as part of a grid, select the Xgrid option.

MORE INFO ▶ For more information about Xgrid, visit www.apple.com/server/macosx/features/xgrid.html.

Protecting Your Mac with the Mac OS X Firewall

Because other people can access your computer when it's on a network, you should protect it from unauthorized traffic. Mac OS X includes firewall software you can use to block unwanted network connections and prevent unauthorized network access to your computer. The firewall uses the BSD utility ipfw (IP Firewall) to block network traffic on specific IP ports.

The firewall included in Mac OS X is separate from network firewalls or network security devices that network administrators use to protect against attacks from outside the network, but it has the same function: it protects your computer from attacks or unwanted intrusion. If your computer is on a network that has a firewall, you should still use the Mac OS X firewall to protect against the possibility of attacks from other computers on the network.

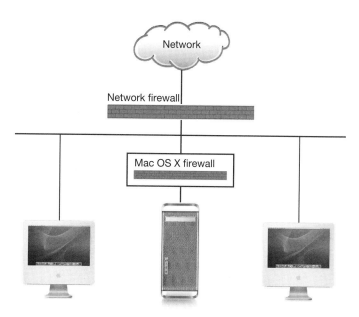

TIP All Mac OS X computers connected to the Internet, including those behind network firewalls, should enable the firewall.

To enable the firewall, click Firewall in Sharing preferences and then click the Start button. The Mac OS X firewall blocks traffic to specific IP ports. IP ports specify network services, such as Apple File Service (port 548) and web services (port 80). By preventing incoming traffic from reaching certain port numbers, you can prevent many types of unauthorized access to your computer.

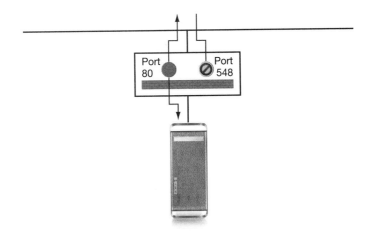

When you enable the firewall, all ports other than the ones checked in the list will be blocked. Blocking ports may disrupt services such as iChat Bonjour browsing and iTunes music sharing, so be sure to block only those ports you know are not in use.

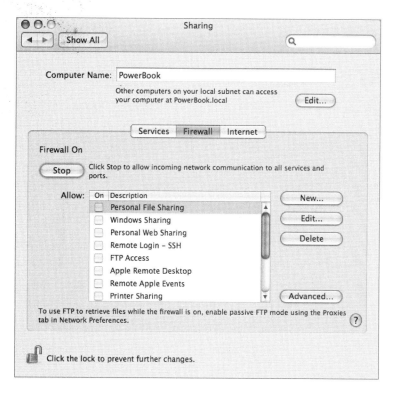

When you turn on a network service in the Services pane of Sharing preferences, Mac OS X automatically allows that service in the Firewall pane. This allows authorized traffic to pass and other traffic to continue to be blocked.

If you are curious about the ports typically used for certain services, open /etc/services file. To read the file contents, either use the command line or navigate to /etc using Go to Folder (Command-Shift-G) in the Finder, and use TextEdit to view the file contents.

You cannot change the settings for the default ports listed in the Firewall pane; however, you can specify additional ports to be opened as follows:

1 Click New.

A configuration sheet appears.

2 From the Port Name pop-up menu, choose one of the defaults and click OK, or choose Other.

Defaults have port numbers already assigned. If you choose Other, you must specify the port number to use.

3 Enter a port number, range, or series to open.

4 Enter a description of the port.

5 Click OK.

NOTE ▶ If you are using iTunes for Windows, refer to Knowledge Base document 93396: "iTunes for Windows: Music Sharing With Windows Internet Connection Firewall."

Advanced Firewall Settings

To set additional firewall options, click the Advanced button in the Firewall pane of Sharing preferences. There are three advanced options:

▶ Block UDP Traffic — This can be helpful in preventing hackers from using your computer as part of a denial of service attack.

▶ Enable Firewall Logging — Keeps a log that shows which traffic the firewall has allowed or denied.

▶ Enable Stealth Mode — Prevents a sender from receiving any information about denied traffic. If someone is trying to get into your computer, they won't even know that you're preventing them from doing so (which makes it harder for them to know if an attack is working).

Sharing Your Internet Connection

If your Mac OS X computer is connected to the Internet, you can share its Internet connection with other computers on your local network.

For example, if your computer accesses the Internet using a DSL (digital subscriber line) modem connected to Ethernet, and your Macintosh also has an AirPort Card installed, you can share the DSL connection with other AirPort–equipped computers. Complete instructions for doing so are included with AirPort products.

When you select the checkbox to share your Internet connection using Built-in Ethernet, a warning appears about the possibility of causing a network problem. If your network already has a DHCP server, enabling Internet Sharing will add a second DHCP server, confusing other computers on the network.

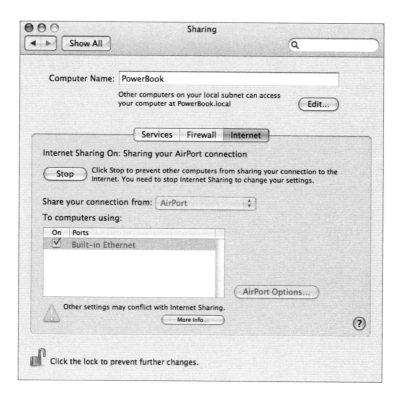

Internet Sharing uses a technology called Network Address Translation (NAT). With NAT, your computer handles the Internet traffic for the computers you're sharing your connection with. Your computer uses a single public IP address while distributing private IP addresses to other computers using DHCP.

> **NOTE ▸** On many networks, enabling Internet Sharing, and therefore DHCP services on the subnet, may interfere with other DHCP servers on the same subnet. In most cases, Internet Sharing should only be enabled in controlled environments.

> **NOTE ▸** If your Internet connection and your local network use the same port (built-in Ethernet, for example), investigate possible side effects before you turn on Internet Sharing. In some cases (if you use a cable modem, for example), you might unintentionally affect the network settings of other ISP customers, and your ISP might terminate your service to prevent you from disrupting their network. Internet Sharing works best if you receive services on one port, such as Ethernet, and provide services on another, such as FireWire or AirPort.

Sharing your Internet connection over AirPort is similar to the functionality provided by an AirPort Base Station. To share over AirPort, open the Internet pane of Sharing preferences, choose Built-in Ethernet from the "Share your connection from" pop-up menu, choose AirPort from the "To computers using" pop-up menu, then click Start to share the connection.

When sharing over AirPort is enabled, click the AirPort Options button to configure the AirPort network options, including the name of the network and its security level. When Wireless Encryption Protocol (WEP) is enabled, all data transmitted over AirPort is encrypted and you must enter a password to gain access to the AirPort network.

Although it is not recommended, you can simultaneously create and share an Internet connection with the Ethernet network port. However, you cannot connect to the Internet and receive client (shared) connections over the same AirPort or modem port.

Troubleshooting Network Services

There are three services in Sharing preferences that are likely to need trouble-shooting if problems occur: file sharing, firewall access, and Internet Sharing. For example, file sharing is a robust and easily-configured service, but because it "just works," it can be hard to know where to start troubleshooting. This section provides some guidance to direct your troubleshooting efforts.

Troubleshooting File Sharing

If users are unable to connect to your computer, try the following:

▶   Verify that the appropriate file sharing service is enabled in the Services pane of Sharing preferences.

▶   If the appropriate service is enabled, but users are still unable to connect, there could be a networking problem such as an incorrect setting in Network preferences or a broken connection in the network.

  •   Check the IP address and DNS settings in Network preferences. If an IP address starts with 169.254, it was self-assigned and therefore is accessible only to computers on the local subnet.

  •   Use Network Utility to check whether or not the two computers are able to communicate using ping. For more information on trouble-shooting network connectivity issues, see Lesson 8, "Networking Configuration and Troubleshooting."

  •   If users are able to connect but not authenticate, verify that they are using a valid user account on the computer and that they are using the correct password.

  •   Some networks and routers may block specific protocols. If the pre-ceding strategies did not resolve the problem, check with your net-work administrator to see if that might be the case.

▶   If a user is able to connect and authenticate but is unable to access files, check to make sure that the permissions for the files the user is trying to access and all of the folders that encompass the files are set to allow access for the user. If just one encompassing folder doesn't have at least read per-mission for the user, the user will be blocked from accessing the files, regardless of how the files' permissions are set.

Troubleshooting the Firewall

Using the firewall protects your computer from potential exploits, and is essential in any network environment that is directly exposed to the Internet. However, it is designed to protect your computer by blocking access, and it can block network services that you want to share. If you share a service and it is not available to other computers on your network, check the firewall service.

You can specifically open ports for services and programs to which you want to allow access, such as iTunes, iPhoto, or iChat. You can also open ports for network-aware games, or even to provide special access to particular services. Keep in mind that every open port is a potential source of intrusion into your computer.

The ipfw.log file is very useful for troubleshooting firewall issues, because it can show all types of firewall usage, including denied port requests that might indicate some kind of attack.

Troubleshooting Internet Sharing

If you use the firewall, clients of your shared Internet connection may receive an IP address from your computer, but find that they cannot browse websites. Enable Personal Web Sharing in the Services pane of Sharing preferences to open a firewall port and allow computers sharing your connection to browse the web.

> **MORE INFO** ▶ Refer to Knowledge Base document 107653, "Mac OS X 10.2 or Later: Firewall Blocks Internet Sharing."

Internet Sharing with WEP may not allow Windows wireless computers on the network. WEP has two methods to authenticate. Windows defaults to "Open," whereas Mac OS X uses "Shared." AirPort Extreme and AirPort Express Base Stations support both modes. Windows systems may be able to use "Shared" or "Auto/Both." Check the advanced configuration options in Windows wireless software.

What You've Learned

- You enable AFP, SMB, and FTP file sharing in the Services pane of Sharing preferences.

- File sharing on Mac OS X requires users to log in with a user name and password.

- File permissions protect your files and folders from unauthorized access by network users as well as local users.

- The volumes that are available over AFP may differ for administrators and standard users.

- Personal Web Sharing allows users with a browser to connect to your computer's main website and to users' websites.

- You enable Remote Login and Remote Apple Events in the Services pane of Sharing preferences. These services have significant security implications.

- The Mac OS X firewall protects your computer from unwanted network traffic. You can allow certain types of traffic to support network services for applications like iTunes, iPhoto, and iChat.

- Internet Sharing allows you to share one IP address with multiple computers.

References

The following Knowledge Base documents (located at www.apple.com/support) will provide you with further information regarding file and Internet Sharing in Mac OS X.

File Sharing

- 106461, "Mac OS X: About File Sharing"

- 107086, "Windows File Sharing will not start, stay on, or allow workgroup name change in Mac OS X 10.2"

Windows (SMB)

▶ 106660, "Mac OS X: Sharing your files with non-Apple computers"

▶ 93396, "iTunes for Windows: Music Sharing With Windows Internet Connection Firewall"

Internet Sharing

▶ 107653, "Mac OS X 10.2 or Later: Firewall Blocks Internet Sharing"

▶ 108058, "Choosing a password for networks that use Wired Equivalent Privacy (WEP)"

URLs

Visit the following website for more information.

▶ Xgrid: www.apple.com/server/macosx/features/xgrid.html

Lesson Review

Use the following questions to review what you have learned:

1. What are the preconfigured share points on Mac OS X?

2. Where do you enable AFP, SMB, and FTP file sharing?

3. Where is your computer's main web page located?

4. What URL would you use to access the web page for user nancy on the computer client.example.com?

5. If users are unable to access files on your computer over the network, what should you check?

Answers

1. A standard user can mount only user home folders. An administrator user can mount their own home folders as well as any mounted file system (the entire hard drive, CD-ROM, disk image, and so on).

2. You enable AFP, SMB, and FTP file sharing in the Services pane of Sharing preferences.

3. Your computer's main web page is located in /Library/WebServer/Documents. If you selected English as your language during installation, the name of the file is index.html.en.

4. You would enter http://client.example.com/~nancy followed by a Return.

5. Verify that the appropriate file-sharing protocol is enabled; verify network connection between the two computers; if using Windows, verify that the account is allowed to log in; check permissions.

11

Time   This lesson takes approximately 1 hour to complete.

Goals   List device classes or types used in Mac OS X 10.4 to categorize
peripherals

List the types of drivers used in Mac OS X to communicate with
peripherals

Use System Profiler to identify what USB and FireWire devices
are connected and recognized by the system

Use System Profiler to isolate and resolve a peripheral issue in
Mac OS X 10.4

Perform basic troubleshooting of peripheral issues

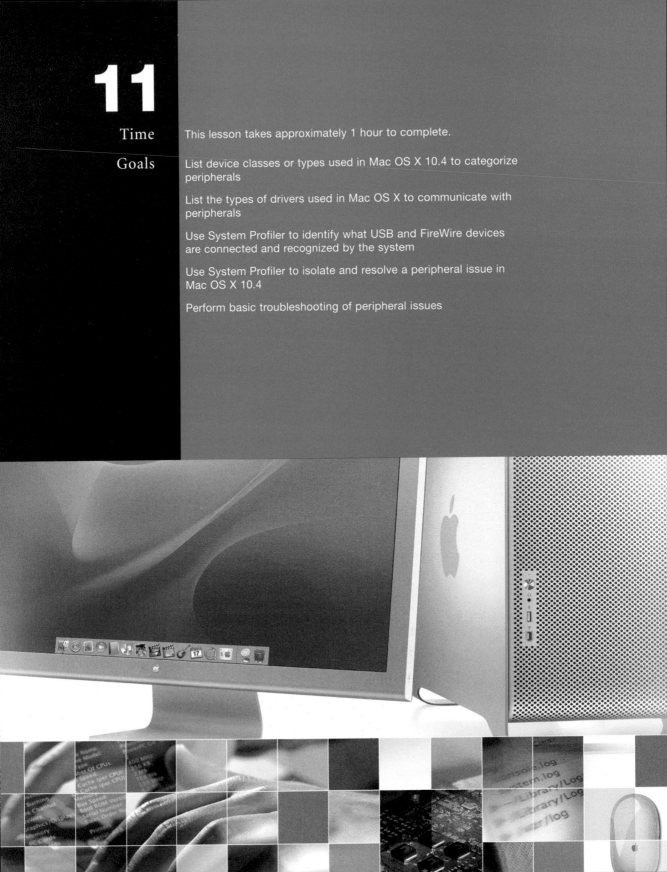

Lesson 11
Peripherals

Macintosh computers come from the factory with a wide range of necessary and useful hardware components, from internal hard disks and optical drives to keyboards and mice. In addition, Macintosh computers have options for adding internal and external peripherals such as expansion cards, printers, and scanners.

Mac OS X supports connectivity to a wide variety of devices. It also includes several applications designed to interact with and manage connected devices, such as Disk Utility, iPhoto, and Image Capture.

Each device is defined by its connection *bus* and *device class*. For example, you might use a FireWire printer or a Bluetooth keyboard. This lesson will discuss how peripherals are supported in Mac OS X 10.4, including the various peripheral buses and device classes, as well as how to troubleshoot issues when working with peripherals.

Understanding Buses

A *peripheral bus* provides connections for peripheral devices. Different types of buses support the communication requirements of different types of peripheral devices. For example, a keyboard sends very small amounts of information to the computer, while a video camera or a hard drive sends much more information. Mac OS X supports a large number of industry-standard buses.

Plug-and-Play Buses

The two most commonly used plug-and-play buses for connecting peripheral devices to Macintosh computers are Universal Serial Bus (USB) and FireWire. Bluetooth is less common, but is gaining popularity. Plug-and-play buses allow you to connect, use, and disconnect devices while the device and the computer are powered on (hot-swapping), without the need to install special drivers or software for the devices to function.

USB 1.1/2.0

Universal Serial Bus (USB) is a plug-and-play interface for external add-on devices such as audio players, joysticks, keyboards, phones, scanners, and printers. You can connect USB devices directly to your computer or to other USB devices. For example, you can connect your USB mouse to your USB keyboard, which is then connected to your computer. You can also purchase USB hubs that allow you connect several USB devices to a single port on your computer.

USB 1.0/1.1 is the original version of the USB specification, still in use in many environments where maximum data transfer is not needed. Its maximum speed is 12 Mbit/s. The most recent USB version, USB 2.0, supports data transfer speeds of up to 480 Mbit/s, and is better suited for high-speed peripherals, such as storage devices and digital cameras. USB 2.0 devices can be plugged into a USB 1.1 port, but the device will operate at the slower bus speed. Also, USB 1.1 devices can be plugged into a USB 2.0 bus, but that will force all devices on the bus to operate at the slower speed.

USB devices operate at three speeds. High-speed devices are designed for a data rate of 480 Mbit/s. Full-speed devices are designed for a data rate of 12 Mbit/s. Low-speed devices are designed for a data rate of 1.5 Mbit/s. High-speed and low-speed devices can both operate at their rated speed as long as the bus version is the same. Whenever possible, segregate USB devices by bus version.

While USB ports provide power, the maximum power is very low (5 volts and .5 amps). While a low-power device, such as a mouse or keyboard, can be plugged into any USB port, a device that requires more power, such as a scanner, needs to be plugged into a powered port directly on the computer or on a powered USB hub. A *self-powered* USB device requires its own separate power supply.

USB Error Messages

Most USB issues occur because a device is not properly powered or the correct driver software is not installed. There are four categories of USB error messages:

▶   Not Enough Power to Function — A device is drawing too much power, or the device requires its own power cord.

▶   Not Enough Power for All Functions — There is enough power to supply some, but not all, of the functions the device is designed to provide.

▶   The USB Driver Needs to be Updated. Would you like to search for the update on the Internet? — Mac OS X detects an out-of-date driver.

▶   No Driver Found — Mac OS X detects no driver for the device, and cannot use the generic driver for the device class.

Troubleshooting USB Issues

To troubleshoot USB issues, try the following:

▶   Make sure all USB cables and power cords are plugged in properly.

▶   Make sure you have installed any software that was included with the device. Check for updates to software required by the device. Visit the manufacturer's website to get the latest software for your device.

▶   If the device doesn't have a power cord and is plugged into another USB device that doesn't have a power cord, try plugging the device directly into your computer or to a USB device that does have a power cord.

FireWire 400/800

All current Macintosh computers have one or more FireWire 400 (IEEE 1394a) ports that transfer data at up to 400 Mbit/s. Some also have a FireWire 800 (IEEE 1394b) port that transfers data at up to 800 Mbit/s.

FireWire ports can provide bus power to FireWire devices (more power than USB; up to 30 volts and 1.5 amps). This is enough power to operate webcams, hard drives, or other devices; if your device can run on bus power, it does not need a separate AC adapter.

FireWire devices have 4-pin, 6-pin, or 9-pin connectors. The 4-pin connectors do not provide bus power, but are popular on digital video cameras due to their compact size. On Macintosh computers, FireWire 400 ports have 6-pin connectors, and FireWire 800 ports have 9-pin connectors. You must use a FireWire cable that has the correct connector for your computer on one end, and the correct connector for the device on the other end. So if you have a device with a 4-pin connector and you want to plug it into your computer's FireWire 400 port (which accepts a 6-pin connector), you need a 4-pin to 6-pin cable.

> **MORE INFO** ▶ Visit http://developer.apple.com/devicedrivers/firewire/ index.html or refer to Knowledge Base document 30520, "About FireWire 400 Technology."

Starting in Target Disk Mode

Most Mac OS X computers that have built-in FireWire have the capability to start in Target Disk Mode (TDM). Instead of booting the operating system, the computer (target) in disk mode acts as a hard drive that can be used by the host Macintosh with a FireWire connection. Essentially, this gives the host computer full access to the master internal hard drive of the target computer.

NOTE ▶ Blue and White G3 computers do not support Target Disk Mode.

Target Disk Mode is useful whether or not the computer can boot. You may opt to use TDM on a fully-functioning computer as an alternative to file sharing over a network if you have a large amount of data to transfer between computers. You can also use Target Disk Mode to migrate user accounts and home folders from one computer to another using the Migration Assistant during setup. You can even install software on a computer in TDM (for example, to get around Mac OS X 10.4's requirement for a DVD drive).

Target Disk Mode is especially useful when a computer is unable to boot. You can use TDM to try to fix the problem with Disk Utility or third-party tools running on another computer. If that fails, you may still be able to copy or recover files from the nonbooting computer before erasing.

Target Disk Mode can be a big security risk. There are multiple ways to use TDM to access a system without knowing the system's password. If someone has physical access to a system, he or she can access files on the system. One method to lock out TDM is to use the Open Firmware Password utility (which you can download from Apple) and give the hardware itself a password.

To experiment with Target Disk Mode, you need two Macintosh computers with FireWire ports and a single FireWire cable. If you don't have access to the necessary hardware, you can still follow along with these instructions:

MORE INFO ▶ Refer to Knowledge Base document 58583, "How to Use FireWire Target Disk Mode."

1   Unplug all other FireWire devices from the target computer (the one whose hard drive you want to access) prior to using Target Disk Mode. Do

not plug in any FireWire devices until after you have disconnected the two computers from each other, or have stopped using Target Disk Mode.

2   Shut down the target computer.

3   Start up the target computer and immediately press the T key until the FireWire logo appears, indicating that the target computer is now in Target Disk Mode.

   NOTE ▶ Startup Disk preferences in Mac OS X 10.4 has a new Target Disk Mode button that restarts the computer in TDM.

   NOTE ▶ If you are using a laptop as the target computer and battery power becomes completely drained during this process, disk corruption can occur. For this reason, it's highly recommended to use an AC adapter when in Target Disk Mode.

4   Make sure the host computer is fully booted into the Finder in Mac OS X.

5   Connect the target computer and the host computer using a FireWire cable.

   After a few seconds, Mac OS X adds the target computer's hard drive to the Sidebar. In some cases, the hard drive may not appear right away because the operating system may be busy verifying the disk.

6   Use the target computer's hard drive as you would any other volume.

7   When you are done with the target computer's hard drive, unmount it by selecting its icon in the Finder and choosing File > Eject (Command-E).

8   Disconnect the FireWire cable from the host computer and the target computer.

9   Press and hold the power button to turn off the target computer.

10 Turn on the target computer without pressing any keys at startup to return it to normal operation.

Troubleshooting FireWire Issues

To troubleshoot FireWire issues, try the following:

▶ Make sure each FireWire device is turned on and connected to AC power (if device is not bus-powered).

▶ Make sure all cables and power cords are plugged in. Make sure the cables match the requirements for the FireWire connection protocol (for FireWire 400, cables no longer than 15 feet; for FireWire 800, cables no longer than 300 feet).

▶ Make sure you have installed any software that came with the device. Check for updates to software required by the device. Visit the manufacturer's website to get the latest software for the device.

▶ If the device still doesn't work, try quitting and restarting any applications that use the device.

Bluetooth

Bluetooth is a short-range wireless connection protocol used by desktop and portable computers, personal digital assistants, mobile phones, printers, scanners, digital cameras, and even some home appliances. It uses a globally available frequency band (2.4 GHz) for worldwide compatibility. Because Bluetooth uses a radio frequency to transmit data, Bluetooth devices communicate with any devices in range, even those that are not in line of sight. Although Bluetooth uses the same frequency as AirPort, they can both be enabled at the same time.

With Bluetooth, you can link your Palm OS-based handheld device, Bluetooth–enabled mobile phone, and other peripherals to your Bluetooth–equipped computer within a 30-foot range. Once linked, you can synchronize data, such as contacts and schedules, between your Macintosh and Bluetooth–enabled mobile phones and PDAs, or even use your Bluetooth–enabled mobile phone as a wireless mobile modem. While Bluetooth is not intended as a replacement for AirPort, it can be used for simple computer-to-computer communication. Mac OS X includes the Bluetooth File Exchange application (/Applications/ Utilities) to transfer files between two Bluetooth–enabled computers.

To use Bluetooth, you must either have a computer with Bluetooth preinstalled or install a Bluetooth adapter, such as the D-Link DWB-120M Bluetooth USB adapter. You can use Bluetooth preferences to pair up with a device configured to be discoverable and set a passkey to authenticate connections with the device. Bluetooth preferences presents a list of all Bluetooth devices within range that are configured to be discoverable. Once you select the Bluetooth device in the list and click the Pair button, you're connected.

Configuring Bluetooth Preferences

To experiment with Bluetooth devices, you need two Macintosh computers, both with built-in Bluetooth or with Bluetooth adapters. If you don't have access to the necessary hardware, you can still follow along with these instructions.

Before you can use Bluetooth to connect your computer to another Bluetooth device, you must perform some configuration, including setting a unique name for your computer:

1 Log in to your computer as Apple Admin.

2 If you are using a computer that does not have built-in Bluetooth support, plug a Bluetooth USB dongle into a free USB port.

3   Open System Preferences.

You should see a Bluetooth icon in the Hardware section.

4   If you do not see the Bluetooth icon, quit System Preferences and reopen it.

5   Click the Bluetooth icon to open Bluetooth preferences.

6   Click the Settings button.

The Bluetooth Device Name is the computer name set in Sharing preferences.

Bluetooth preferences include the option to open the Bluetooth Setup Assistant automatically when you start your computer and a cabled keyboard and mouse are not detected. This allows you to configure a computer that shipped from the factory with a Bluetooth keyboard and mouse, for example.

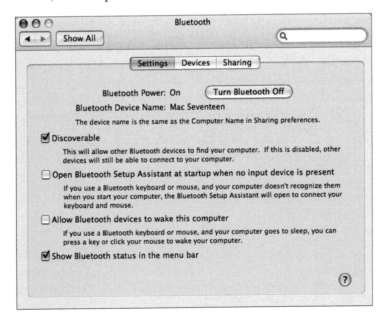

7   If Bluetooth Power is off, click Turn Bluetooth On.

8   Select "Show Bluetooth status in the menu bar."

This adds a Bluetooth menu extra at the right of the menu bar.

9   If it is not already enabled, select the Discoverable checkbox.

10 Repeat steps 1 through 9 on a second Bluetooth–capable Macintosh, making sure that it has a unique computer name set in Sharing preferences.

Exchanging Files Using Bluetooth

To use the Bluetooth File Exchange application to exchange files between Bluetooth–enabled computers, follow these steps:

1   In Bluetooth preferences on your computer, click Sharing.

The Sharing pane determines how files are transferred using Bluetooth. Use the defaults for this exercise.

2   From the Bluetooth menu extra, choose Send File.

3   Select a small sample file on your computer, then click Send.

The Bluetooth File Exchange application opens and displays the Send File window listing previously-paired devices.

4   Click Search to find the Bluetooth–enabled computers within range.

You might have to click the Search button multiple times to find your other computer.

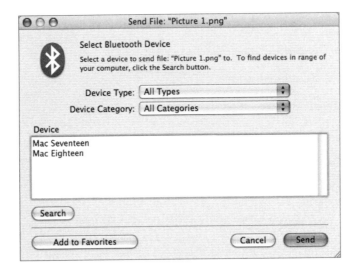

By default, your computer will accept single file transfers in this manner, unless you turn off Discoverable access for Bluetooth or deselect Bluetooth File Exchange in the Sharing pane of Bluetooth preferences.

5   Select the name of the computer you want to send files to from the list, and then click Send.

A dialog will appear while Bluetooth File Exchange negotiates the transfer and waits for acceptance.

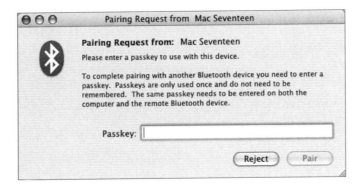

6   On the receiving computer, click Accept to receive the file.

If you select the "Accept all without warning" checkbox, all files sent via Bluetooth will automatically be placed in your Documents folder.

7   When the file transfer is completed, the receiving computer displays a dialog listing the file transferred.

8   Click the Find button (the magnifying glass) to open the folder containing the sent file.

NOTE ► The default location for accepted items is specified in the File Exchange pane of Bluetooth preferences.

9   Quit Bluetooth File Exchange.

Pairing Two Devices Using Bluetooth

When you want two devices to communicate automatically, they must be paired so they can identify and authenticate each other. Normally you would pair your computer with a Bluetooth device such as a phone or PDA; however, this exercise has you pair two computers. The task is very similar to pairing with a phone or PDA.

1   On your computer, click Devices in Bluetooth preferences.

2 Click "Set up new device."

The Bluetooth Setup Assistant prompts you for the device type.

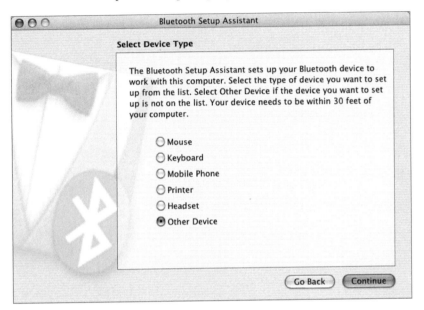

3 Select Other Device, and click Continue.

Bluetooth searches for Bluetooth–enabled devices within range.

At first all other in-range Bluetooth–enabled devices are displayed as their MAC addresses, but after a few seconds, these numbers are replaced with their DNS names or local hostnames.

4   Select the device (your other computer) that you want to pair with, and click Continue.

You will see a six-digit passkey on your computer while a pairing request dialog appears on the other computer.

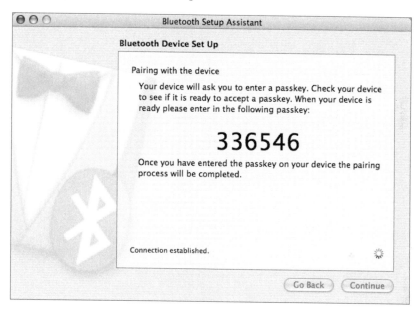

5   On the other computer, enter the passkey and click Pair.

If you enter an incorrect passkey, no error appears, and you will have to try again. If you enter the correct passkey, the Bluetooth pair is created and remembered, and the paired computers appear in each other's Bluetooth Devices lists in the Devices pane.

6 On the other computer, the Devices pane of Bluetooth preferences should look something like this:

You have established a secure connection to a known device. Note that the device address is visible in this dialog, along with the device name.

7 Quit Bluetooth preferences.

Paired devices and computers will automatically attempt to connect to your computer if they are within range of the Bluetooth receiver. Therefore, pairing allows devices such as PDAs, mobile phones, keyboards, and mice to work seamlessly with your computer, and you can delete specific pairings or create temporary pairings as needed.

Using Additional Buses

Mac OS X supports several other buses for connecting a wide variety of peripherals, including video cards, audio cards, and internal and external hard drives.

PCI and PCI-X

Peripheral Component Interconnect (PCI) cards are expansion cards that are installed inside desktop computers after turning off power. Because of their very high throughput compared to the plug-and-play connection buses, PCI cards are often used to add display capabilities, hardware RAID, or high-end analog video capture and compression. PCI cards are available to add a SCSI bus as well as additional USB and FireWire buses. PCI supports bus speeds up to 66 MHz, and PCI-X supports bus speeds up to 133 MHz. Note that PCI buses are present even in Macintosh models that lack slots, such as the iBook and PowerBook.

AGP

Accelerated Graphics Port (AGP) is a standard video card connection bus used by many graphics card manufacturers. It is a faster connection bus than PCI, making it ideal for high-performance video. Current Power Mac G5 computers have an 8x AGP Pro slot for the primary video card.

PC Card

Also known as CardBus or PCMCIA (Personal Computer Memory Card International Association), the PC Card bus is used primarily on laptop systems. The thickness of PC Cards is indicated as Type I, Type II, or Type III. Although support for PC Cards was included in Mac OS 9, the use of PC Cards in Mac OS X requires a version higher than 10.0.3.

ATA and Serial ATA

Advanced Technology Attachment (ATA), also referred to as Parallel ATA, is an internal bus used to connect storage devices, such as hard disks and CD-ROM drives. Most Mac OS X–compatible computers prior to the Power Mac G5 incorporated ATA buses for internal storage and optical drives. As ATA performance has improved, other names have appeared for ATA connections, which describe ATA bus speeds such as "ATA-100." All ATA buses are built on the Parallel ATA protocol.

Serial ATA is the next-generation industry-standard storage interface that replaces the standard ATA interface for the hard drives in the Power Mac G5. Serial ATA supports 1.5 Gbit/s throughput (equivalent to a 150 MB/s data rate). Since each Serial ATA drive is on an independent bus, there's no competition for bandwidth as with Parallel ATA.

Macintosh computers that ship with Serial ATA buses include an ATA bus to connect slower storage devices such as optical media drives.

SCSI

Small Computer System Interface (SCSI) is a high-speed bus used mostly for storage devices. Due to the comparatively higher cost of SCSI drives and interfaces, ATA drives are used more commonly for internal storage. SCSI bus devices usually are reserved for systems that require high-performance data transfer. Current Macintosh systems do not have SCSI built in, and they require the addition of a PCI card to connect SCSI devices.

Viewing Peripherals with System Profiler

The Hardware section of the Contents list in System Profiler displays reports for various hardware components, including buses supported by Mac OS X (for example, USB, FireWire, and PCI). After clicking a bus type, the upper-right pane of System Profiler displays a hierarchical view of the bus and devices connected to the bus. Clicking a device in the upper-right pane displays information about the device in the lower pane.

NOTE ▶ System Profiler in Mac OS X 10.4 is significantly improved from the previous version. It now supports many more plug-ins, such as Power, Fonts, and Bluetooth, and reports far more information about devices on peripheral buses.

If you find that a connected peripheral is not functioning, use the Hardware section of the Contents list in System Profiler to see if the device is recognized by the system. If a device appears in System Profiler but isn't working properly, the problem is probably related to the device driver and support software not being installed and configured correctly. If the device is not listed, there may be a physical problem with the device or its connection to the computer.

System Profiler can generate reports of all the devices connected to a computer. To see what devices are connected to your computer, follow these steps:

1 Open System Profiler (/Applications/Utilities).

The System Profiler window displays the Hardware Overview.

The Contents list at the left lists the types of reports that System Profiler can generate.

2 If the Hardware item in the Contents list is not expanded, click the disclosure triangle to list all of the hardware reports.

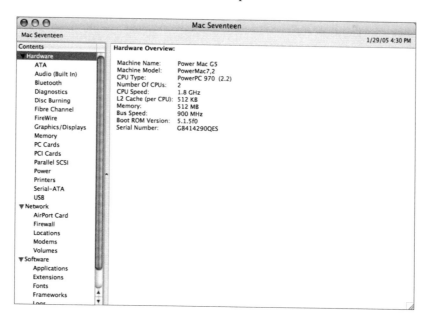

3   Select USB in the Contents list.

Hierarchical lists representing the USB buses are displayed in the upper-right pane. The built-in Bluetooth port, if available, appears on the USB bus.

Devices connected to a bus are listed beneath the bus and indented. In the preceding screenshot, nothing is connected to the first USB bus, and a hub is connected to the second bus. The lower-right pane displays details about the currently selected bus or device.

If a device is connected to a hub, it is listed beneath the hub and indented. In this example, a Studio Display is connected to the first hub. The mouse and keyboard are connected to the keyboard's hub.

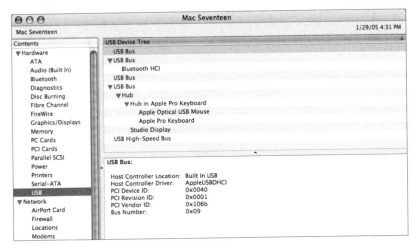

NOTE ▶ Do not be confused by the fact that the keyboard is listed under a hub, which is located inside the keyboard itself. If a device allows other devices to be connected to it, it is actually a hub with the device (the keyboard in this case) connected to that hub.

4   Locate and select the mouse in the USB report for your computer.

Details about the mouse are displayed in the lower-right pane.

5   Being careful not to click the mouse, unplug the mouse and move it to a different USB port, such as to a different free port on the computer, keyboard, or monitor.

6   Choose View > Refresh (Command-R).

7   Locate the mouse in the report to verify that it has changed places.

8   Move the mouse to yet another free USB port and refresh the report.

   If you are using a monitor with built-in USB ports, try moving the mouse to one of them or try plugging the mouse into a free USB port on the back of the computer.

9   Locate the mouse in the report.

10   Plug the mouse back into its original USB port.

11   Select ATA in the Contents list.

12   The report window now lists all of the ATA buses in the computer and any devices connected to each bus.

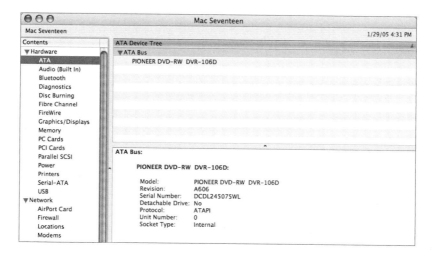

In this example, there is one ATA bus with a Pioneer DVD drive connected. Note the model number, which can be useful in researching driver versions.

13 Select a hard disk in the report. Depending upon your computer configuration, you might need to select ATA or Serial-ATA.

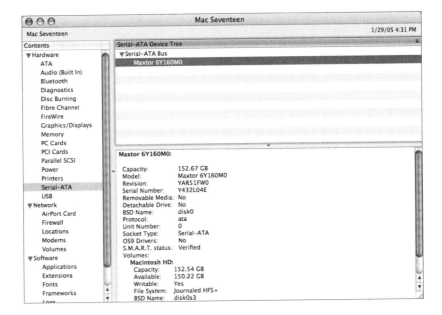

The lower pane lists details about the disk drive, including the drive's capacity, serial number, and model number. It also lists the disk drive's partitions and details about each partition.

14 Select Parallel SCSI in the Contents list.

Unless a Parallel SCSI card has been installed in your computer, the report pane displays "No information found."

15 Select Graphics/Displays in the Contents list.

Here you will see details about your video card.

16 Quit System Profiler.

Understanding Device Classes

Mac OS X groups devices into device classes, or types, to determine how to interact and support the devices' functionality.

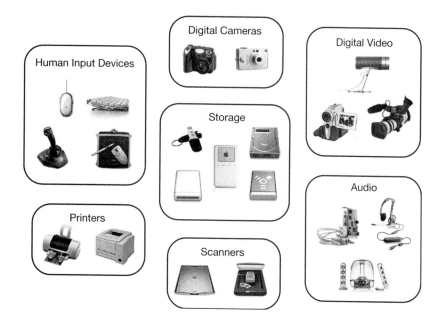

Most applications are not concerned with what buses' devices are connected. All they need to know are the types of devices connected. The operating system handles interaction across the various buses. For example, when using the Finder, you are able to retrieve files from a storage device whether the device is connected via FireWire, USB, or ATA.

The three most common types of devices are human input devices, digital cameras and scanners, and storage devices.

Human Input Devices

One of the most common device types connected to a Macintosh computer is a human input device, part of the human interface device (HID) class. The HID class includes all of the devices that allow you to input data or control the computer. Some of the devices in this class include mice, keyboards, joysticks, and graphics tablets.

Digital Cameras and Scanners

To support digital cameras and scanners, Mac OS X includes the Image Capture framework. When you plug in a supported digital camera, or press a scanner's Scan button, Mac OS X detects the action and opens an appropriate application to handle the camera or scanner. By default, iPhoto (/Applications) opens for cameras, and Image Capture (/Applications) opens for scanners. You can specify alternate applications in the Preferences menu in the Image Capture utility.

Mac OS X supports digital cameras in three ways: it directly supports those that implement Photo Transfer Protocol (PTP); it uses the mass storage driver to access those that emulate a storage device and mount automatically on the desktop; and the Image Capture utility connects to cameras that have an Image Capture plug-in (/Library/Image Capture/Devices).

The Image Capture application also supports scanners that have installed either an Image Capture or TWAIN plug-in or module. In either case, the plug-in acts like a driver, providing software to allow the application to control the scanner. Image Capture modules for scanners also are installed in /Library/Image Capture/Devices, and TWAIN modules are stored in /Library/Image Capture/ TWAIN Data Sources.

> NOTE ▶ You can use Image Capture to share your digital cameras and scanners with computers on the same subnet. Choose Image Capture > Preferences and click Sharing. Select the "Share my devices" checkbox, and then select the device or devices you want to share. To find other devices on your network, choose Devices > Browse Devices. You will see the Image Capture Devices window, where you can select a network imaging device.

Storage Devices

Mac OS X supports a wide variety of storage devices, from SCSI hard disk drives to USB floppy drives and keychain flash drives. In most cases, no additional drivers are required: if the device complies with storage device specifications for the connection bus, Mac OS X has built-in drivers that allow it to be used. Some device manufacturers may include a driver or other software to provide additional functionality, such as password protection and encryption.

When removable drives or media are mounted, Mac OS X makes the files contained on the media accessible to the user by temporarily setting ownership of all the items on the disk to the current user. For more information on how Mac OS X assigns permissions to removable media, see Lesson 5, "Permissions."

Understanding Device Drivers

Drivers are programs that enable a computer to access and interact with hardware devices. Traditionally, drivers are thought of as existing at the lowest levels of the operating system. However, Mac OS X has three distinct types of drivers: kernel extensions, plug-ins or modules, and applications.

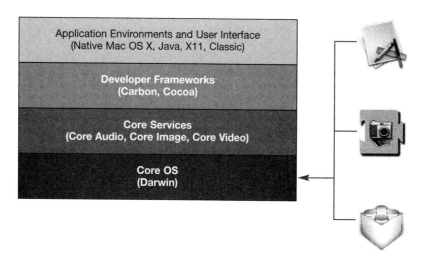

Kernel extensions (KEXTs) are pieces of software, provided in .kext files, that add functionality to the operating system kernel (Darwin). They are not the same thing as extensions in Mac OS 9. By default, kernel extensions are stored in /System/Library/Extensions. One type of kernel extension is a device driver. Mac OS X uses device drivers to provide system-wide or low-level functionality for a connected device, such as being able to read and write storage devices or read mouse movements.

Mac OS X includes a wide range of kernel extensions, allowing many devices to be used without installing extra software. However, if a device supports device-specific functionality, such as a disk drive providing password protection, you may need to install an extension provided by the developer of that device.

Some drivers are provided as plug-ins or modules for frameworks in Mac OS X. For example, support for cameras and scanners is provided with Image Capture modules. Printer drivers are provided as plug-ins to the printing architecture.

For some devices, a driver is not provided as an addition to the operating system; rather, it is included as part of an application. For example, a backup utility could include a driver to control a tape drive, since Mac OS X doesn't include native support for it.

Viewing Extensions with System Profiler

Because kernel extensions can be stored in several different Library folders, System Profiler provides the Extensions item under the Software section of the Contents list. Clicking the Extensions item lists all of the installed kernel extensions available in the system, along with other information such as their version numbers and modification dates in the upper-right pane of the System Profiler window. Clicking a kernel extension in the upper-right pane displays the Info strings (additional text that is displayed in the Finder's Info window) in the lower-right pane of the window.

Not all kernel extensions are drivers. In addition to controlling devices, kernel extensions provide other low-level services such as file system and networking support. Unfortunately, aside from the name and possibly the Get Info string, there is no way to distinguish between the different types of kernel extensions in either the Finder or System Profiler.

To use System Profiler to generate a list of all installed kernel extensions:

1   Open System Profiler.

2   Click the disclosure triangle next to Hardware to collapse the list, and click the disclosure triangle next to Software to expand it. You will see the Extensions item beneath Software in the Contents list.

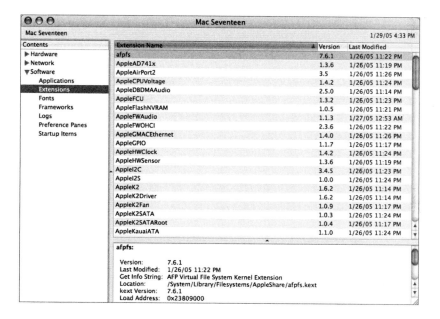

System Profiler scans the system and generates a list of all installed kernel extensions. Remember, Mac OS X extensions are not the same thing as Mac OS 9 extensions. Mac OS X extensions are enhancements to the Kernel, including hardware drivers, support for networking protocols, and file system enhancements.

3   Locate the driver for the BSD Kernel extension. The name of the extension is BSDKernel.

4 Identify the version of the extension.

5 Quit System Profiler.

Configuring Universal Access

Some users have difficulty using some of the input and output peripheral devices included with Mac OS X computers, such as the display, keyboard, and mouse. Mac OS X includes built-in software that helps users who need assistance viewing the screen, hearing, using the keyboard, or using the mouse. You can turn on these features in the Universal Access pane of System Preferences.

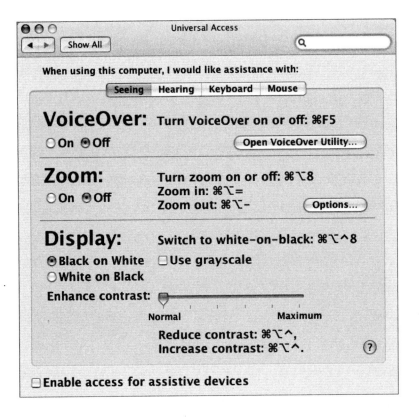

In addition to the universal access features built in to Mac OS X, specially designed peripheral devices can provide alternative methods of controlling the computer.

To use special equipment to control your computer, select the "Enable access for assistive devices" checkbox in Universal Access preferences. Selecting this option also enables User Interface (UI) scripting with AppleScript.

MORE INFO ▶ For more information on Universal Access, visit www.apple.com/accessibility.

Synchronizing Information with iSync

iSync helps you manage contact and calendar information across your Mac OS X computer and devices, such as an iSync-compatible Bluetooth mobile phone, a Palm OS device, or an iPod. To see if your device is compatible with iSync, visit www.apple.com/macosx/features/isync/devices.html.

iSync compares the Address Book contact and iCal calendar and To Do information on your computer with the address and contact information on your other devices, and then updates your computer and devices to have the same information. Some fields, including custom fields in Address Book, do not synchronize with all devices. Search the Knowledge Base for information about fields that may not sync with your device.

iSync 2.0 is part of Mac OS X 10.4, and includes the Palm conduit. To enable Palm syncing, install Palm HotSync software (www.palmsource.com), then choose Enable Palm Syncing from the Devices menu.

> **NOTE ▶** .Mac synchronization settings are available in .Mac preferences. If you click the .Mac icon in iSync, you're directed to .Mac preferences.

Troubleshooting Peripherals

Here are some strategies for identifying and fixing problems with peripherals connected to your computer:

▶ Verify that the operating system recognizes that the device is connected. Use System Profiler's Hardware section of the Contents list to locate the device. If you cannot find the device listed, you probably have a hardware problem, such as a broken device or loose connection.

▶ Unplug and reconnect the cables, making sure the connections are tight. Be sure the cables are not too long. USB 1.1 cables, for example, should be a maximum of 4.5 meters long. Try a different cable to connect the device to make sure the cable isn't defective.

▶ Try plugging the device into a different port. If the device doesn't have a power cord and is plugged into another USB device that doesn't have a power cord, try plugging the device directly into your computer or to a USB device that does have a power cord.

▶ Try unplugging all other devices to make sure that there isn't a conflict between devices.

▶ Reset parameter random-access memory (PRAM) by pressing Command-Option-P-R during startup until you hear the startup sound twice. When you reset PRAM, all connection buses are reset to their default values.

▶ If you are able to find the device listed in System Profiler, you probably have a software problem. Check with the manufacturer and install the latest version of the drivers.

What You've Learned

- ▶ Buses, such as USB and FireWire, are used to connect devices to the computer.

- ▶ Devices are categorized into classes based on their functionality.

- ▶ Drivers are pieces of code that allow the system or a user to interact with a device. Drivers can be kernel extensions that provide functionality at a very low level in Mac OS X (such as plug-ins), higher-level system components (such as printing and Image Capture frameworks), or applications that are used to control specific devices.

- ▶ System Profiler provides information about connected devices and available drivers. The Hardware section of the Contents list in System Profiler lists the buses built into your computer. For each bus, System Profiler lists the connected devices. The Extensions item in the Software section of the Contents list lists all of the kernel extensions installed on your system.

- ▶ Universal Access preferences provides options to allow easier access for users with difficulties using I/O devices such as keyboards, mice, and monitors.

- ▶ To troubleshoot issues with peripherals, use System Profiler to determine whether a device is connected, plug the device into a different port, unplug other devices, or update drivers.

References

The following Knowledge Base documents (located at www.apple.com/ support) will provide you with further information regarding peripherals in Mac OS X.

External Devices

- ▶ 25403, "Mac OS X 10.4: About compatible devices and peripherals"

- ▶ 25527, "Mac OS X: Files With Leading Period Appear on a Windows-Compatible PC"

- ▶ 58648, "Mac OS X: Do Not Connect USB Printer to Apple Pro Keyboard"

- ▶ 106403, "Mac OS X: 'No Driver for this platform' Message"

USB

▶   31116, "USB Cable: Maximum Cable Length"

▶   43005, "USB: Hub Description"

▶   61237, "What to do if a USB device isn't working"

FireWire

▶   30520, "About FireWire 400 Technology"

▶   58583, "How to use FireWire target disk mode"

URLs

Visit the following websites for more information.

▶   FireWire: http://developer.apple.com/devicedrivers/firewire/index.html

▶   Universal Access: www.apple.com/accessibility

▶   iSync devices: www.apple.com/macosx/features/isync/devices.html

Lesson Review

Use the following questions to review what you have learned:

1.   What is the difference between a bus and a device class?

2.   What can you use to determine if a device's nonfunctionality is caused by software in the operating system or by a bad physical connection?

3.   What is FireWire?

4.   What is USB?

5.   What is Bluetooth?

6.   What quick fixes are particularly useful to consider when troubleshooting peripherals issues?

7.   What is the function of Universal Access preferences?

8.   What are the three types of drivers discussed in this lesson?

Answers

1. A bus connects a device to a computer and carries data between the device and the computer. A device class is a grouping of devices by their functionality.

2. System Profiler will list all devices that are connected to a bus. If a device is not listed, there is a physical connection problem between the device and the computer.

3. FireWire is a high-speed bus most frequently used to connect external digital video cameras and storage devices.

4. USB is a low-speed bus, most frequently used to connect external input devices and printers.

5. Bluetooth is a wireless bus used to connect between a computer and mobile phones, PDAs, and other computers.

6. Use System Profiler to locate the device; try a different port; disconnect other peripherals; update drivers.

7. Universal Access preferences allow the system to be configured to allow easier access to the computer for users who have difficulty viewing the screen, hearing, using the keyboard, or using the mouse.

8. Kernel extensions, which reside in the kernel; plug-ins or modules; and drivers included as part of an application.

12

Time   This lesson takes approximately 1 hour to complete.

Goals   Describe the printing process on Mac OS X

Configure Mac OS X for printing and Printer Sharing

Configure Mac OS X for fax support

Lesson 12
Printing

Mac OS X includes a powerful printing architecture that provides support for a wide variety of printers. In many cases, users can connect a printer to their computer and print to it without having to do any configuration. Mac OS X will detect a newly connected printer and automatically configure itself to print to the printer.

Although Mac OS X provides automatic configuration, it doesn't work for all printers. You will still need to understand how Mac OS X prints and the tool you use to configure the print service and printers so that you can manually add printers and troubleshoot problems.

Understanding the Printing Process

When you print from an application in the Mac OS X graphical interface, the application uses the Mac OS X imaging frameworks to create a PDF spool file that is passed off to the Common UNIX Printing System (CUPS), a cross-platform open-source printing solution. When you print from the command line, the spool file might be in a different format, such as text or PostScript. CUPS allows you to print to PostScript and raster printers, whether they are connected directly to your computer or shared over a network.

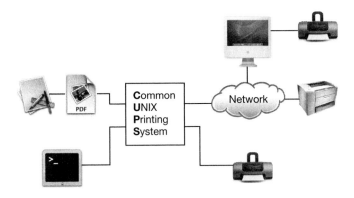

Spool files created by Mac OS X applications or by the command-line utilities are placed in the directory /var/spool/cups. The CUPS daemon then finds each spool file and passes it through a set of filter processes known as the print chain. These processes convert the file to a format that the printer understands, and then send the output file to the printer.

CUPS contains many features that are beyond the scope of this book. You can also learn more about CUPS by accessing online help in the built-in CUPS web server by entering the following URL in a web browser running on Mac OS X: *http://127.0.0.1:631.*

> **MORE INFO** ▶ Refer to Knowledge Base document 75413, "Mac OS X Server 10.2: How to Set Up Print Load Balancing Using CUPS."

Configuring Printers

The primary utility for configuring the print service is Print & Fax preferences, which has been substantially revised in Mac OS X 10.4. Its settings determine which printers are listed in the Print dialog, which printer is selected by default in the Print dialog, and the default paper size selected in the Page Setup dialog.

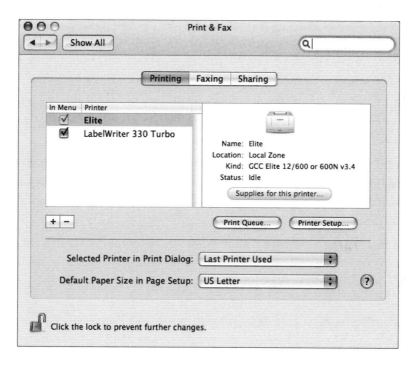

In addition to configuring the print service, Print & Fax preferences acts as a gateway to other print utilities. To open a printer's queue, select the printer and click Print Queue. When you click the Add Printer button (+) or Printer Setup, System Preferences opens Printer Setup Utility.

Adding Printers

You use Printer Setup Utility (/Applications/Utilities) to add and configure printers in Mac OS X. The standard Mac OS X installation includes printer drivers for Brother, Canon, Epson, EFI, Hewlett-Packard, Lexmark, Ricoh, and Xerox printers, so users can easily connect to the most common printers.

However, you should always check with the manufacturer to see if updated printer drivers are available for your particular printer. Mac OS X also includes Gimp-Print drivers, which are open-source printer drivers that support many older printer models for which the manufacturer might not have the Mac OS X driver.

> **NOTE ▶** Gimp-Print drivers vary in quality. Some Gimp-Print drivers are better than the vendor's and use less disk space. More often, the vendor-supplied drivers offer more functionality. Gimp-Print drivers are most useful for customers who have very old printers or printers that are not supported by the vendor, and for customers who do custom, high-end printing.

To add a printer, click the Add Printer (+) button in Print & Fax preferences or the Add button in the Printer List in Printer Setup Utility. Both methods open the Printer Browser window, which provides three methods for adding a printer. You can select a printer by browsing a list of discovered printers (click Default Browser), manually specifying the IP address of a networked printer (click IP Printer), or adding a printer by selecting the printer's connection method and PPD (click More Printers).

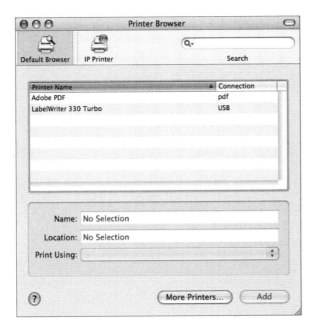

Regardless of the method you use to add a printer, a PostScript Printer Description (PPD) file describing the features of the printer is created in the hidden directory /etc/cups/ppd. The file is created regardless of whether or not the printer uses PostScript. The PPD file is copied or generated from files that were installed along with the printer driver. PPD files for standard CUPS and Gimp-Print drivers reside in /usr/share/cups/model and /usr/share/cups/model/C, respectively. PPD files for Mac–specific drivers provided by printer manufacturers reside in subfolders of /Library/Printers/PPD.

> NOTE ▶ If a printer feature, such as duplex printing, isn't available or functioning, make sure the correct PPD is selected for the printer and the option is selected in the Installable Options pane in the printer's Show Info dialog in Printer Setup Utility.

A PPD file describes the features offered by the printer. PPD files provided by printer manufacturers usually include more printer features than those provided with CUPS or Gimp-Print. After you click the Add button, you might be presented with a sheet asking you to identify the printer's options. These are printer features the manufacturer supports with the PPD, even if they are not installed in your printer. Select only those options you have installed.

> NOTE ▶ If you are encountering persistent printing problems or are moving the computer to a new location, you can choose Printer Setup Utility > Reset Printing System. This command resets the printing system to its default state, deleting all added printers and print jobs. You can then start over and add the necessary printers.

Adding a Printer Using the Default Browser

In the Default Browser pane, Printer Setup Utility lists all of the printers that it was able to discover. These include networked printers discovered through AppleTalk or Bonjour, and local printers that use the standard USB and FireWire drivers provided by Apple.

NOTE ▶ Printer Setup Utility will only display AppleTalk printers in the Default Browser when AppleTalk is enabled in Network preferences. Because AppleTalk is turned off by default, you might not see all network printers. If you do not see a specific network printer listed in the Printer Browser, try turning on AppleTalk in Network preferences or click More Printers and choose AppleTalk from the topmost pop-up menu. This will also enable AppleTalk and show any AppleTalk printers available on your network.

After you select a printer, Printer Setup Utility will query the printer to determine the appropriate PPD file to use. Some networked printers do not return enough information to enable Printer Setup Utility to select a PPD. In those cases, Generic PostScript Printer will be selected and you can choose a more appropriate PPD with the Print Using pop-up menu.

Adding a Printer in the IP Printer Pane

If the desired networked printer is not listed in the Printer Browser window, click the IP Printer icon in the toolbar to open a pane in which you can add a printer by specifying its IP address. Quite often, IP printers are part of a printer queue, or print server that provides printing services for a small or large network. IP printing allows you to add printers that use the LPD (Line Printer Daemon), IPP (Internet Printing Protocol), and Socket (HP Jet Direct) protocols.

Adding a Printer Using the More Printers Sheet

When you click the More Printers button at the bottom of the Printer Browser window, a sheet appears. The topmost pop-up menu in this sheet lets you specify the method your computer uses to access the printer. Choices include:

▶ AppleTalk — For network printers that use the AppleTalk protocol.

   NOTE ▶ Although AppleTalk is turned off by default, choosing AppleTalk from this pop-up menu automatically turns on AppleTalk, even if you do not select an AppleTalk printer.

▶ Bluetooth — For Bluetooth–enabled printers.

▶ Windows Printing — For shared printers using the SMB protocol.

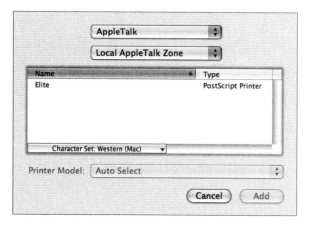

The lower portion of the pop-up menu lists manufacturer-specific connection methods. Some third-party printer drivers include their own USB, FireWire, or network connection drivers. You need to use the More Printers sheet to add these printers.

To add a Windows-shared printer, in Printer Setup Utility click Add, click More Printers, and choose Windows Printing from the pop-up menu. You can list printers by Windows workgroup or domain. Select the one you want, and then click Add.

Adding a Networked PostScript Printer

Directly-connected USB printers are discovered and added to the list of available printers automatically. For networked printers, you can select the auto-configured Bonjour printers, network print servers, or add networked PostScript printers manually in Printer Setup Utility. In this exercise, you'll add a networked printer to the Printer List for use with Mac OS X applications. If you don't have a networked printer, just read these steps so that you understand the procedure:

1   Open Printer Setup Utility (/Applications/Utilities).

    Printer Setup Utility opens and briefly displays the printer list. If you have no printers configured, it immediately prompts you to add a printer.

2   Click Add.

    Printer Setup Utility then displays the Printer Browser. The Default Browser displays any Bonjour-enabled printers or print servers.

    To set up printers that do not support Bonjour discovery, to add printers that are not configured on a print server, or to add printers on different subnets, you need to manually configure the printer.

3   Click the IP Printer icon in the toolbar.

4   From the Protocol pop-up menu, choose the protocol for the networked printer.

5   In the Address field, enter the networked printer's host name or IP (Internet Protocol) address.

    To obtain this address, you may need to contact your network administrator or check the printer's documentation to determine how to generate a configuration page.

6   Leave the other settings at their default values and click Add.

    Printer Setup Utility will redisplay the printer list with your network printer added. Note that the default queue name is the same as the printer's address. A URL or IP address does not help a typical user identify a printer. You can change the local name of the printer in the Printer Info dialog.

7   In the Printer List window, select the printer you just added.

8   Press Command-I to display the Printer Info window.

9   Change the Printer Name to something a bit more descriptive.

10 Enter a description of the printer's physical location in the Location field.

    The printer's location is very useful information in large workgroups. It is especially effective when new printers are added to your network, existing printers are moved, or when new users need to locate printers. It is also handy when dispatching technicians for maintenance or service.

11 Click Apply Changes, and close the Printer Info dialog.

12 Quit Printer Setup Utility.

Printing to a Networked Printer

Now that you have added a printer in Printer Setup Utility, make sure you can print to it.

1   Open any text document in TextEdit (/Applications).

2   Choose File > Print (Command-P).

    The print dialog appears.

3   From the Printer pop-up menu, choose the printer that you named in step 9 of the previous exercise.

4   Click Print.

5   Quit TextEdit.

Sharing Printers

Printer Sharing allows other Mac OS X and Windows users on the network to print to USB printers connected to your computer. In Print & Fax preferences, click Sharing, then select the "Share these printers with other computers" checkbox (you can also turn on Printer Sharing in Sharing preferences). Once you have enabled Printer Sharing, select which printers you wish to share in the Sharing pane of Print & Fax preferences.

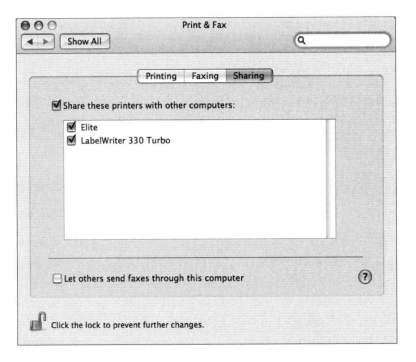

Although intended primarily for sharing local USB printers, you can also use Printer Sharing with network printers. This allows you to monitor and manage jobs sent to the network printer, assuming that other users' print jobs pass through your computer instead of bypassing your system and going directly to the network printer. There are two disadvantages to resharing network printers:

▶   You will increase network traffic. Instead of users sending the print jobs directly to the printer, they will send print jobs to your machine and then your machine will send them to the printer.

▶   Your machine will have to handle the increased load of processing all print
    jobs sent to the network printer.

Shared printers appear in the following two places on other Mac OS X computers on the local network:

▶   In the Printer Browser list in Printer Setup Utility

▶   In the Printers > Shared Printers pop-up menu in applications' print
    dialogs

Users might not have the required print drivers installed on their computers
for printers shared over the network. In this case, Mac OS X downloads the
PPD file of the printer from the computer sharing the printer and provides the
client computer with details on the shared printer's capabilities. This process
happens automatically and does not require any action on your behalf, but
may cause a slight delay when a shared printer is first chosen.

Printing to a Shared Printer from Windows

As was explained in "Adding a Printer Using the More Printers Sheet," your
Mac can access printers shared by Windows computers on your network.
Conversely, if you've enabled Printer Sharing on your Mac, it's possible for
Windows users to access your shared printers.

If you turn on Windows Sharing in Sharing preferences, you are enabling the
SMB protocol, which allows Windows computers to see your Mac OS X computer in Network Neighborhood. A Windows user can browse for your
Mac OS X computer under its workgroup (you can change the workgroup
of your Mac OS X computer in Directory Assistant). If the Windows user
double-clicks the Mac OS X computer's icon in Network Neighborhood, the
user sees whatever services you are sharing on your Mac. To use a shared
printer, the Windows user must double-click the printer's icon. A dialog will
prompt for the necessary driver, which can be downloaded from the Internet.

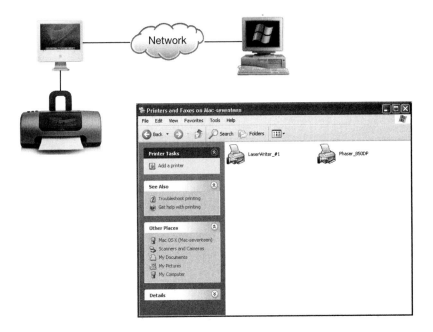

Managing Print Queues

Each printer that you have set up has a queue associated with it. A *queue* is a list of *jobs* sent to the printer by users. When you share a printer, all jobs sent to that printer are sent to that printer's queue on your computer, so it's important not to shut down your computer or put it to sleep, otherwise networked users will not be able to use your printer.

You can view and manage a printer's queue from within Printer Setup Utility by double-clicking the printer entry in the print list. A window will open displaying the printer's queue and the current print status. Individual print jobs can be paused, restarted, or deleted from the queue by selecting the print job and clicking the Hold, Resume, or Delete buttons, respectively. The Stop Jobs button stops the print queue completely until the Start Jobs button is clicked, after which the print jobs in the queue will resume printing.

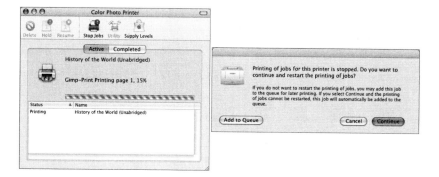

If a queue is stopped and someone tries to print to it, a dialog will ask them to add the job to the queue and wait for the queue's owner to turn it on, or to restart the queue and print the job.

If you are resharing a network printer, you can conveniently monitor and manage what is being sent to the printer using the network printer's queue.

> **NOTE ▶** You can drag print jobs between print queues. If you are drag-
> ging between different printer models or from a laser printer to an inkjet
> printer, any print jobs that require printer-specific features such as duplex-
> ing or special resolution settings will be printed with generic settings instead.

Setting Printer Info

It may be difficult to accurately identify printers in Printer Setup Utility's Printer List window, especially IP printers that may be identified by only an IP address. Fortunately, you can modify any entry and change the name to something more descriptive and useful. You can also provide location information to help others find where the printer is physically located. To modify printer information, select a printer in the Printer List window and choose Printers > Show Info (Command-I).

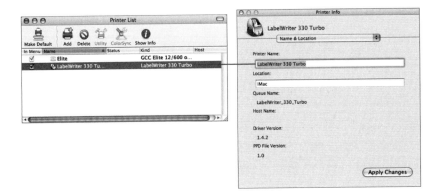

Printing Documents

Once you have added a printer using Printer Setup Utility as explained earlier in this lesson, all Mac OS X applications can print to that device using a simple process and a consistent interface.

Printing from Mac OS X Applications

Almost all Mac OS X applications that create or edit documents have Page Setup and Print commands in their File menus. If you've never printed from a particular application, the first step is to configure Page Setup because each application maintains its own settings for this dialog.

Configuring the Page Setup Dialog

The Page Setup dialog in Mac OS X applications allows you to change the appearance of pages to be printed. The choices for settings depend upon the application you are printing from and the printer you are using to print.

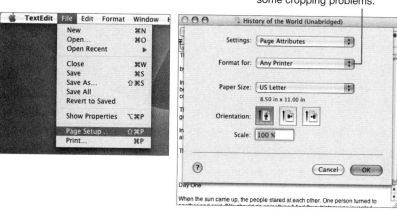

Choose your printer to avoid
some cropping problems.

Because the printable area on a page varies for each type of printer, it is important to use the Page Setup dialog to choose the intended printer so that the application does not attempt to exceed the printable area of the printer. The configuration in Page Setup is used by the application to determine the printable area.

The "Format for" pop-up menu is subtle in how it affects the page. Each printer has different page boundaries. Some can print closer to the top and bottom edges of the page; others can print closer to the left and right edges. Choose Any Printer from this pop-up menu to specify a lowest common denominator for the printable area, one that just about any printer can handle.

> NOTE ▶ If you find that headers or footers are cropped when printed from your computer, but not from another computer, check the printer chosen in Page Setup. If Any Printer is already chosen, try choosing the correct printer manually.

The default items in the Paper Size pop-up menu in Page Setup are country-specific. For example, if you selected United States as your country in Setup Assistant when you configured your computer, the Paper Size menu items will include US Letter and US Legal.

Configuring the Print Dialog

The Print dialog is the main interface for printing from any Mac OS X application. Printers that are configured in Printer Setup Utility can be chosen from the Printer pop-up menu on the Print dialog. Options such as number of copies and pages, layout, output, paper feed, and error handling can be configured and saved as settings. Additional options depend upon the printer driver being used and might be configurable in the Printer Setup Utility on the Show Info pane.

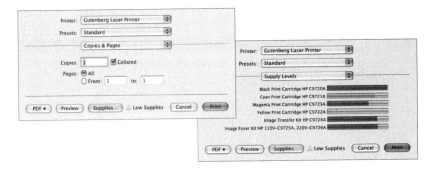

New in Mac OS X 10.4, if Mac OS X is able to detect that a printer is low on supplies, the Supplies button turns golden and a warning message appears next to the button. Click the warning message to display the Supplies pane to see what supplies are low. Click the Supplies button to visit the Apple Store webpage that contains supplies for your printer.

NOTE ▶ Not all printer drivers report supply levels to Mac OS X. Also, the information displayed in the Supplies pane will vary depending upon the printer.

Printing Using Desktop Printers

If you create a desktop icon for a printer, you can quickly print documents by dragging and dropping document icons onto the printer icon in the Finder. You can also double-click the desktop printer icon to open the printer's queue window and monitor jobs while they print.

To create a desktop printer, either select the printer in the Printer Setup Utility and choose Printers > Create Desktop Printer (Command-Shift-D), or drag the printer's name from the Printer List to the Finder's desktop.

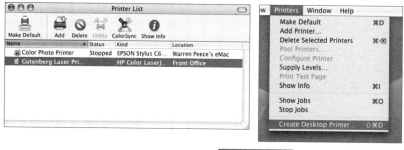

Using Other Print Options

Mac OS X has some unique options for outputting documents that don't involve printing, but they utilize the same interface because the process is virtually the same as printing.

Saving Documents as PDF Files

In Mac OS X, it is easy for you to save a document as a PDF file. All you need to do is choose File > Print (Command-P), and then in the Print dialog, click the PDF button. This reveals a menu from which you can choose Save as PDF. Enter a name and location for the PDF file, then click Save. You can open a PDF file with Preview (/Applications/Utilities) or any of Adobe's Acrobat applications on any platform, making PDF the perfect vehicle for sharing documents when retaining formatting is important.

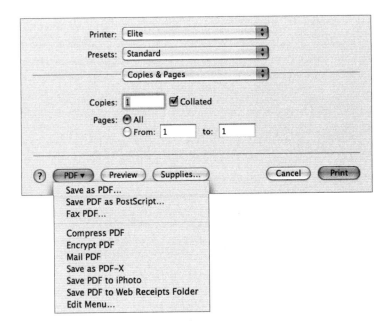

NOTE ▶ Mac OS X 10.4 adds the following PDF menu options: Compress PDF, Encrypt PDF, Mail PDF, Save as PDF-X, Save PDF to iPhoto, and Save PDF to Web Receipts Folder.

The ability to save any document as a PDF file is very useful. It can be extended almost infinitely through the PDF Workflow feature, which enables you to specify how you will prepare the PDF and what to do with it after creation. A PDF workflow is any AppleScript script, Automator action, or application that can open a PDF file. For example, you can create a script that applies a Quartz filter to a PDF file, or you can specify that the PDF file be opened by Adobe Acrobat immediately after it's created.

To use a PDF workflow you have set up, open a document and choose File > Print. Then choose your workflow from the PDF pop-up menu. Your document is converted to a PDF file, and then the PDF file is immediately opened by your workflow.

To add or delete a PDF workflow, choose Edit Menu from the PDF pop-up menu in the Print dialog. Then you can add or delete scripts, applications, or actions in the Printing Workflows list. The Edit PDF Menu window adds a copy of the workflow to the ~/Library/PDF Services folder, which enables the workflow for the current user account. If you want to add a workflow for all user accounts on that computer, you need to create a PDF Services folder in /Library and manually add items to it. Workflows can also be located in /Network/Library/PDF Services.

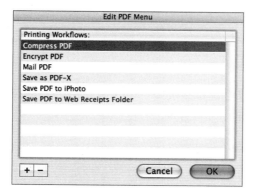

Working with Documents in PostScript Format

Although Quartz, the imaging model in Mac OS X, is based on PDF, it includes support for creating, viewing, and printing PostScript documents.

Creating PostScript Documents

Several Mac OS X applications, such as Adobe Illustrator and Adobe Photoshop, have the ability to create and edit PostScript documents. The Mac OS X printing system allows any Mac OS X application to create a PostScript file as well. In the Print dialog, choose "Save PDF as PostScript" from the PDF pop-up menu and the document will be "printed" to a PostScript file.

Viewing PostScript Documents

In addition to creating PostScript documents, the Mac OS X imaging system also includes a PostScript interpreter to allow users to view PostScript documents. If you double-click a PostScript document in the Finder, it will be opened in Preview by default. You can also use the ColorSync utility to open a PostScript file and apply Quartz filters such as Sepia Tone or Lightness Decrease.

Printing PostScript Documents

Once you have a PostScript file on your computer, you can print it on either a PostScript or a raster printer by dragging the file's icon to the desktop printer alias. You can also print a PostScript file from the command line. (You could open the PostScript file in Preview and print from there, but Preview would convert the file to PDF for printing, which might degrade the quality.)

Faxing Documents

With Mac OS X 10.4, you can "print" a document to a fax machine using your computer's internal modem and any Mac OS X application that can print to a normal printer.

Sending Faxes

To fax a document, open it with its default application, then choose File > Print. In the Print dialog, choose Fax PDF from the PDF pop-up menu and a configuration sheet appears.

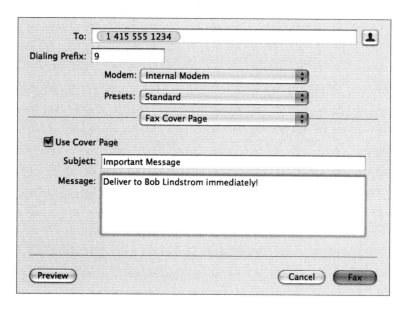

In the To field, enter the phone number of the receiving fax machine. Alternatively, click the icon to the right of the To field to choose a recipient from your Address Book. All other fields in the configuration sheet are optional. When you are ready to send your document, click Fax. Mac OS X transmits the document as a fax through the chosen modem, which must be connected to a working phone line.

Like printing, the application creates a fax job and adds it to a fax queue. You can view a list of fax jobs to be sent and jobs that have been sent in Printer Setup Utility. Choose View > Show Fax List, select the fax modem, and click Show Info.

Receiving Faxes

You can also set your system to receive faxes by selecting the appropriate checkbox in the Faxing pane of Print & Fax preferences. In addition to specifying how many times the phone should ring before the fax modem answers, you can specify how the received fax should be handled: save it as a PDF in a folder, email it, or print it on a specified printer.

TIP If you don't want to leave your computer on all the time to receive an occasional fax, you can put it to sleep. But before doing so, in the Options pane of Energy Saver preferences, select the "Wake when the modem detects a ring" checkbox.

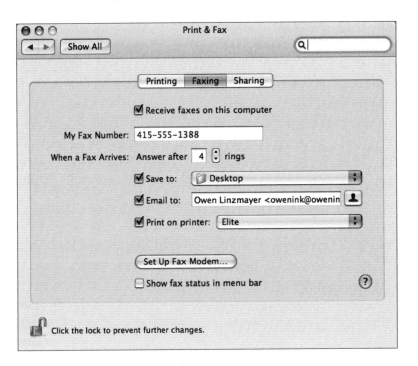

Fax Sharing

You can also share your fax/modem with other computers so they can fax through your computer, the same way you can share a printer. Click Sharing in Print & Fax preferences, and select the "Let others send faxes through this computer" checkbox. Your fax/modem will show up under Shared Fax in the Modem pop-up menu in the Fax PDF sheet.

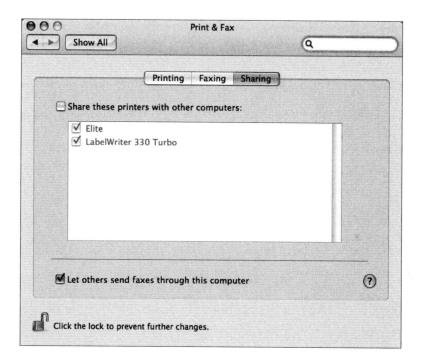

Note that when you are sharing your fax/modem, other computers on the network using your machine to send faxes will spool their print jobs to /var/spool/fax on your computer, at which point your computer will handle the faxing. It's important not to shut down your computer or put it to sleep, otherwise networked users will not be able to use your fax/modem.

Faxing Status

When the "Show fax status in menu bar" checkbox is selected in the Faxing pane of Print & Fax preferences, a fax status menu extra is added to the menu bar. The icon displays status information when your computer sends or receives a fax.

You can also control some fax functions through the menu extra. For example, you can answer an incoming call and treat it as a fax by choosing Answer Now from the fax status menu extra. If you need to hang up on an incoming fax, choose Hang Up Now.

Troubleshooting Mac OS X Print Services

Printing is a fundamental task in any networked office environment, and every support professional is called on to perform printer support at some point. These exercises address the logical structure of troubleshooting, the tools you use to set up printers and troubleshoot problems, and the location of files used by the printing system.

You will view file locations used by the printing system in Terminal, then use Printer Setup Utility to reset the printing system. After resetting the printing system, you will review the CUPS log to see the results of your actions.

In Mac OS X, fax services are designed for robustness and require very little attention. With background-receive features and print-to-fax functionality built into the operating system, most fax troubleshooting will involve phone line issues. Printing issues will take significantly more of your troubleshooting time, so this material focuses on that subject.

Identifying File Locations

In Mac OS X, CUPS is the printing engine that manages and executes print jobs. CUPS stores its configuration files in several locations. You will use Terminal to view some of the essential configuration files.

1   In the Finder, choose Go > Go to Folder (Shift-Command-G).

2   Enter */etc/cups* and press Return.

This shows you a list of the CUPS configuration files. In the /etc/cups folder, you will see several important configuration files that you can use for advanced troubleshooting, such as printers.conf and cupsd.conf. For now, it is sufficient to know that these files exist.

3   Double-click printers.conf.

You will see a message that there is no default application specified to open printers.conf.

4   Click Choose Application, and navigate to TextEdit (/Applications) to open the file.

You will see an error message that you do not have sufficient privileges to view the file. Many configuration files are protected with administrator-only editing permissions. As an administrator, however, you might need to edit those files on a user's computer.

5   Open Terminal (/Applications/Utilities).

Terminal automatically opens a terminal session with the active user account. You will use the su (switch user) command to change your terminal session login from your Chris Johnson user account to the Apple Admin administrator account.

6   At the prompt, enter *su apple* and press Return.

7   Enter the Apple Admin password and press Return.

Now you can use sudo to view the contents of a configuration file.

8   At the prompt, enter *sudo more /etc/cups/printers.conf* and press Return.

9   Enter the password for Apple Admin when prompted.

You will see your configured printers.

Due to the restrictive permissions on these files, you must use sudo to view their contents, even when you log in as an administrator. Many files in the printing system are protected from direct manipulation, because you can use Printer Setup Utility to do the maintenance tasks with less chance of errors that might result in printing system problems.

10 Enter *exit*, and press Return.

This command logs you out of your administrator terminal session. Whenever you use su to perform administrative tasks on a user's computer, you should always use exit to log out the administrator user when you are done.

11 Quit Terminal.

Reviewing Activity in the CUPS Log

Your actions in Printer Setup Utility are logged in the CUPS log in Console. This log can be invaluable in identifying the actions that led to any problem you encountered.

1   Open Console (/Applications/Utilities).

2   Click the Logs button in the toolbar to show the list of logs.

3   Click the disclosure triangle next to /var/log.

4   Click the disclosure triangle for CUPS.

You will also see the fax log in the /var/log list. This is where you can perform fax system troubleshooting if needed.

5   Select error_log in the CUPS list. You can see all of your printer setup work in the log contents at the right. To show only the pertinent entries, use the Filter field to limit the log display.

6   Enter *queued* in the Filter field.

The log display is truncated to show only the log entries for queued print jobs.

7   Quit Console.

Resetting the Print System in Printer Setup Utility

You use Printer Setup Utility for most of your initial printer troubleshooting, because it can easily resolve many basic printing problems. If a problem is especially troublesome or persistent, you might find that it's easier to reset the printing system entirely.

1   Open Printer Setup Utility (/Applications/Utilities).

    Printer Setup Utility opens and displays the printer list.

2   Choose Printer Setup Utility > Reset Printing System.

    Printer Setup Utility will display a warning dialog that you are deleting all of your printers and print jobs. This command removes all setup files, configuration files, and pending or completed spool jobs. It does not remove print drivers or PPDs, so you can use this without needing to rein-stall drivers for printers that require them.

3   Click Cancel to leave your computer unchanged.

    If you click Reset, you must authenticate as an administrator.

4   Quit Printer Setup Utility.

Using Strategies for Print Troubleshooting

Here are some strategies for identifying and fixing problems with printing:

▶   If there are problems with the format of the printed documents, make sure that you formatted the page for the correct printer in Page Setup. Also, attempt to print to a different printer, if one is available, to see if the prob-lem is with the printer. Try printing from a different application to see if there is an application setting that is interfering with the print formatting.

▶   Try removing and then re-adding the printer in Printer Setup Utility.

▶   For USB printers, try adding them manually. If you are unable to locate the printer in Printer Setup Utility, use the troubleshooting techniques suggested in Lesson 11, "Peripherals," to identify if you have a hardware or software issue.

▶ For network printers, use the networking troubleshooting techniques you learned in Lesson 8, "Networking Configuration and Troubleshooting," to make sure that your network settings are correct and your connection to the network is functioning properly.

▶ If you've verified that it isn't a hardware problem, but you can't see the printer listed in Printer Setup Utility, reinstall the printer's driver. Since the installation of printer drivers is optional while installing Mac OS X, it could be that the drivers were never installed. Also, check the manufacturer's website to get the latest version of the printer driver. Even if your printer came with Mac OS X printer drivers, they may be out-of-date.

▶ Use Console to read the log files related to printing. They are access_log, error_log, and page_log, all located in /var/log/cups. They serve as the best source of information for any problems you may encounter.

▶ A new feature in Mac OS X allows you to reset the printing system. You can reset the printing system if you suspect that there are problems with a number of different printer queues or printing components. This deletes all print queues and custom drivers. In Printer Setup Utility, choose Printer Setup Utility > Reset Printing System.

▶ Keep in mind that you might not have control over problems that occur with network printers and print servers. You should coordinate with the administrators of those computers and printers to resolve problems.

▶ Occasionally, you might have to call the printer vendor to resolve a problem.

MORE INFO ▶ Refer to Knowledge Base document 25407, "Mac OS X: About Third-Party Printer Compatibility."

What You've Learned

- ▶ Mac OS X printing is based on the Common UNIX Printing System (CUPS).

- ▶ The primary utilities for configuring printing are Print & Fax preferences for configuring the print and fax services, and Printer Setup Utility for adding and deleting printers and managing print queues.

- ▶ You can share locally connected printers over a network by turning on Printer Sharing in the Services pane of Sharing preferences or in Print & Fax preferences. Shared printers can be used by Mac OS X 10.2 or later and Windows computers.

- ▶ Mac OS X includes a powerful printing architecture that allows you to print documents to a fax/modem. Mac OS X can also receive faxes and have them printed, stored as PDF files, or emailed.

References

The following Knowledge Base documents (located at www.apple.com/support) will provide you with further information regarding printing in Mac OS X.

External Devices

- ▶ 58648, "Mac OS X: Do Not Connect USB Printer to Apple Pro Keyboard"

- ▶ 106403, "Mac OS X: 'No Driver for this platform' Message"

Printing

- ▶ 25407, "Mac OS X: About Third-Party Printer Compatibility"

- ▶ 25609, "Mac OS X 10.3, 10.4: Printer Sharing shares both printers and faxes"

- ▶ 75216, "Mac OS X: USB Printer Drivers No Longer Available"

- ▶ 75413, "Mac OS X Server 10.2: How to Set Up Print Load Balancing Using CUPS"

- ▶ 106706, "Mac OS X: How to Print"

▶ 106707, "Adding a printer to your printer list in Mac OS X"

▶ 106789, "How to access third-party ink jet printer utilities (Mac OS X)"

▶ 106714, "Troubleshooting printing issues in Mac OS X"

▶ 107060, "Mac OS X 10.2, 10.3: Sharing a printer with Mac OS 9 computers"

USB

▶ 31116, "USB Cable: Maximum Cable Length"

▶ 61237, "What to do if a USB device isn't working"

URLs

Visit the following website for more information:

▶ CUPS: http://127.0.0.1:631 (Accessed on a computer running Mac OS X 10.2 or later)

Lesson Review

Use the following questions to review what you have learned:

1. What utilities are used to configure and control printing in Mac OS X?

2. What methods are used to connect and control a printer in Printer Setup Utility?

3. What printer information do you need to correctly select and print to a printer connected to the network via IP?

4. What quick fixes are particularly useful to consider when troubleshooting printing issues?

Answers

1. Print & Fax preferences and Printer Setup Utility are used to configure and control printing in Mac OS X.

2. AppleTalk, IP Printing, Open Directory, Bonjour, USB, and Windows Printing are used to connect and control a printer in Printer Setup Utility.

3. You need the printer's IP address or URL and the printer type/model. In addition, choosing the printer make and model will enable you to take advantage of printer-specific options.

4. Verify that the printer is listed in Print & Fax preferences and Printer Setup Utility; verify that the correct printer is selected in the Page Setup dialog in the application from which you want to print.

13

Time

This lesson takes approximately 1 hour to complete.

Goals

Identify the processes that run at system startup

Identify the location of important files and scripts used by the startup sequence

Identify the different stages of the startup sequence and their corresponding visual or auditory cues

Troubleshoot startup issues, including startup items and login items

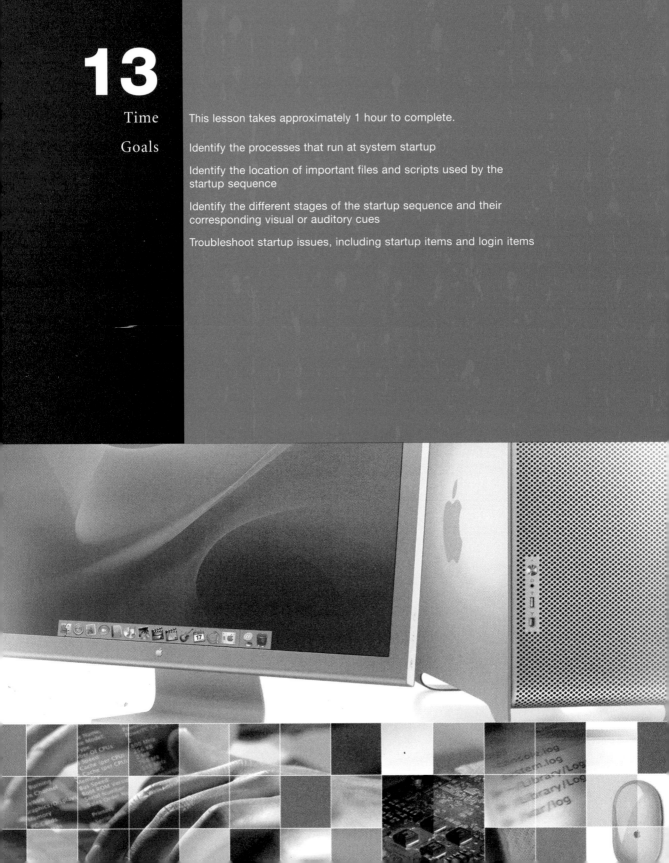

Startup Sequence

Most Macintosh users turn on their computers and wait for the Finder or login window to appear. That's all normal users need to know to begin working on a Macintosh computer. But power users and administrators benefit from understanding what goes on behind the scenes to run Mac OS X.

When the power is turned on, Mac OS X performs a series of tasks to prepare the system for operation. Visual and auditory cues help you follow the startup sequence. If something goes awry during startup, those cues can provide clues as to where the problem is and how to fix it. The following pages explain the Mac OS X startup sequence.

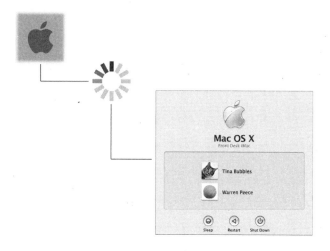

Understanding BootROM

BootROM is a hardware component that contains the startup (boot) programs, which are the first processes that run when the computer is turned on. These programs include the Power-On Self Test (POST) and Open Firmware.

POST

The Power-On Self Test checks basic hardware components for functionality. POST sets components such as the processor, random access memory (RAM), and crucial hardware interfaces to states expected by the system. In addition, POST verifies that the RAM is functioning to operating specifications.

If the system fails POST, the following error beeps occur:

▶ One beep — No RAM installed

▶ Two beeps — Incompatible RAM types

▶ Three beeps — No good memory banks

▶ Four beeps — No good boot images in BootROM

▶ Five beeps — Processor is not usable

Error beeps may vary, depending upon the computer model. If no sound is present, some models will flash an LED to indicate a failure. Search the Knowledge Base for the specific hardware error messages.

If the system passes POST, you will hear the normal startup chime.

Open Firmware

Open Firmware initializes the rest of the hardware, builds the initial device tree (a hierarchical representation of devices associated with the computer), and selects the operating system to use.

Open Firmware also checks whether startup modifier keys have been pressed, and takes the appropriate action.

Startup Modifier	Action
Command-Option-O-F	Start up in Open Firmware
Command-Option-P-R	Reset parameter RAM
Command-Option-Shift-Delete	Bypass startup volume
Option	Open the Startup Manager
X	Force Mac OS X startup
C	Start up from an optical disc
mouse or trackpad button	Eject optical disc
N	Start up from a network server
R	Reset PowerBook screen
T	Start up in Target Disk Mode
Shift	Start up in Safe mode
Command-V	Start up in Verbose mode
Command-S	Start up in Single-User mode

Tracking BootX

When the Open Firmware startup program in BootROM locates and selects the Mac OS X operating system, it transfers control to BootX (a process that Open Firmware starts from /System/Library/CoreServices on the startup disk). The primary task of BootX is to initialize the kernel environment and the drivers (such as the drivers for I/O buses) needed to boot the system. In addition, BootX starts up the kernel initialization process.

When Open Firmware attempts to find BootX, one of the following icons will appear, indicating these results:

▶ Metallic Apple logo — Found BootX

▶ Circle with slash — Could not find BootX on the startup volume

▶ Flashing square with globe — Looking for BootX on a remote disk via the network

▶ Small metallic spinning globe — Found BootX on the network
▶ Flashing question mark over a folder or floppy disk icon — Open Firmware did not find a startup disk (locally or on the network)

MORE INFO ▶ Refer to Knowledge Base document 58042, "A flashing question mark appears when you start your Mac."

If Mac OS X components have been renamed or moved from the root level of the startup disk, a broken folder icon will appear. A black belt may appear around a folder icon if a Mac OS 9 restore has been installed incorrectly using the Restore discs that came with the computer.

MORE INFO ► Refer to Knowledge Base document 106294, "Mac OS X: Reinstalling Mac OS 9 or recovering from a software restore."

When loading the kernel environment, BootX first attempts to load a previously cached set of device drivers. If this cache is missing or corrupt, BootX searches /System/Library/Extensions for drivers and other kernel extensions whose OSBundleRequired property is set to the appropriate value for the type of boot. (This is either a local or network boot, depending upon the current selection in Startup Disk preferences.) You can recognize this stage by the metallic Apple logo and the spinning gear that appear on the screen.

Understanding Kernel Tasks

The kernel initializes the Input/Output Kit (I/O Kit), which controls input and output devices. The I/O Kit links the loaded drivers into the kernel based upon the device tree previously created by Open Firmware.

The kernel starts the launchd process, and the launchd process is then responsible for bootstrapping the rest of the system.

launchd

New in Mac OS X 10.4, the launchd process manages daemons, both for the system as a whole and for individual users. A *daemon* is a continuously running program, which exists for the sole purpose of managing service requests that the computer system expects to receive. The daemon forwards the requests to the appropriate processes. launchd manages daemons, both for the system as a whole and for individual users.

During startup, launchd scans the LaunchDaemons and LaunchAgents folders in both /System/Library and /Library for plist files. Each plist file represents a process that launchd needs to manage. The contents of the plist file specify the location of the code that should be run and when the process should be launched.

Unlike startup items, which are always launched during in the initial startup sequence, launchd items are intended to launch only when needed. This reduces the number of processes running, which, in turn, helps increase system performance and reduce initial startup time.

Viewing the Process Hierarchy

The launchd process is an essential part of Mac OS X 10.4, because it is initiated by the kernel task during startup, and launches a series of background processes. It is important to understand that there is a hierarchy of tasks in the core operating system, because it can be important in the event of a problem to identify parent tasks, such as launchd, that spawn several child tasks. In this exercise, you will learn how to use Activity Monitor to gather information about processes.

1   Open Activity Monitor (/Applications/Utilities).

2   Choose "All Processes, Hierarchically" from the pop-up menu at the top of the window.

3   Click once on the Process ID column heading to sort the processes in ascending order.

4   Use the disclosure triangles to reduce the view to just kernel_task and launchd.

You can see that in the Process ID column, kernel_task is listed as process 0. It is the first operating system process that launches after the hardware initialization. You can also see that launchd is process 1, meaning that it is the second task that launches. All other processes will be numbered sequentially above these core tasks. However, to understand the task hierarchy, you need more information than the task name and ID.

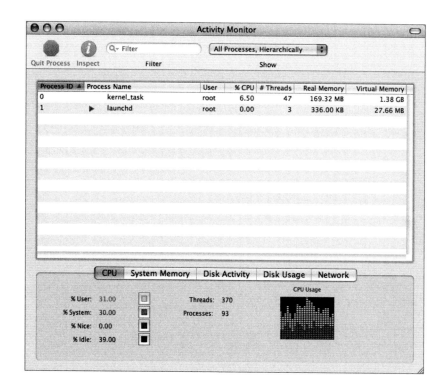

5 Select launchd, and click the Inspect button in the toolbar (Command-I).

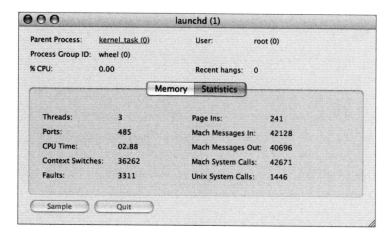

When inspecting a process, the name of the window will be the name of the process followed by the process ID in parentheses. The parent process is shown in this window, which is helpful when you are trying to evaluate processes during troubleshooting.

Note that you can click the parent process and open an inspector for that task as well. This is very useful when you are working with higher-numbered tasks and you are tracing the process hierarchy backward.

6   Close the Inspect window.

7   Click the launchd disclosure triangle.

You will see the list of processes and daemons currently running on your computer.

8   Click the WindowServer disclosure triangle.

You will see the current list of user applications and background processes.

Check the WindowServer process for unexpected processes that might affect the user environment. For example, this list contains applications that were launched as login items for the current user, but hidden at startup. It also shows a disclosure triangle for processes that have sub-processes, allowing you to view all running tasks.

9   Quit Activity Monitor (Command-Q).

10 Shut down the computer.

Startup Scripts and Startup Items

After launchd executes successfully, it runs the /etc/rc script to perform basic system initialization tasks. These initialization tasks include a file-system consistency check (fsck) and starting a process called SystemStarter, which launches the startup items.

Startup items are processes that run during the last phase of the startup sequence to prepare a Mac OS X system for normal operation. Startup items consist of programs, including customizable shell scripts, which perform tasks such as starting additional system daemons.

System startup items are located in /System/Library/StartupItems, and consist of folders each containing (at a minimum) one program (typically a shell script) whose name matches the folder's name, and a configuration property list (plist) file that the shell script reads when the startup item loads.

> **NOTE** ▶ Administrator users should not add startup scripts to /System/Library/StartupItems. However, you can create and store custom startup items in /Library/StartupItems.

As mentioned earlier, launchd items are intended to replace startup items. However, Mac OS X 10.4 still supports startup items to provide compatibility with existing software.

Launchd items, startup items, and any applications that launch before the loginwindow process are referred to as *system processes*. These applications provide services to all users of the system and are usually *children* of launchd. (A *child process* is a process that is started by another process, which is called its *parent*.) Processes created after the launching of loginwindow are referred to as *user processes*. User processes are always associated with a particular user session, and are usually children of the session's Window Manager process. You specify which user processes to launch after login in the Login Items pane of Accounts preferences, as discussed in Lesson 3, "User Accounts."

Many startup scripts rely on system configuration information stored in /etc/hostconfig. Some entries in hostconfig specify whether certain services should be started when the computer starts up. For example, when you turn on Personal Web Sharing, the Services pane of Sharing preferences sets an entry in hostconfig:

WEBSERVER=-YES-

When the Apache startup item executes during system startup, it checks whether the WEBSERVER value is set to YES, and if so, it starts the Apache web server.

A number of processes are already running by the time the user logs in to a Mac OS X system. Most of these processes are daemons or processes created by the system that run in the background. In addition to those started by launchd and startup scripts, a handful of processes are created on behalf of the user by the loginwindow process and the Window Manager daemon.

The loginwindow Process

Login occurs after system initialization with the appearance of the login window. The loginwindow process coordinates the login process and the individual user's session, calling on other system services as needed. Depending upon the user's login preferences, the login window may prompt the user for a valid login name and password, or may use cached values to log in the user automatically. When the user's login name and password have been authenticated, loginwindow proceeds to load the user environment.

When the user logs in, loginwindow does the following:

► Loads the user's computing environment, including preferences, environment variables, device and file permissions, keychain access, and so on

► Launches the Dock, Finder, and SystemUIServer

▶ Launches the Setup Assistant if an installation is in progress

▶ Automatically launches applications specified in the Login Items pane of Accounts preferences

When all of these applications are launched and running, the login procedure is complete.

The loginwindow application uses Launch Services to launch all applications, including the Finder, Dock, SystemUIServer, and user-specified applications. Most applications in the user session run as child processes of the Window Manager process. They are not owned by loginwindow.

Once the user session is running, loginwindow monitors the session and user applications in the following ways:

▶ Manages logout, restart, and shutdown procedures

▶ Manages the Force Quit window, which includes monitoring the currently active applications, responding to user requests to force quit applications, and relaunching the Finder

▶ Displays alert dialogs when a notification is received from hidden applications (applications not visible in the user interface)

▶ Writes any standard error (stderr) output to /Library/Logs/Console/*user*/console.log (where *user* is the short name), which is then used as input by the Console application

▶ Saves a limited archive of logs in console.log.# files within the same folder, where # is a number from 0 through 9, which are all viewable in the Console application under /Library/Logs/Console/user

NOTE ▶ If your computer is set to automatically log in, and you need to display the login window to log in as another user, press the Shift key when the blue screen appears during startup until the login window appears. If you were already pressing the Shift key to enter Safe mode, continue pressing it until the login window appears.

Viewing User Environment Setup

Mac OS X requires user authentication prior to accessing the system. Although the loginwindow process manages the user authentication process, it does not itself authenticate the user. The loginwindow process passes the information specified in the login window to Open Directory for authentication. When Open Directory authenticates the user, loginwindow initiates the user session and displays the status bar, along with the text "Logging In."

NOTE ► If you select the "Automatically log in as" option in the Login Options pane of Accounts preferences, the loginwindow process does not prompt you for login information.

When a user logs in to the system, the loginwindow process sets up the user environment and records information about the login. It also configures the mouse, keyboard, and system sound using the user's preferences, and retrieves the user record from Open Directory.

Troubleshooting the Startup Sequence

To troubleshoot issues during startup, try the following techniques.

Start the Computer in Verbose Mode

Start the computer in verbose mode (press Command-V at startup) to get more details on startup issues.

Start the Computer in Open Firmware Mode

You can boot into Open Firmware by pressing Command-Option-O-F during startup. The Open Firmware environment can be intimidating, because even the user prompt is simplified. The following five commands are useful in Open Firmware mode:

▶ mac-boot (starts loginwindow and completes startup normally)

▶ shut-down (shuts down the computer)

▶ reset-all (resets the NVRAM, all ports, and the processor)

▶ reset-nvram (resets the NVRAM)

▶ eject cd (ejects the optical drive tray, or optical media in a slot-loading drive)

Start the Computer in Safe Mode

Safe mode is the state Mac OS X is in after a Safe Boot (press Shift at startup)—a special way to start Mac OS X when troubleshooting. Starting up into Safe Mode simplifies the startup and operation of your computer in the following ways:

▶ It forces a directory check of the startup volume and runs fsck. Running fsck in this way takes extra time because it performs more extensive checks.

▶ It loads only required kernel extensions (some of the items in /System/Library/Extensions).

▶ It loads only launchd items located in /System/Library/LaunchDaemons and /System/Library/LaunchAgents.

▶ None of the items in /System/Library/StartupItems or /Library/StartupItems are run.

Starting in Safe mode is useful when you are trying to isolate the cause of a problem that may be caused by third-party kernel extension conflicts or startup items that cause the machine to act erratically. If the problem goes away, then you can narrow your troubleshooting focus to find out which startup item could be causing the problem.

Identifying Startup Item Locations

In this exercise, you will view three locations where your computer identifies startup items that are affected by Safe Boot. When you troubleshoot problems, it's important to understand that Safe Boot is simply a way to turn off a number of items. If the computer boots properly in Safe Boot, your understanding of where those items are located is essential for you to perform a split-half search (removing items that might be problematic) to determine what has caused the problem.

1   In the Finder, navigate to /Library/StartupItems.

   Third-party applications will often place startup items here. The folder may be empty if you haven't installed any third-party applications, but this is an important place to check when troubleshooting startup problems.

   If you find that a problem is user-specific, go to ~/Library/StartupItems.

2   In the Finder, navigate to /System/Library/LaunchDaemons.

   These are preferences for the tasks that are run at startup by launchd. It's important to know that these exist, because these will still launch in Safe Boot.

   In this folder, troubleshooting is very straightforward: if a daemon with a file here seems to cause the problem, remove the file and allow it to be recreated on the next startup. If the problem persists, that might indicate a problem with the daemon itself, something serious enough to require you to reinstall Mac OS X.

3   Scroll the /System/Library folder to see StartupItems.

4   Select the StartupItems folder to see its contents.

This folder contains the system scripts that run on a normal startup. During a normal startup, the rc script goes through this folder recursively and runs each of these scripts. Some start background processes, some check for particular hardware components, and some perform configuration steps and stop executing.

Items in this folder that are not critical for system operation or security are disabled by a Safe Boot. For example, you can see the folders for cron and CrashReporter, which are important for everyday use, but not as important when you are doing startup troubleshooting.

When you troubleshoot startup problems, remember that your computer checks several places for its startup scripts.

Prevent Login Items from Launching

If you suspect that a login item (an application that launches automatically at login, as specified in the Login Items pane of Accounts preferences) is preventing successful login, you can prevent startup items from launching as follows:

1   Start the computer.

2   As soon as you see the blue background followed by the Mac OS X progress window, press and hold the Shift key.

By pressing Shift at this point, you prevent Mac OS X from logging in automatically, giving you the option of logging in as any user.

3   When the login window appears, release the Shift key, log in, then immediately press the Shift key again.

4   Release the Shift key after the Finder's menu bar appears.

Examine Logs in Single-User Mode

Start your Mac OS X computer in single-user mode (press Command-S at startup), and when the command-line prompt appears, examine the system log by entering

less /var/log/system.log

If the startup sequence is hanging, the system log shows where the process stops.

Remove Corrupted Preferences in Single-User Mode

Corrupted system, loginwindow, or directory services preferences can cause long delays and possibly stop the machine from completely starting up. Delete these preferences by starting your computer in single-user mode, moving them to a temporary location, and restarting. These preferences are located at

▶ /Library/Preferences/SystemConfiguration/preferences.plist

▶ /Library/Preferences/com.apple.loginwindow.plist

▶ /Library/Preferences/DirectoryService

▶ ~/Library/Preferences

Restore /mach_kernel, /etc, /var if Deleted

If you start in Mac OS 9 (Macintosh models introduced after January 2003 don't boot in Mac OS 9) or another partition that has a version of Mac OS X installed and you delete key files and folders required for Mac OS X to function properly, you will need to repair the system before your drive is able to boot properly. Key files to be aware of are /mach, /mach-sym, and /mach_kernel. Other key files are actually symbolic links to important system folders required for the underlying UNIX subsystem. These symbolic links are /etc, /var, and /tmp, which are all symbolic links to folders of the same name, but located in /private. Note that most of these files and folders are set to be invisible when viewed from the Finder in either Mac OS 9 or Mac OS X.

If you deleted the /mach_kernel file, restart the computer from another drive and copy the mach_kernel file from the root level of the Mac OS X Install DVD to the root level of the Mac OS X startup volume.

If you deleted the /etc or /var links, start your computer in single-user mode, run fsck (use fsck -f to force fsck to run on journaled systems), mount the file system, and enter the following to re-create the /etc and /var links:

ln -s /private/etc etc

ln -s /private/var var

NOTE ▶ Even though /etc, /var, and /tmp tend to be referred to as folders, they are actually symbolic links to their respective folders in /private.

MORE INFO ▶ Refer to Knowledge Base documents 106908, "Mac OS X: Issues after removing 'etc' and/or 'var' directory alias when started up from Mac OS 9" and 107396, "Mac OS X: Cannot print, use Classic, start file sharing, burn discs, or update software if /tmp missing."

Single-User Mode and Network Troubleshooting

In this exercise, you will enter single-user mode, verify networking, then continue booting to the login window.

1   Boot into single-user mode by pressing Command-S immediately after turning on your computer.

   When your computer reaches the prompt for single-user mode, notice that Mac OS X 10.4 displays instructions on how to continue booting the system, but stays in single-user mode. This is useful for troubleshooting issues with the network or user environment.

2   Try to run the ping command. Enter

   ping 17.254.0.91

   and press Return. Because networking is not enabled at this point, you will not be able to access Apple's server.

3   Press Control-C to exit the ping command.

4   To continue booting in single-user mode, enter

   sh /etc/rc

   and press Return. Your system will remain in single-user mode, but it will mount the local file system, start virtual memory, and enable networking.

5   After you see the "Link is up" message, press Return to return to the command prompt.

6   Run the ping command again. Enter

ping 17.254.0.91

and press Return.

7   Press Control-C to exit the ping command.

You should now be able to verify the network connection between your computer and Apple's server.

At this point in troubleshooting, you could also verify network status by testing DNS or verifying the packets received from your DHCP server.

8   Enter

host 17.254.0.91

and press Return. You will see that DNS resolves because networking is now enabled.

You will now proceed by exiting single-user mode and booting to the login window.

In Mac OS X 10.4, the boot sequence occurs much faster than in previous versions. Be prepared to watch carefully after you press Return in the next step.

9   Enter

exit

and press Return.

The computer will exit single-user mode, initialize the user environment, and show the login window so that you can log in normally.

10   Log in as Chris Johnson when the login window appears.

Using Logout and Shutdown

The procedures for logging out, restarting the system, and shutting down the system have semantics similar to those for logging in. The foreground process usually initiates these procedures in response to the user choosing an item from the Apple menu; however, a process can also initiate the procedure programmatically by sending an appropriate Apple event to the loginwindow process. The loginwindow process carries out the procedure, posting alerts and notifying applications to give them a chance to clean up before closing.

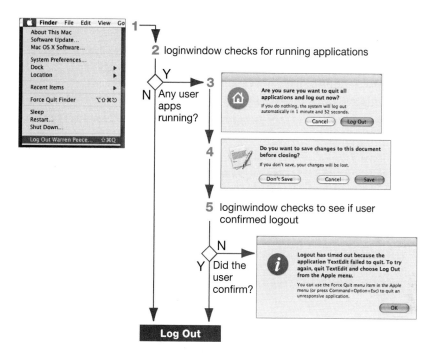

A typical logout/restart/shutdown procedure is as follows:

1　The user chooses Log Out, Restart, or Shut Down from the Apple menu.

2　The foreground application initiates the user request by sending an Apple event to the loginwindow process.

3　The loginwindow process displays an alert to the user asking for confirmation of the action.

4　If the user confirms the action, loginwindow sends a Quit Application event (kAEQuitApplication) to every foreground and background user process.

NOTE ▶ An unresponsive application can prevent a user from logging out or shutting down the computer. After 45 seconds, loginwindow automatically aborts the termination sequence. In this case, force quit the application and try logging out or shutting down again.

5   The loginwindow process closes out the user session and continues with one of the following actions:

▶   On a logout action, loginwindow dequeues all events in the event queue, starts the logout-hook program (if one is defined), records the logout, resets device permissions and user preferences to their defaults, and returns the user to the login window.

▶   On a restart, loginwindow sets the device permissions and user preferences to their defaults, powers off the system, and then powers it back on to start the startup process.

▶   On a shutdown, loginwindow powers off the computer.

What You've Learned

In this lesson you learned the basic description of the various stages of the Mac OS X startup sequence. The following table lists these stages. For each stage, the table lists the corresponding visual and auditory cues. Once you have identified the stage where startup is failing, you can isolate the cause and fix it.

Startup Sequence Stage	Cue
Power On	Black screen
BootROM-POST	Flashing lights and LEDs, and activity sound as POST mounts all devices, including hard disks and removable media
	One beep — No RAM installed
	Two beeps — Incompatible RAM types
	Three beeps — No good memory banks

Startup Sequence Stage	Cue
	Four beeps — No good boot images in BootROM
	Five beeps — Processor is not usable
BootROM-Open Firmware	Startup chime
BootX	Metallic Apple logo — Found BootX
	Circle with slash — Could not find BootX on the startup volume
	Flashing square with globe — Looking for BootX on a remote disk via the network
	Small metallic spinning globe — Found BootX on the network
	Flashing question mark over a folder or floppy disk icon — Open Firmware did not find a bootable OS
	Broken folder icon — Missing Mac OS X components
	Folder icon with a black belt around it — Restored Mac OS 9 incorrectly on a drive with Mac OS X installed
kernel	Gray screen with Apple logo and spinning gear
launchd	Blue screen
loginwindow	Login window appears
User Environment Setup	The text "Logging In" appears in login window along with a progress bar upon successful login
	Desktop and Dock appear

In comparison to starting up, the process of logging out or shutting down is simpler. After a user chooses Log Out, Restart, or Shut Down from the Apple menu and confirms the action, loginwindow quits all of the user's applications, and if appropriate, resets hardware and restarts or shuts down the computer.

References
The following Knowledge Base documents (located at www.apple.com/support) will provide you with further information regarding the startup sequence in Mac OS X.

▶ 42642, "'To continue booting, type mac-boot and press return' Message"

▶ 58042, "A flashing question mark appears when you start your Mac"

▶ 75459, "Mac OS X keyboard shortcuts"

▶ 106294, "Mac OS X: Reinstalling Mac OS 9 or recovering from a software restore"

▶ 106388, "Mac OS X: How to Start up in Single-User or Verbose Mode"

▶ 106464, "Your Mac won't start up in Mac OS X"

▶ 106805, "Mac OS X: 'Broken folder' icon, prohibitory sign, or kernel panic when computer starts"

▶ 106908, "Mac OS X: Issues after removing 'etc' and/or 'var' directory alias when started up from Mac OS 9"

▶ 107392, "What is Safe Boot, Safe Mode? (Mac OS X)"

▶ 107393, "Mac OS X: Starting up in Safe Mode"

▶ 107394, "Mac OS X: Safe Boot Takes Longer Than Normal Startup"

▶ 107396, "Mac OS X: Cannot print, use Classic, start file sharing, burn discs, or update software if /tmp missing"

▶ 14438, "You hear 'breaking glass' or 'musical beeps' when you turn on your Mac"

Lesson Review

Use the following questions to review what you have learned:

1. What do one beep, two beeps, three beeps, four beeps, and five beeps at startup signify?

2. List the possible scenarios that may occur during the BootX sequence.

3. Describe what happens during the Kernel Load stage.

4. What is the major difference between a startup item and a launchd item?

5. State three tasks that loginwindow performs after a user has logged in.

6. Identify the six visual or auditory cues that are displayed during the Mac OS X boot process.

Answers

1. One beep: no RAM installed; two beeps: incompatible RAM types; three beeps: no good memory banks; four beeps: no good boot images in BootROM; five beeps: processor is not usable.

2. Kernel found

   System not found

   Network boot

   No startup disk found

3. Loads device drivers, initializes I/O Kit, loads and starts launchd.

4. Startup items are always started during the startup process whether they will be used or not. A launchd item ideally is only launched when needed.

5. Loads the user's computing environment; launches the Dock, Finder, and SystemUIServer; and automatically launches applications specified in the Login Items pane of Accounts preferences.

6. Black screen, start-up chime, gray screen, gray screen with Apple logo and spinning gear, blue screen, login window.

14

Time	This lesson takes approximately 1 hour to complete.
Goals	Gather information about a computer problem and verify the problem
	Use online tools such as Knowledge Base and Apple Help to research a problem and its possible solution
	Use the Apple General Troubleshooting Flowchart to trouble-shoot Mac OS X problems
	Describe the difference between quick fixes and other types of fixes
	Troubleshoot top Mac OS X issues
	Perform a Knowledge Base search to identify known issues with a given system

Lesson 14
Troubleshooting

In this lesson, you'll learn about the troubleshooting process and see how the process can be applied to real-world situations you might encounter using Mac OS X.

There are two goals in troubleshooting: fix the problem properly, and fix it quickly.

To fix a problem properly, you must:

▶ Follow systematic troubleshooting procedures

▶ Use up-to-date references and tools

▶ Not create new problems

Another element in proper problem resolution is documenting your work. If you are in a shared support environment, or if you rely on outside contractors, documenting your fix for a particular problem is a very effective way to ensure that your team does not have to start from scratch every time they approach a problem. Each organization prioritizes documentation differently, but as a technician, if you take some time to organize and review your notes, you will be able to make them a useful part of your toolbox.

Using appropriate troubleshooting procedures will help you fix problems quickly. You should be sure to complete the troubleshooting steps that are applicable to the problem. (A quick fix does not necessarily mean a shortcut.) Time is an asset, so you must be complete and efficient, without rushing things in a way that might result in careless or sloppy work. It is easy to introduce problems by rushing your work.

Using Good Troubleshooting Techniques

Here are some tips that you should keep in mind throughout the trouble-shooting process.

Take Notes

What starts out as a simple troubleshooting job can sometimes unravel into a major task. Start taking notes from the very beginning of the troubleshooting process, even if it seems like a simple problem. After you complete the fix, review your notes to see where you might have been more effective.

Write down the following:

▶ Each piece of information you gather

▶ Each test that you perform (along with the results)

▶ Your proposed solution (to preserve a record of what you tried) each time you think you know what's wrong

Consult Resources

Consulting with available resources is a great way to find information about the product and problem you're troubleshooting. Even if you're not sure what you're looking for, browsing through references such as the Knowledge Base can be helpful when you don't know what to try next. You might come across a document related to the issue you're trying to resolve. Don't hesitate to ask questions of coworkers or other reputable technical authorities, because they can provide valuable clues.

Consider the Human Factor

When you have been working long and hard on a problem that has you stumped, try taking a break.

Frustration can impair your ability to think logically and rationally. You may be surprised how often a short break can allow you to think of solutions that you previously overlooked.

Don't fall prey to "confirmation bias." When you believe you have solved a problem, confirmation bias causes you to favor factors that confirm that solution, and to ignore or misinterpret factors that contradict that solution. The more intelligent an individual, the more skillful he or she can be at reinforcing a confirmation bias. Keep an open mind and don't be trapped by assumptions.

Another human factor to consider is whether the user should be present while you troubleshoot. Having the user present can be useful for gathering information about problem causes. However, having the user peer over your shoulder while you troubleshoot may also pressure you into making hasty and possibly bad decisions.

Additionally, users may later try to repeat some of the techniques on their own. Without adequate understanding of the techniques, users can cause irreparable damage. You can warn them not to try these techniques without a support person present. Unfortunately, people do not always pay attention to warnings.

Following a Methodical Order of Elimination

Approaching a problem methodically is efficient and cost-effective. Most problems can be categorized and eliminated with careful troubleshooting.

While troubleshooting, you should generally check for problems in the following order:

1. User-related problems
2. Software-related problems
3. OS-related problems
4. Hardware-related problems

Statistically, most problems are user-, software-, or OS-related. Also, this order usually represents the least expensive to the most expensive repairs. If you approach your problem-solving in this order, you will be as efficient and cost-effective as possible.

What could be causing this problem?

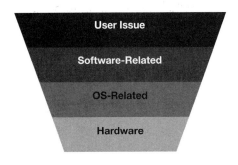

User Issue	1 "I don't know what happened, it just stopped working."
Software-Related	2 "This program always crashes when I click a button."
OS-Related	3 "My computer can't see the Internet."
Hardware	4 "It makes a strange noise when it boots."

Troubleshoot to eliminate possible sources following the most likely reasons for a problem.

User-Related Problems

Check for user-related problems while gathering information, duplicating the problem, and trying quick fixes. These include incorrectly set preferences, inadvertent errors, incompatibilities, and incorrect assumptions.

Software-Related Problems

Software can cause symptoms that look like hardware problems. Always check for software problems before assuming the problem is hardware-related. Report bugs if you find them (this is an instance where your notes will be helpful).

OS-Related Problems

You can identify OS-related problems from general symptoms that affect all applications, or from specific symptoms, such as problems that prevent the startup process from completing. Most of this lesson focuses on OS-related problems.

Hardware-Related Problems

When you're convinced that the problem is not user-related, software-related, or OS-related, you should troubleshoot it as a hardware issue. Hardware problems are beyond the scope of this book; Apple's Knowledge Base at www.apple.com/support is an invaluable resource, as is the Peachpit Press book "Apple Training Series: Desktop and Portable Systems, Second Edition."

If you isolate the problem to hardware, and you are an Apple–authorized service technician, follow the appropriate service procedures. Otherwise, contact an Apple–authorized service provider for repairs.

Troubleshooting Systematically

Troubleshooting is a process. If you go about it systematically, you'll greatly improve your chances of success. Even in those instances where you can skip a step, it's important to evaluate the process in its entirety to ensure that you are not missing something obvious.

The following illustration shows the main steps of the troubleshooting process. The first row includes steps that help you assess the problem, the second row shows steps where you identify the cause and troubleshoot so that you understand it completely, and the third row is about fixing the problem and wrapping up the issue.

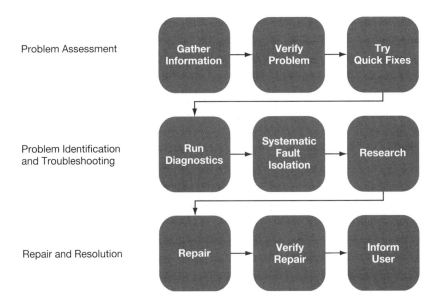

As you go through the process, keep in mind:

▶ The two goals of troubleshooting: fix the problem properly, and fix it quickly.

▶ Tasks such as keeping notes that are important in every stage.

▶ You are troubleshooting to eliminate potential causes and determine appropriate solutions. When you find the answer, you can move on to the next stage.

Every support person uses some type of troubleshooting process, and many organizations formalize their process to ensure that their technicians don't inadvertently skip troubleshooting steps. The troubleshooting process in the following illustration is used by the AppleCare support group, in order to make sure all issues are properly handled and accurately tracked. Your organization may have a similar process, and you may already be familiar with steps in this process flowchart.

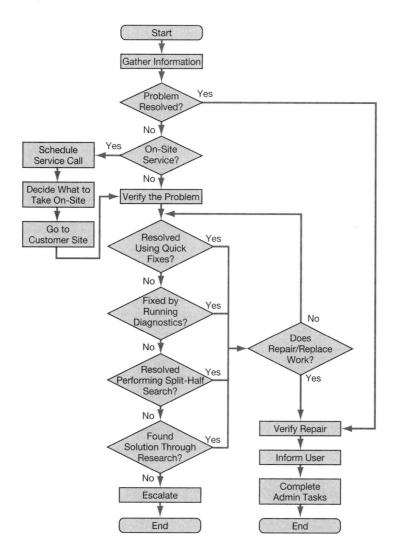

The flowchart describes a series of loops you perform until you return the system to normal operation. Let's say you're a desktop support technician called to work on a malfunctioning computer. According to the flowchart, the first step is to gather information. You immediately encounter a decision point: was it a simple problem, and did gathering information alone resolve the problem? If it doesn't, you then verify the problem, that is, you see if you can reproduce it, and you try a quick fix. (You can skip the on-site service decision, since you already have the computer in front of you.) Let's say you think you have identified the problem, so you skip to repair or replace. (In a software context, this choice can be stated as "troubleshoot or reinstall.")

After completing the repair (often a quick fix is a repair), you ask yourself if the problem is resolved. No? Then you loop back to trying quick fixes. You may try a number of quick fixes before either resolving the problem or deciding that no more quick fixes apply and you need to go on to running diagnostics. You may realize that you have exhausted your knowledge and need to research. You may decide that it is time to escalate the problem to a senior technician. Or, you may determine that the problem is fixed and enter the documentation/notification stage.

Gathering Information

Your most powerful tool in troubleshooting is your ability to ask smart, probing questions. Good probing questions can center around the description of the equipment being used and the steps to reproduce the issue.

The first thing you should find out is: What exactly is the problem? Getting a clear picture of what is not working is crucial if you want to find the solution. Try to get as complete and specific a picture as possible about what problems are occurring, when they occur, and what error messages are displayed. Search the Knowledge Base if you think this might be a common problem.

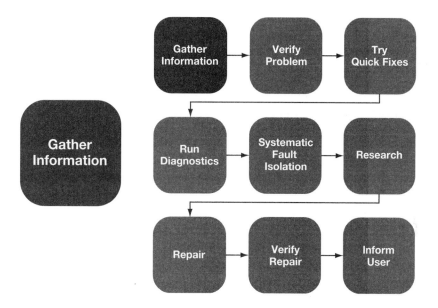

Identifying the Problem

1 Start with open-ended questions such as "What is the issue?" or "What is happening onscreen?" Open-ended questions generally start with words like *how, why, when, who, what,* and *where.* They can't be answered by yes or no. You usually gather more information this way, even if some of it is not exactly pertinent to the problem at hand.

2 Let the user explain uninterrupted and in their own words what they have experienced. The explanation may help you avoid assumptions about the source of the problem, because you may hear that more things are broken than you expected.

3 As you begin to understand the basics of the problem, start using closed-ended questions that require more limited, specific answers. "What version of the operating system are you using?" and "Is there an icon on your Desktop?" are closed questions. The user can either tell you the version or tell you that he or she doesn't know (in which case, you would guide the user to the information). Closed-ended questions often can be answered by yes, no, or a value such as "10.4."

4   Verify your understanding of what the user has told you. Restate what you
have been told and get the user's agreement that you understand the problem. An example of restatement would be, "Okay, so what's happening is
that when you do X, Y happens. Is that correct?"

5   If the user agrees that you understand, continue to gather information. If
the user does not agree that you understand, clarify what you misstated
and again verify your understanding. Do not continue with troubleshooting until the user agrees that you understand the problem.

Asking Helpful Questions

Here are some questions to ask a user before you continue to troubleshoot:

▶   What are the problems and symptoms?

▶   What were you (the user) doing when the problem occurred? (Very useful
when you try to reproduce the problem.)

▶   Has this feature or functionality ever worked? (Is the user trying to burn
DVDs in a Combo drive?)

▶   What exact system hardware, Mac OS version, and exact versions of software are involved? (Important when you try to reproduce the problem,
and later when you verify the repair.)

▶   Was any hardware or software recently added or removed?

▶   Are there environmental considerations? (Is the computer close to a
heater, window, or an electrical device?)

Sometimes, just looking at menus or standard dialogs gives you important information. For example, the quickest way to check for basic network connectivity
is to check the Network Status pane in Network preferences. You don't need to
begin your troubleshooting by restarting all of your company's network routers
or calling your network administrator to complain about connectivity.

Using Tools and Techniques to Gather Information

When you are gathering information, three useful resources are System Profiler, which provides information about the current state of your computer, Apple Remote Desktop, which helps you to gather information from remote computers, and Mac OS X logs, which serve as a chronological diary of everything that has happened on your computer.

System Profiler

Use System Profiler (/Applications/Utilities) to gather information about your computer's current state and configuration. System Profiler gets its main information from the device tree that Open Firmware builds at startup time, but it updates dynamically when plug-and-play bus devices are connected, so FireWire and USB devices will appear in System Profiler even if they are connected after startup. Unlike many other applications or utilities, System Profiler does not use a preference file (.plist), so its behavior cannot be corrupted by invalid or corrupted preferences.

Use System Profiler for situations where the operating system, or an application running on it, refuses to recognize hardware that is known to be connected to the system. You can also run System Profiler after booting from the Mac OS X Install DVD, or from a remote computer over the network.

System Profiler provides information about the configuration of the system, including the computer type and speed, the version of firmware, the version of Mac OS running, the amount of memory installed, and the types of network connections.

If you need to gather information remotely, you can use tools like Apple Remote Desktop or log in to the other computer via ssh and run System Profiler from the command line. If it's not appropriate for you to directly manipulate the other computer, you can have the user run System Profiler, save the generated report, and email it to you. If you don't have access to a Mac OS X computer, the user can export the report in a plain-text or rich-text format.

Apple Remote Desktop

Apple Remote Desktop is a real-time screen sharing and desktop management tool that allows system administrators to configure remote systems, distribute software, and provide direct assistance. With the Apple Remote Desktop administration software, you could access your office computer from home as if you were sitting at your office computer. In a classroom, Apple Remote Desktop enhances the learning experience by allowing the instructor to monitor and control students' computers. In a corporate environment, it provides a solution for managing remote systems, reducing administration costs and increasing productivity.

The client for Apple Remote Desktop is included with Mac OS X 10.4 and can be enabled from the Services pane in Sharing preferences. The Apple Remote Desktop administration software can be purchased separately.

You can also use third-party tools that provide some of the functionality of Apple Remote Desktop. Virtual network computing (VNC) programs like Chicken of the VNC can provide this functionality.

> **MORE INFO** ▶ For more information on Apple Remote Desktop, visit www.apple.com/remotedesktop.

Mac OS X Logs

You can use the Console utility (/Applications/Utilities) to view log files on a Mac OS X computer. To do so, open Console and click Logs in the toolbar to display a list of available logs in the Logs list at the left. To view the contents of a log, select the log in the list. Console displays the contents of the log in the Contents pane at the right. If you prefer to view log files using the command line, or with another program, the log files for Mac OS X are stored in /var/log, /Library/Logs, and ~/Library/Logs.

For installer errors, look in the installer log (install.log) under /var/log in the Logs pane. Among other things, this log lists the files that were copied, any errors, and the installed partition. If you suspect there have been Software Update errors, look in the Software Update log under /Library/Logs. For application and system process errors, look in console.log. To view system messages in Console, click system.log. Console updates its log display dynamically as events take place.

To simplify viewing particular logs, the File menu in Console has commands to open console.log and system.log, as well as an "Open Quickly" submenu you can use to navigate directly to a particular log. The logs are identical regardless of the method you use to view them.

When using Console, you can either manually note the date and time on the last entry, or click Mark in the toolbar to add a time marker after the last entry. You can then look at actions that occur after that date and time. When commands execute in Mac OS X, messages appear in Console. Typically, the first part of a system message gives you the date and time stamp. The next part names the owner of the process. After that, you see the process and the process ID. After the process ID, you see the actual error or message. In this example, the only information is a repeat of the date, showing that the iCal helper will relaunch in an hour.

2005-04-28 14:48:48.906 iCal Helper[516] Launch of helper planned at : 04/28/05 15:48:48

Log viewing is most helpful when there is no apparent error in the user interface, and you cannot figure out why an application is no longer working. In that case, Console might show you an error message that will direct your troubleshooting.

Verbose Mode

If you encounter a problem during the startup of Mac OS X, you can use verbose mode to gather information. To use verbose mode, press Command-V when you hear the startup chime. Verbose mode shows what's happening in the startup process in a command-line interface. The startup sequence will stop if there is a problem, and you may be able to see the items or processes that are involved with the problem.

Messages during startup are stored in the system.log file. Any kmod destroy messages that you see in the verbose mode are harmless. These are simply indications that Mac OS X is unloading kernel modifications that do not apply to your particular platform.

MORE INFO ▶ Refer to Knowledge Base document 106388, "Mac OS X: How to Start up in Single-User or Verbose Mode."

Problem Scenario—Gather Information

It's important to be thorough in the information-gathering stage. Users tend to notice only the parts of the problem that affect them directly. As a result, they don't always provide a complete or accurate description of the problem.

Here's an example. A user says that she can no longer access the Internet from home. She's using an AirPort Base Station and a DSL modem. She says she hasn't made any changes to her settings and she has a strong AirPort signal. Her DSL modem status lights indicate that she has a DSL connection.

As you gather information, you ask if there are other wireless networks in range. Checking the AirPort menu extra, you see that there are a number of wireless networks (she lives in an apartment). You notice that the network she has joined is called "linksys." This strongly suggests that the network she's on is provided by a Linksys wireless router. When you ask her about it, she mentions that it is not the name of her AirPort Base Station. She reveals that a few days before, she had inadvertently unplugged her AirPort Base Station. She hadn't realized it was unplugged because her Internet connection continued to work fine. When she discovered it was unplugged, she plugged it back in, but still can't connect.

When her AirPort Base Station was unplugged, her computer joined another wireless network. The base station that provided services to the new network also gave her an IP address, so she continued to have Internet access. Now it appears that the owner of that network is restricting the distribution of IP addresses, so her Internet access seemed to disappear without her intervention. Switching back to her AirPort network, now that it is properly plugged in, restored her Internet service.

If you hadn't asked for details about how it was working, you probably would not have discovered that she was using the wrong wireless network until you had spent a significant amount of time troubleshooting her network settings.

Verifying the Problem

Verifying the problem means reproducing the symptoms the user describes and observing the problem for yourself.

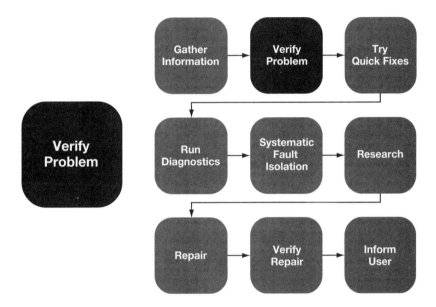

Verifying the problem is important for several reasons:

▶ Sometimes you can solve the problem by observing what the user does to recreate the symptoms. It's possible that he or she is doing something wrong that can be corrected.

▶ It often yields more information about the circumstances of the problem. (This information can differ from the description provided by the user.)

▶ It helps ensure that you don't jump to a conclusion, or waste time trying to troubleshoot a nonexistent or poorly-defined problem.

Problem Scenario—Verification

Verify the following problem to make sure you're working on the right thing.

A user calls and says that he can't get into his computer. He sees a message on his screen that will only let him restart or shut down. On the surface, this sounds like it could be the kernel panic message, but to verify the problem, you ask him to power on the computer and describe what the computer is doing as it starts up. The user is reluctant to do this, because he has seen the problem happen every time, and someone has told him that the problem is a kernel panic. He wants you to recommend steps to him to address the kernel panic. You tell him that reproducing the problem while you're speaking with him will help solve his problem more quickly.

He describes a normal startup sequence, and then the "message" appears on screen that will only let him restart or shut down. When you ask him to read everything in the message, it becomes clear that he's describing the login window. You ask him to click on his name and log in.

Further questioning reveals that he had recently added another user account for someone else to use the computer. Because he had only used the computer with one user before, he had never seen the login window before. (He was not aware that he could click the user names in the login window, because they did not clearly look like buttons.)

Trying Quick Fixes

An effective troubleshooter quickly and systematically eliminates areas to explore and continually isolates likely solutions. Trying quick fixes is one of the most effective steps in this process.

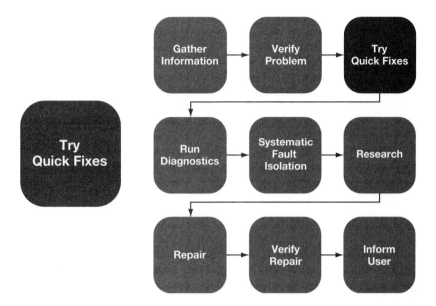

A quick fix is a repair action that:

▶ Can be performed quickly

▶ Involves little or no risk of harm to the system

▶ Has little or no cost

NOTE ▶ A quick fix is not temporary or substandard.

A quick fix is not necessarily the most likely solution to the problem, but because it's easy to perform and takes little time or expense, it's worth trying. Trying quick fixes gives you valuable information about where the problem is not.

For convenience, we divide the quick fixes applicable to troubleshooting the operating system into three increasingly invasive levels.

NOTE ▶ Whether you try a quick fix or some other type of fix, try one at a time so that you know which fix corrected the problem.

Trying Quick Fixes—Innocuous

For software-related problems, there are several quick fixes you can try that do not alter the system (refer to "Mac OS X Quick Fixes" in Appendix A, "Apple General Troubleshooting Flowchart"):

▶   Use System Profiler. For instance, you can use System Profiler to verify that the system detects a connected FireWire drive in situations where the volume doesn't appear on the Desktop.

▶   Start up from a known good operating system (such as the Mac OS X Install DVD), restart, or power off. If you press the Option key when you start up the system, the computer will display the Startup Manager screen, which lists drives and partitions with System folders. From this list you can select a different volume to boot from. The underlying goal is to start up using a known good operating system, thereby narrowing the problem to the original operating system (if the startup succeeds) or eliminating the operating system (if the startup fails).

> **MORE INFO** ▶   Refer to Knowledge Base document 107199, "Mac OS X: If your computer stops responding, 'hangs', or 'freezes.'"

▶   Use Disk Utility to verify and repair hard disk directory damage.

Trying Quick Fixes—Less Innocuous

Less innocuous quick fixes alter the user's system in some minor way. For example:

▶   You can create a new administrator user to test whether faulty user settings or preferences were causing the original problem—although this will not resolve issues with system-wide preferences or the local NetInfo database. Or, when troubleshooting an application such as iMovie, you can eliminate the possibility of a corrupt preferences file (plist file) by moving or renaming the application's preferences file.

> **MORE INFO** ▶   Refer to Knowledge Base document 25398, "Mac OS X: How to troubleshoot a software issue."

▶ As mentioned in Lesson 6, "Application Environments," you can force quit an application if it is not responding or is causing problems. If the application works fine after restarting, no further action is required. However, if the application continues to be problematic, you need to continue troubleshooting.

▶ You can try logging in as a different user. You may find that another user account works fine, allowing the user to complete any urgent tasks. You can then compare the working user account against the nonfunctional one to find out what difference is causing the problem.

▶ You may need to update the firmware on the computer. You can determine the current firmware version by running System Profiler (if the computer is functional enough), or by restarting into Open Firmware (restart while pressing Command-Option-O-F until the Open Firmware message appears).

MORE INFO ▶ Refer to Knowledge Base document 60351, "Determining BootROM or Firmware Version."

▶ Use the Verify/Repair Disk Permissions in Disk Utility. As mentioned in Lesson 3, "User Accounts," erratic system behavior could be caused by incorrect permissions set on the boot volume.

Trying Quick Fixes—Invasive
Invasive quick fixes, such as reinstalling the operating system, are more risky, because they alter the computer in some way. Before attempting invasive quick fixes, complete each of the following tasks, as appropriate:

▶ Make a backup of user data. You must do this before updating, reinstalling, or otherwise modifying the software on a system. This backup ensures that you can restore the system to its original state if you need to do so. If the system is unable to boot and you have a FireWire–enabled system, you may be able to start up the system in Target Disk Mode, which allows you to connect it to another system and copy critical data files.

▶ Make sure you are using only known-good software to modify the system. Avoid introducing new problems while trying to solve the original one.

▶   Look for the latest versions of software that you intend to update or rein-
    stall. Be careful not to add new software components that can adversely affect
    applications and other software that the user has placed on the system.

If the problem occurs only with a single application, reinstalling the application may fix the problem. It is possible that key components for the application had been deleted or corrupted.

If the computer is having difficulties in the BootROM startup sequence, you
may wish to reset the parameter random-access memory (PRAM). Resetting
the PRAM will reset any Open Firmware variables that may have been incorrectly entered. Resetting the PRAM also resets the non-volatile random access
memory (NVRAM).

> **NOTE** ▶ Mac OS X does not store as much information in PRAM as Mac
> OS 9. For more information, refer to Knowledge Base document 86194,
> "Mac OS X: What's stored in PRAM?"

Reset PRAM by pressing Command-Option-P-R during startup until you hear
the startup sound twice. To reset NVRAM independently, start into Open
Firmware and enter

reset-nvram

> **MORE INFO** ▶ Refer to Knowledge Base document 42642, "'To continue
> booting, type mac-boot and press return' Message."

These changes are invasive in that changes to the system are required and
could have repercussions later. For example, resetting NVRAM immediately
after a kernel panic erases potentially useful log information.

Problem Scenario—Quick Fixes

After you've verified the problem, trying relevant quick fixes can save time and
provide more information.

Here's an example. A home user is having a problem with his Internet connection. It worked fine yesterday, but today he cannot connect to any sites from Safari.

After verifying that he has not made any changes since his connection was working, you have him check network settings. It appears that he is getting a correct IP address and can even communicate between two machines on his home network. Because his local settings seem to be unchanged from yesterday and his home network seems to be working, you have him cycle power to his cable modem. After the cable modem powers up, he is able to connect. While incorrect network settings frequently cause home networking problems, resetting base stations, cable modems, and routers are also common fixes.

Running Diagnostics

If the system is still not functioning correctly after you've gone through the quick fixes, you should try running diagnostics. Diagnostic tools are software packages that allow you to check the performance of a system (refer to "Mac OS X Diagnostic Tools" in Appendix A, "Apple General Troubleshooting Flowchart").

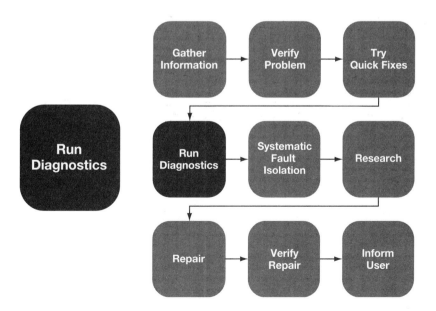

If you can open Network Utility or access Network Diagnostics, you can diagnose basic networking issues. Also, if you have the Mac OS X Install DVD, you can boot from that disc and run System Profiler or Terminal to verify that the hardware is operating correctly.

If you are trying to diagnose and repair disk problems with the boot drive, you'll need to boot from the Mac OS X Install DVD and run Disk Utility. If you don't have access to an Install DVD, you can boot into single-user mode, and at the prompt use the fsck command to test and fix the disk:

```
# /sbin/fsck -y
```

```
# /sbin/mount -uw /
```

You can also use a virus scanner to check whether the system has become infected, but virus infections very seldom cause problems on the Macintosh.

Problem Scenario—Diagnostics

An employee who works in your group complains that her computer has been running really slowly and that she can't customize her applications to work the way she wants them to.

You're able to work with her computer yourself, and you verify that it's performing slowly. You also determine that her applications are not retaining changes made to the preferences. Restarting the computer does not change the behavior.

You decide to run Disk Utility, and in doing so you find that her hard disk is almost full. You work with her to identify several items she no longer needs and delete them. After freeing up a significant amount of disk space, applications retain their settings and the computer is performing much better.

Performing a Split-Half Search

A split-half search is a technique for systematically isolating the source of a problem. You start by temporarily eliminating roughly half of the variables that could be part of the problem, and try to recreate the problem. Then at each subsequent step, you split your set of potential problem items in half. You continue halving your search group until you find the source of the problem. Then after you identify the source, you can remove it permanently and restore all of your eliminated items.

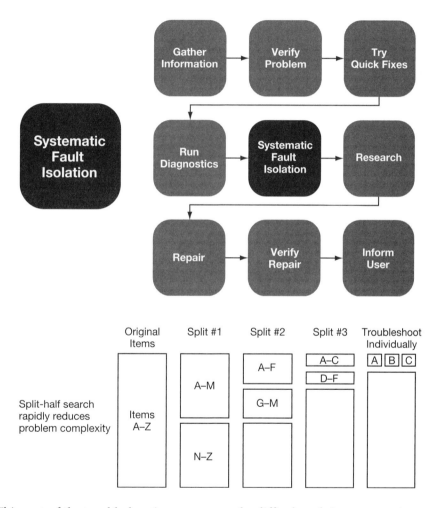

This part of the troubleshooting process can be difficult and time-consuming. Exhaust the tools and techniques in the earlier steps of the flowchart before performing a split-half search, and consider whether it would be faster just to reinstall.

By pressing Command-S while you start up the computer, you start Mac OS X in single-user mode and eliminate all of the multiuser processes from the picture. You can then determine if the issue arises just when you are running in multiuser mode or if it occurs whenever the operating system is running. Starting in single-user mode and then using the exit command to return to the normal multiuser mode can sometimes quickly fix a startup issue. Single-user mode is only innocuous as long as no other commands are entered.

Pressing the Shift key while the computer starts up puts the system in Safe Mode. In Safe Mode, the system does not load items from the StartupItems folders. For more information about Safe Mode, see "Start Computer in Safe Mode" in Lesson 13, "Startup Sequence." If the problem does not occur in Safe Mode, you can narrow your split-half search to determine which items in /Library/StartupItems or /System/Library/StartupItems could be causing the problem.

Similarly, if you press the Shift key right after you log in, you enter Safe Login mode. The system will not open the items that were activated in the Login Items pane of Accounts preferences. If the problem goes away while doing the Safe Login, you can narrow your split-half search to find out which login item is causing problems.

If you think the problem is account-based, and auto-login has been set for the problem account, you can disable auto-login for the current startup. While your computer is starting, after the kernel has completed building, press the Shift key when you see the Apple logo and progress bar. (Do not press the Shift key through the entire startup sequence, or your computer will enter Safe Mode.)

If you have properly pressed the Shift key, login will stop at the standard login window so that you can log in to a different user account. This allows you to test a different account without having to open Accounts preferences. If you don't see the login window, restart and try it again.

You can also systematically kill or forcibly quit processes using the Activity Monitor or the kill command in Terminal. Again, this eliminates possible causes of an issue until you get to a process that has an impact on that issue.

Sometimes the problem you are encountering is caused by a hardware device. By systematically unplugging peripherals from the system, you can track down a device that is causing problems.

In situations in which you're trying to determine if the issue is with the computer system or with the network, you can run Network Utility.

As you try to eliminate potential causes, you might find it useful to compare the computer to another computer that is working correctly. By focusing on the differences between the two systems, you can cut down on the trouble-shooting time.

Problem Scenario—Split-Half Search

A student says all his programs are crashing. He's restarted the computer and you verified the crashing problem in a word-processing application. Relevant quick fixes have not changed anything.

As part of a split-half search, you use Safe Mode to see if the problem is related to something in the StartupItems folders. The computer seems to work fine in Safe Mode.

Now you know that the problem probably lies with an item in one of the StartupItems folders, so you start another split-half search. Because the /System/Library/StartupItems folder contains only Apple items, you assume it's more likely that the problem is caused by a third-party extension in /Library/StartupItems. So you remove all the items from /Library/StartupItems and restart (not using Safe Mode). Everything works fine this way, so you return one item to the /Library/Startup Items folder and restart again. You keep returning items and restarting until you see the problem again. When you see the problem again, you know that the item you just added is the source of the problem.

Researching Problems

If you have completed the steps described so far and still can't determine the source of the problem, it is time to use additional resources to research the problem.

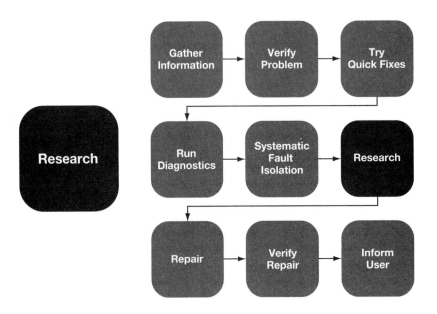

Check This Source:	For Information On:	Where
Read Me files	Last-minute compatibility and installation	Installation disks and installation directories
Mac Help	Basic features, functions, and use, as well as relevant Knowledge Base documents if you have a working network connection	Help > Mac Help in the Finder

Check This Source:	**For Information On:**	**Where**
User manuals	Product-specific troubleshooting and installation information	Product installation disks and installation folders
Network Utility	Computer's network interfaces, access to specific hosts or IP addresses (Ping), network performance statistics, IP addresses and host names, user information, and active TCP ports	/Applications/ Utilities
Console	Messages about the system and log files	/Applications/ Utilities
Apple Support web page	Top support questions, downloads, and updates (information is organized by product)	www.apple.com/ support
Knowledge Base	Technical articles, Read Me files, symptom/cure charts, specifications, late-breaking information, error codes	www.apple.com/ support or AppleCare pane in Sherlock
Service Source	Hot issues, product specification database, Apple Software Updates, troubleshooting symptom/cure charts	Available from Apple to Apple–authorized service providers and AppleCare Technician Training customers only

Check This Source:	For Information On:	Where
Email lists	Service that sends you information via email (messages sent to a mailing list are delivered to your email address so you can keep up with the discussion throughout the day)	http://lists. apple.com
Discussion lists	Message board where you post messages to forums, view messages by thread, and find solutions to issues that you are troubleshooting (can create bookmarks to postings that you want to return to later, customizing the Bookmarks page as your own personal support page)	http://discussions. info.apple.com

One of the first research resources you should use is the Mac OS X built-in Help feature. You may find that the operating system is functioning correctly and the user is not following the correct steps to enable a particular feature to work. An index for help topics is new to Help in Mac OS X 10.4.

The Knowledge Base (www.apple.com/support) gives you detailed examples of issues and their resolutions. The Knowledge Base makes use of an extensive set of keywords. These terms give you shortcuts to specific types of information. You can use keywords to assist you in making Knowledge Base searches. For example, using the keyword *kmosx* will list documents that cover Mac OS X issues.

MORE INFO ▶ Refer to Knowledge Base document 75178, "Knowledge Base: How to use keywords."

In addition, the Knowledge Base provides search options to help you narrow down the search. For example, you can specify exact phrases to look for or limit the search to a certain product.

If you've isolated the problem to a startup issue, you can search the Knowledge Base for *Mac OS X startup*. The results include Knowledge Base document 106464, "Your Mac won't start up in Mac OS X."

Discussion forums are also available. Discussion forums give you the advantage of interacting with other users who are doing similar things with Mac OS X and, perhaps, running into similar issues.

NOTE ▶ If the troubleshooting process has not resolved the issue, you might have to escalate. This might mean contacting a third party or Apple for help as appropriate. AppleCare, the service and support organization, provides a variety of online and phone-based support services as well as support plans for different consumer segments. The service and support options for AppleCare are described at www.apple.com/support.

Searching the Knowledge Base

The following steps take you to Apple's service and support web page.

1   Open Safari (/Applications).

2   Go to www.apple.com/support.

    You will see the main Apple Service & Support page.

At the left, you will see guided search options for different Apple product families. At the right, you will see products and services and links to status pages. At the bottom left, you will see recent software updates.

At the top right, you will see a search field with an advanced search link.

3   Click the Advanced Search link.

You may be prompted to sign in with your Apple ID. This is a single user name that you can use to connect to Apple services. You may have skipped this step when you installed Mac OS X following the instructions in this book, but you can create an Apple ID at any time.

4   Log in with your Apple ID and you will see the Advanced Search page.

5   In the search field next to "with all of the words," enter

iPod update Mac OS X

and press Return.

You will see a list of documents with the search results.

6   At the right, click the link for "Sort By Date."

The most recent results display first. Experiment with another search value to get a feel for the search feature.

Searching Mac Help

You can use the Mac Help viewer in Mac OS X 10.4 to find documents stored in the local help database and in the Knowledge Base.

1   In the Finder, choose Help > Mac Help (Command-?).

You will see the Mac Help window, with hyperlinked topics at the right.

2   In the search field at the top right, enter *firmware* and press Return.

You will see both local help topics and Knowledge Base documents returned from your search. This is a very effective method for getting quick answers when you need to do research.

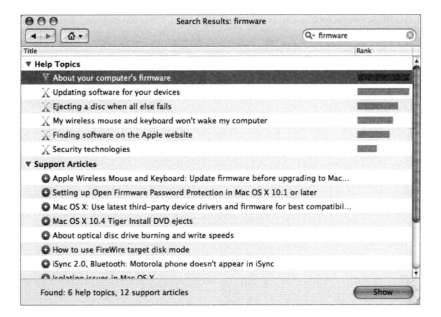

Problem Scenario—Research

Sometimes there are known issues that are resistant to traditional troubleshooting. If you're unable to identify the cause of the problem through systematic fault isolation, take some time to use your resources to research the issue.

A customer calls to complain that her iMac displays a negative image. She says she hasn't changed any settings, and that everything seems to work fine, it's just that everything on the screen is negative.

After gathering information, verifying the problem (making sure she describes how the desktop appears), trying some quick fixes (restarting, etc.), you're unable to isolate the fault any further. You search the Knowledge Base with the words "negative image on screen."

The first document you find on this search is document 107329, "Mac OS X: Unexpectedly Displays Negative Image (White on Black, Reverse Type)." It indicates that if someone or something presses the Control-Option-Command-8 key combination, the computer may display a negative image, and that this is a feature of Universal Access preferences. Pressing the same key combination toggles the feature off, so you have the customer press these keys to solve the problem.

Repairing the System

Once you've located the problem, you must fix it.

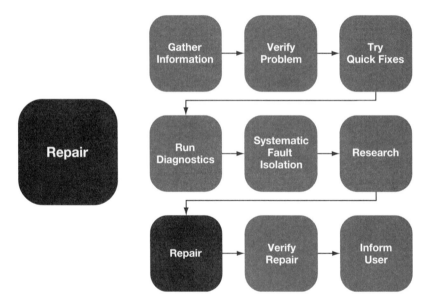

Before you replace software or hardware:

▶   Make a backup of user data. You must do this before updating, reinstalling, or otherwise modifying the software on a system. This backup ensures that you can restore the system to its original state if you need to do so. If the system is unable to boot and you have a FireWire–enabled system, you may be able to start up the system in Target Disk Mode, which allows you to connect it to another system and copy critical data files.

▶ Make sure you are using only known-good software to modify the system. Avoid introducing new problems while trying to solve the original one.

▶ Look for the latest versions of software that you intend to update or reinstall. Be careful not to add new software components that can adversely affect applications and other software that the user has placed on the system.

Refer to "Mac OS X Repair/Replace" in Appendix A "Apple General Troubleshooting Flowchart." This section groups the repairs from simplest and involving least consequences, to more difficult and/or time-consuming and involving greater consequences. Always consider the repairs from the innocuous section first, then less innocuous, then invasive, unless you are certain what repair will solve the problem.

Notice that some of these repairs are also quick fixes. You will not necessarily try every quick fix while troubleshooting a particular problem. For example, it may be appropriate to use the tools in the First Aid pane of Disk Utility during the Try Quick Fixes step while solving one problem, but it may not be appropriate until the Repair step for another problem.

You might need to reinstall the operating system and, if necessary, reconfigure it. This can be made less drastic if you do not select the erase option in the Installer. Without selecting the erase option, the Installer will fix system files with incorrect checksums (corrupted files), user/group, permissions, or location (files that have been moved or deleted) by comparing the receipt for what is being installed with the receipt that is already on the hard disk. If you have upgraded Mac OS X since installing it, go to /Library/Receipts and delete the update packages for Mac OS X before reinstalling. After you reinstall Mac OS X, use Software Update preferences to update the software again.

On computers that ship with Mac OS X preinstalled, you can use the Erase and Install option on the Mac OS X Install DVD to get the computer running again. While this ensures that Mac OS X will be installed as it was when the computer was shipped, it does erase everything on the computer first. If Mac OS X was not included on your computer when it shipped, you can start up from the Mac OS X Install DVD and run the Installer. If you decide to erase the contents of the disk before installing Mac OS X, you will guarantee a fresh installation of Mac OS X, but you will also lose everything that was on the computer.

If you still have problems after you perform an Erase and Install, it's possible that your drive has other problems that can be fixed by using the Erase Disk command in Disk Utility to completely reformat the drive. Disk Utility is included on the Mac OS X Install DVD so that you can perform this task as needed.

If you determine that the issue is not software related, you will need to investigate possible hardware issues. For example, although hard disks are very reliable and solid-state electronic devices are very durable, they sometimes fail. You should remove or replace any additional hardware, such as peripherals or PCI cards, and see if the issue persists. If you still cannot resolve the issue, you might need to have the Apple hardware repaired by an Apple authorized service provider.

Problem Scenario — Repair/Replace

A customer calls to say he is following training materials for his new Mac mini and that certain keyboard commands aren't working, specifically when using keyboard shortcuts. As you gather information, you ask him if he has ever seen this work. He says no. (Because it has never worked, it's possible that the end user has inadvertently turned on a Universal Access feature or the number lock function, but more questioning can help narrow that down.) You ask the customer which keys do not work, and it appears that none of the Command key equivalents work, although he says Control-click works fine.

You ask your user to click on the Desktop and try entering Command-N to open a new Finder window, and the end user is confused, saying that there is no Command key on the keyboard. This is a vital clue. The Mac mini does not include a keyboard, so you ask if he's using a keyboard that he previously used with a Windows computer. He says that he is. That's the answer. Most USB keyboards will work with a Macintosh, but many USB keyboards do not have the exact keys that you would see on Apple keyboards, which can be confusing for users. He was able to Control-click because he was using the right mouse button, as he would on his PC, but he reported to you that he was using Control-click.

The solution is to use the Alt key in place of the Option key, and the Windows key for the Command key, or use key remapping software that will substitute the keys for you. So in this case, the simplest repair is to inform the user that he can continue to use the keyboard with some instruction on how to use the keys, and long-term, to recommend either a standard Macintosh keyboard or key remapping software.

Verifying the Repair

A repair is not complete until you make sure the computer is functioning correctly. Sometimes you may fix one problem only to find another.

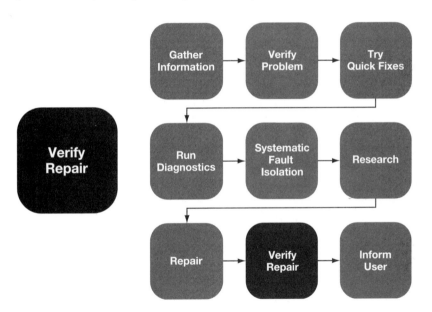

These are the criteria to use to determine if a problem has been fixed:

▶ The entire problem has been resolved.

▶ No new problems have been introduced during the troubleshooting and repair.

▶ All elements of the system work correctly together.

To verify the repair, try to recreate the problem:

▶ Restart the computer. See if the problem recurs.

▶ Open all affected applications and files.

▶ Run MacTest Pro, Apple Hardware Test, or Apple Service Diagnostic (if available) to test the entire system, even if only one part of the system was repaired. If possible, run looping tests for several hours, to catch any intermittent problems. Use Verify Disk and Verify Disk Permissions in the First Aid pane of Disk Utility. Use Network Utility to test networking.

▶ Run System Profiler to review the before and after state of connected devices. This ensures that you did not fix one problem device and introduce another.

▶ Review logs in Console. Use the filter in Console to check for error messages.

▶ After you have finished validating the fix, print reports for your end user, if possible. User notification is important to help with the human factor: If the person using the computer is not convinced that the repair was successful, he or she might be more likely to report "phantom problems" (normal computer behavior that the end user interprets as a problem, or minor transient issues).

Problem Scenario—Verify Repair

You've solved a problem with erratic performance by the invasive quick fix of an Archive and Install of Mac OS X.

When the installation completes, you verify the repair by having the customer open some applications she uses often. Double-clicking some of them causes them to appear briefly, then disappear. Also, some other applications are behaving erratically.

Because you archived and reinstalled the system, this suggests that a possible explanation is an application/framework mismatch. Application/framework mismatches are often caused by performing an Archive and Install without performing Software Update afterward.

An Archive and Install archives the operating system (including frameworks) and bundled applications. However, newer applications than the version being installed are not archived. So, you may have, for example, a newer version of Safari than the WebKit framework installed from your Mac OS X Install DVD. Using Software Update and updating to the current version of the operating system should resolve this.

To solve the problem completely, you need to make sure the customer completes the necessary software updates.

Informing the User

The last steps in troubleshooting a problem are to explain to the user what you did and why, and to complete other administrative tasks.

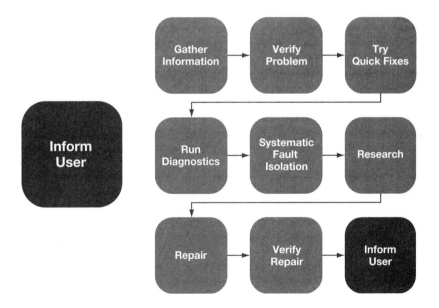

The following are useful tips for informing the user:

▶ Write and deliver a report to the user. Include the initial problem report, any steps involved in the troubleshooting, any hardware repairs or replacements, and your conclusions.

▶ Print diagnostic reports (done at the end of the Verify Fix step), and show the reports to the user. If possible, try to deliver "before" and "after" reports.

▶ Explain any steps the user can take to avoid having problems recur. For example:

• If the user has shut down the Macintosh incorrectly, explain the hazards of not shutting down properly.

• If the user's system was corrupted by disconnecting a hard drive without ejecting, advise the user how to avoid such problems in the future.

• If the user has lost data, describe backup techniques and organizational techniques that might be useful in the future.

The basic idea is to give your users information that improves their computing experience. Taking time to teach users how to avoid future issues adds value and improves their experience.

Problem Scenario—Inform User

Informing the user of what you did, why you did it, and how to avoid the issue in the future is just as important as solving the technical source of the problem.

Here's an example. A user says he has forgotten his password for his computer. You boot the computer from the Mac OS X Install DVD and change the password for him.

He's happy to have his computer back, but soon he contacts you again to say that he can't mount any of the servers he used to use. He says that he hasn't had to log in to them in a while and now he's being asked for a keychain password. When he enters his new user password, it's not correct.

Unfortunately, as you know, he has to create a new keychain and reenter all of his passwords. This is another instance in which it is important to consider the human factor. Informing him that he would encounter this problem after you reset the user password would have prevented him from having to contact you again and made his experience less frustrating.

What You've Learned

This lesson introduced Apple's systematic troubleshooting process. The troubleshooting steps outlined in this lesson are not hard-and-fast rules. They are a recommended, field-tested process. Your organization may already have an established set of troubleshooting guidelines that you follow.

With whatever process you go through, you'll need to be flexible while completing it. Sometimes you'll have to go back and repeat earlier steps. For example, after you research the problem, you may find that you need to go back and try some different quick fixes. It's also possible that your research was incomplete, and a periodic review of your technical resources can ensure that you stay up-to-date.

When you complete your troubleshooting, be sure to complete the task. Review your notes, document the issue as needed, and evaluate your troubleshooting to determine whether you could do things more effectively.

Also, remember the human factors involved. You may be helping someone who is stressed, uncooperative, or inexperienced. You may not be at your best, because you're fatigued or hungry. You and your user are a team for the duration of the troubleshooting, and anything you can do to help things work smoothly will help make you a more effective troubleshooter.

References

The following Knowledge Base documents (located at www.apple.com/support) will provide you with further information regarding troubleshooting Mac OS X:

- ▶   9804, "Mac OS System Error Codes: −299 to −5553"
- ▶   9805, "Mac OS System Error Codes: 0 to −261"

- ▶ 9806, "Mac OS System Error Codes: 1 to 32767"
- ▶ 10182, "Mac OS: Rebuilding Desktop File and Icon Recovery"
- ▶ 25398, "Mac OS X: How to troubleshoot a software issue"
- ▶ 42642, "'To continue booting, type mac-boot and press return' Message"
- ▶ 55743, "Common System Error Messages: What they Mean and What Might Help Resolve the Problem"
- ▶ 60351, "Determining BootROM or Firmware Version"
- ▶ 75178, "Knowledge Base: How to use keywords"
- ▶ 86194, "Mac OS X: What's stored in PRAM?"
- ▶ 106227, "What's a 'kernel panic'? (Mac OS X)"
- ▶ 106388, "Mac OS X: How to Start up in Single-User or Verbose Mode"
- ▶ 106464, "Your Mac won't start up in Mac OS X"
- ▶ 107199, "Mac OS X: If your computer stops responding, 'hangs', or 'freezes'"
- ▶ 107329, "Mac OS X: Unexpectedly Displays Negative Image (White on Black, Reverse Type)"
- ▶ 107396, "Mac OS X: Cannot print, use Classic, start file sharing, burn discs, or update software if /tmp missing"

URL

Visit the following website for more information:

- ▶ Apple Remote Desktop: www.apple.com/remotedesktop

Lesson Review

Use the following questions to review what you have learned:

1. What are the nine troubleshooting steps suggested in this lesson?
2. What defines a quick fix?
3. Identify an innocuous quick fix that can be tried in Mac OS X.
4. Identify a less innocuous quick fix that can be tried in Mac OS X.

5. Identify an invasive quick fix that can be tried in Mac OS X.

6. Identify a diagnostic tool that can be used in Mac OS X.

7. What is a split-half search?

8. What is Console used for?

9. If, after trying all previous troubleshooting steps, you still can't locate and fix the problem, what should you do?

10. Identify three Mac OS X repair or replacement techniques.

11. What are the three characteristics of a verified repair?

Answers

1. Gather information, verify the problem, try quick fixes, run diagnostics, perform split-half search, research, repair/replace, verify repair, inform user/complete administrative tasks. If needed, the problem can also be escalated to a higher level of support.

2. A quick fix is a repair action that can be performed quickly, involves little or no risk of harm to the system, and has little or no cost.

3. Restart/shut down

   Run System Profiler

   Start in Safe Mode

   Start from Install Mac OS, Restoration, or MacTest Pro CD

   Suppress Auto-Login

   Suppress login items

   Use known-good disc (e.g., CD, DVD, Zip) (installation)

   Repair with Disk Utility

   Start in single-user mode

   Start in verbose mode

   Start in another OS

   Relaunch Finder

   Disconnect all external devices

Turn off Screen Saver and Energy Saver (installation)

Verify with other users (network problem)

Connect to another device or volume (network)

Connect to PPP test server (modem)

4. Adjust user settings (Check Firewall setting; check Active Ports setting; check Startup)

Select a different startup disk (startup)

Force quit

Log in as test user

Reset permissions

Move, rename, or delete preferences file

Update printer driver (printing)

Update firmware

Change ports (for example, Ethernet and USB)

Use known-good peripherals (for example, monitor, disk drive, and printer)

5. Perform recommended (default) installation

Perform Archive and Install

Perform Erase and Install

Reinstall suspect application

Reset PRAM

Reset PMU/SMU

Remove non–Apple RAM

6. Digital Color Meter

Disk Utility

Network Utility

Apple Hardware Test

Tech Tool Deluxe (available with purchase of AppleCare Protection Plan)

Display Utilities (available to Apple Authorized Service Providers)

MacTest Pro (available to Apple Authorized Service Providers)

Apple Service Diagnostic (available to Apple Authorized Service Providers and AppleCare Technician Training customers only)

7. A split-half search is a technique in which half of the potential causes of a problem are removed or eliminated to help narrow down the potential cause of the problem.

8. Console is used to show you messages about the system and to view log files.

9. Escalate the problem. It's important to know when to consult another authority.

10. Run -fsck

Update driver

Repair with Disk Utility

Run AirPort Admin Utility

Run Setup Assistant

Use Directory Access

Run UNIX commands

Use Target Disk Mode

Adjust user controls

Reset PRAM

Perform recommended (default) installation

Perform Archive and Install

Erase and restore from Restore CDs

Perform Erase and Install

Repair with Apple Hardware Test

11. The entire problem has been resolved.

No new problems have been introduced during the troubleshooting and repair.

All elements of the system are compatible.

Appendix A

Apple General Troubleshooting Flowchart

This appendix serves as a quick reference to the Apple General Troubleshooting Flowchart.

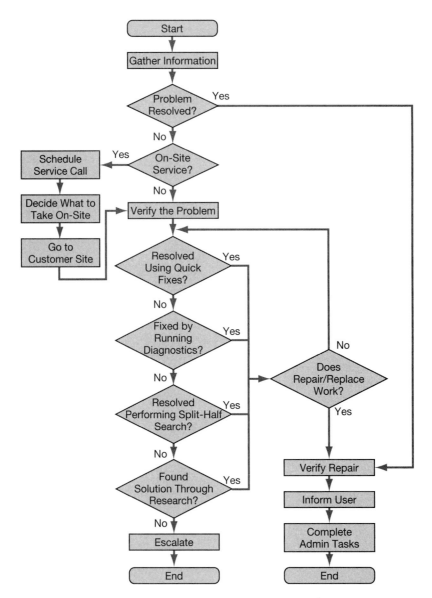

Apple General Troubleshooting Flowchart

Mac OS X Quick Fixes

The quick fixes applicable to troubleshooting the OS are divided into three increasingly invasive strategies, which are discussed in the following sections.

Innocuous Fixes (Consider These First)

The following troubleshooting steps have little or no impact on the computer and Mac OS X, and may fix transient issues:

▶ Restart/shut down

▶ Check Top Support Questions if problem seems familiar (available to Apple Authorized Service Providers)

▶ Repair volume with Disk Utility

▶ Disconnect all external devices

▶ Run Software Update to check for any uninstalled updates

▶ Relaunch Finder

When you begin troubleshooting, these are some innocuous things you might do to assess the problem:

▶ Perform a Safe Boot by pressing Shift immediately on startup until the words "Safe Boot" appear

▶ Run System Profiler

▶ Check with other users to see if they see the same problem (a possible network problem)

▶ Suppress automatic login during startup by pressing Shift when the progress bar appears until the Login window appears

▶ Perform a Safe Login (suppress startup items from launching) by pressing Shift after logging in until the Finder menu appears

▶ Review logs in Console

▶ Start from Mac OS X Install DVD

▶ Start in single-user mode by pressing Command-S during startup

- Start in verbose mode by pressing Command-V during startup
- Start in another operating system
- Try the same task in another application environment (X11 application versus native Mac OS X application, for example)
- Turn off Screen Saver and Energy Saver during installation
- Connect to another device or volume (network)
- Connect to PPP test server (modem)

Less Innocuous Fixes (Consider Next)

The following fixes have a moderate impact on the computer or the end-user operating environment. They are somewhat more time-consuming, so you should use caution and document your work:

- Fix permissions with Disk Utility
- Adjust user settings in System Preferences
- Move, rename, or delete preference file
- Delete cache files from ~/Library/Caches and /Library/Caches files ending in a UID
- Log in as a test user
- Log in as an administrator
- Check the settings in the Firewall pane of Sharing preferences
- In Network preferences, choose Show > Network Port Configurations
- Check the settings in Startup Disk preferences
- Choose Apple > Force Quit if an application is not responding
- Update the printer driver (for printing problems)
- Update firmware
- Change ports (such as Ethernet, USB) in Network preferences
- Use known good peripherals (such as monitor, disk drive, and printer)

Invasive Fixes (Consider Last)

The following fixes have a more drastic impact on the system:

- ▶ Perform Upgrade installation of Mac OS X

- ▶ Perform Archive and Install installation of Mac OS X

- ▶ Perform Erase and Install installation of Mac OS X

- ▶ Reinstall suspect application

- ▶ Reset PRAM by pressing Command-Option-P-R at startup until you hear the startup chime twice

- ▶ Reset Power Manager (See Knowledge Base for reset instructions for your computer)

- ▶ Remove non–Apple memory from your computer

Mac OS X Diagnostic Tools

The following tools are often used for diagnostics on Mac OS X:

- ▶ Activity Monitor

- ▶ Apple Hardware Test (included on disc with most current Macintosh computers)

- ▶ Apple Service Diagnostic (available to Apple Authorized Service Providers)

- ▶ DigitalColor Meter

- ▶ Disk Utility

- ▶ Display Utilities (available to Apple Authorized Service Providers)

- ▶ MacTest Pro (available to Apple Authorized Service Providers)

- ▶ Network Diagnostics

- ▶ Network Utility

- ▶ System Profiler

- ▶ There are several third-party utilities that are useful for troubleshooting, including Tech Tool Deluxe (available with the purchase of an AppleCare Protection Plan)

Mac OS X Split-Half Search Techniques

The following are split-half search techniques:

▶ Start in single-user mode by pressing Command-S during startup

▶ Perform a Safe Boot by pressing Shift during startup

▶ Suppress automatic login during startup by pressing Shift when the progress bar appears until the login window appears

▶ Systematically kill processes

▶ Systematically remove potential problem files

▶ Disconnect peripherals

▶ Run Network Utility to evaluate other devices and computers on the network

Mac OS X Research Resources

The following are common resources to consult for troubleshooting Mac OS X issues:

▶ User documentation

▶ Logs (viewable with Console)

▶ man pages (viewable in Terminal)

▶ Read Me files

▶ Mac Help

▶ AppleCare channel in Sherlock

▶ Knowledge Base (www.apple.com/support)

▶ Service Source (available to Apple Authorized Service Providers)

▶ Internet support communities

Mac OS X Repair/Replace

When choosing to repair or replace items in a system, you can choose from three levels of troubleshooting strategy. The procedures should be used in the order they are discussed here.

First Choices

The following should be tried first when repairing or replacing:

▶   Update drivers using Software Update preferences

▶   Run -fsck in single-user mode to fix disk problems

▶   Repair permissions using Disk Utility

▶   Run AirPort Admin Utility

▶   Run Directory Access and check settings

Second Choices

The following should be tried after the appropriate first choices have been tried:

▶   Adjust user settings in System Preferences

▶   Execute UNIX commands in Terminal

▶   Reset PRAM by pressing Command-Option-P-R at startup until you hear the startup chime twice

Third Choices

The following should be tried after the appropriate first and second choices have been tried:

▶   Perform Upgrade installation of Mac OS X

▶   Perform Archive and Install installation of Mac OS X

▶   Perform Erase and Install installation of Mac OS X

▶   Repair the computer with Apple Hardware Test (included on disc with most current Macintosh computers)

▶   Escalate as needed

Appendix **B**
Networking Technologies

This appendix outlines useful information about some basic network technologies.

802.1X

This is the IEEE standard for network access control. It has these characteristics:

▶ Provides access control for both wired and wireless local area networks

▶ Is based on connection to a network rather than connection to a service

▶ Uses a central authentication server based on Extensible Authentication Protocol (EAP)

Apple Filing Protocol (AFP)

AFP uses a remote volume like a local volume and permits you to

▶ Mount a shared volume from a remote computer

▶ Navigate through the hierarchy for the remote file system

▶ Depending on your privileges, read/write/delete/execute

AFP saves documents and files directly to a remote volume like saving to a local volume. It is used over TCP/IP. (AppleTalk is no longer supported.) It uses URL format to locate servers. For example:

TCP: afp://user:password@server/volume/path

Resources for AFP are located in /System/Library/Filesystems.

AFP can be enabled by turning on Personal File Sharing in the Services pane of Sharing preferences.

AirPort and AirPort Extreme

AirPort and AirPort Extreme are Apple's implementation of IEEE 802.11b and 802.11g wireless protocols (often called WiFi or wireless Ethernet), respectively, and use the same protocols as an Ethernet network.

AirPort networking is enabled in Network preferences and Internet Connect.

Both protocols use WEP (Wired Equivalent Privacy). AirPort has a range of 50 feet. AirPort Extreme has a range of 150 feet. Bridging and amplification can be used to cover longer distances.

Both protocols support TCP/IP, AppleTalk, and PPTP (for VPN connections).

AirPort and AirPort Extreme depend upon kernel extensions in /System/ Library/Extensions. AppleAirPort.kext kernel extensions are stored there.

AirPort utilities located in /Applications/Utilities include:

▶ AirPort Setup Assistant (to set up and configure AirPort)

▶ AirPort Admin Utility (to configure and maintain AirPort network)

Two other AirPort utilities available only with AirPort Extreme Base Stations include:

▶ AirPort Management Utility (to manage multiple AirPort devices)

▶ AirPort Client Monitor (to view client AirPort performance)

Bonjour

Bonjour (formerly called Rendezvous) is Apple's implementation of the Zeroconf (Zero configuration IP Networking) protocol. It is designed to simplify setting up networks with different LAN standards (for example, AppleTalk and NETBIOS networks).

Bonjour has three primary features:

▶ Computers can get dynamic IP addresses with or without a DHCP server.

▶ Computers can translate host names and IP addresses without a DNS server.

▶ Computer users can find network services (printers/servers) without a directory server.

Uses in Mac OS X:

▶ Dynamically assigns an IP address to the computer (which would usually be done by a DCHP server)

▶ Talks to computers and devices via AirPort or Ethernet

▶ iChat and Printer Setup Utility dynamically discover other computers and devices, respectively, in your area without a server to provide information

▶ Limited to finding computer and devices on the same subnet

An administrator user configures the host name in Sharing preferences.

Resources for Bonjour are located in the plug-in to directory services:

▶ /System/Library/Frameworks/DirectoryService.framework/Versions/A/ Resource/Plugins/Bonjour.dplug

MORE INFO ▶ Visit http://developer.apple.com and www.zeroconf.org.

Bootstrap Protocol (BOOTP)

This is the Internet protocol used for booting diskless workstations. Among its functions, BOOTP:

▶ Discovers its own IP address

▶ Discovers the IP addresses of BOOTP servers on the network

▶ Locates a file to be loaded into memory to boot the computer

▶ Enables workstations to boot without a hard drive

The protocol is defined by RFC 951.

BOOTP can be configured in Network preferences.

Dynamic Host Configuration Protocol (DHCP)

DHCP provides a protocol to dynamically allocate IP addresses to computers on a local network.

System administrator assigns a range of IP addresses to DHCP, and LAN clients are granted them upon request. (Client computers receive "leases" that allow them to use the IP address for a fixed period of time, or for the period that they are active on the network.)

DHCP can be configured in Network preferences.

File Transfer Protocol (FTP)

FTP is a simple but unsecure way to transfer files across a network; sFTP is the secure version of the protocol.

FTP uses TCP for reliable delivery of information.

FTP employs login and password to authorize access to folders and files on a remote FTP server, but it transmits data in the clear, and is therefore insecure.

FTP can be enabled by turning on FTP Access in the Services pane of Sharing preferences. Users wishing to log in must have local user accounts.

After choosing Go > Connect to Server in the Finder to access an FTP server, users can see all files on the hard disk, even if they don't have permission to change files/folders outside of shared folders.

HyperText Transfer Protocol (HTTP)

HTTP is a protocol most often used to transfer hypertext markup language (HTML) documents across the Internet.

It uses TCP and is primarily used for retrieving Web pages.

Resources for HTTP are found in /System/Library/StartupItems/Apache.

The Apache HTTP server serves Web pages from your computer.

The Apache HTTP server can be enabled by turning on Personal Web Sharing in the Services pane of Sharing preferences.

Files and folders for Personal Web Sharing are shared from the Sites folder. Files and folders can also be placed in /Library/WebServer/Documents.

IP Addressing (IPv4 and IPv6)

Both IPv4 and IPv6 are Internet Protocol addressing standards supported by Mac OS X. They have common characteristics, as well as several differences that are described here.

IP Addressing

This provides a unique address to identify computers on the Internet.

It routes data when it moves from source to destination.

IP addresses are associated with the media access control (MAC) address of the client.

IPv4 (Internet Protocol version 4)

IPv4 supports up to four billion public addresses.

It defines the use of unique 32-bit addresses.

IPv4 addresses are formatted as four 8-bit fields (4 octets). For example, 192.168.1.2.

Classes are determined by the first octet:

▶   Class A: Large networks 1–127

▶   Class B: Medium networks 128–191

▶   Class C: Small networks 192–223

▶   Class D: Multicast 224–239

▶   Class E: Experimental 240–255

The 127.0.0.1 address is used for loopback or localhost ID.

IPv6 (Internet Protocol version 6)

IPv6 is designed to increase the number of IP addresses, add features, and improve efficiencies of the IP protocol.

In 1995, Apple and Mentat announced that IPv6 was integrated with Apple Open Transport in Mac OS.

It uses CIDR (Classless Interdomain Routing).

It provides increased flexibility in address numbers.

IPv6 allows networks to be flexible in size so IP addresses aren't wasted.

Here are some features of IPv6:

▶   Does not rely on class size to determine network numbers

▶   Translates between IPv4 and IPv6 seamlessly

▶   Uses a 128-bit unique address

▶   Addresses are written in hexadecimal

▶   Uses 16-bit fields separated by colons rather than 8-bit fields separated by decimals

▶   Includes the MAC address of the active network interface

▶   Addresses in URLs are enclosed in brackets [ ]

IPv6 is built in to drivers for various networking interfaces. You can see protocols by using Terminal.

Enter

ifconfig -a

to show active network ports, addresses, and status.

Network Address Translation (NAT)

NAT provides a method of assigning and distributing internal and external addresses and traffic, in the sense that several computers in a workgroup can use the same public address when they are given private addresses by the NAT router.

NAT converts an internal address to a public address.

When set up, NAT has the following characteristics:

▶ Uses one interface (port) for incoming and outgoing external traffic.

▶ Uses one interface (port) for incoming and outgoing internal traffic.

▶ Can be a physical interface (for example, Ethernet-to-Internet and AirPort-to-internal traffic).

▶ Can be a virtual interface (for example, an Ethernet card can be assigned two IP addresses—one external and one internal).

Devices providing NAT (sometimes called gateways) include cable/DSL (Digital Subscriber Line) modems and routers.

NAT can be enabled by selecting the "Share your Internet connection" checkbox in the Internet pane of Sharing preferences. This makes your computer act as a go-between for all information to and from the Internet using your Internet connection.

Point-to-Point Protocol (PPP)

PPP is a standard protocol for connecting a computer to the Internet, usually with a dial-up modem.

PPP provides error-checking features.

PPP sends the computer's TCP/IP packets to a server, which puts packets onto the Internet.

PPP can be configured in Network preferences and Internet Connect.

Resources for PPP are found in /System/Library/ModemScripts.

Point-to-Point Protocol over Ethernet (PPPoE)

This is a specification for connecting users on an Ethernet network to the Internet via a gateway, such as cable or DSL modems and wireless devices.

PPPoE users share a common connection—they're supported by Ethernet in a LAN (multiuser) combined with PPP (serial connections).

PPPoE can be enabled in Network preferences.

Resources for PPPoE are found in /System/Library.

Server Message Block (SMB)

SMB is the basic protocol for file sharing with Windows OS, connecting PC-compatible computers to a LAN.

It uses CIFS (Common Internet File System), a networking standard combining SMB connectivity with Internet file sharing.

Samba (www.samba.org) is an open source application developed to provide compatibility with CIFS and SMB client services.

In the Finder, choose Go > Connect to Server to connect to an SMB server by name. In the Connect to Server dialog, you can browse for servers or choose previously-saved favorite servers. You can also browse for servers by clicking the Network icon in the Sidebar and selecting WORKGROUP (or the name of your local Windows workgroup). SMB is enabled by turning on Windows Sharing in the Services pane of Sharing preferences. The bottom part of the pane provides instructions for other users who want to connect to your computer.

Users wishing to log in must have local user accounts. Furthermore, you must choose which accounts can use Windows Sharing by clicking the Accounts button in the Services pane of Sharing preferences.

Appendix C
The Classic Environment

The Classic environment is an application environment in Mac OS X that allows you to run Mac OS 9–compatible applications. An application environment is a set of libraries, resources, APIs, and API-dependent services. Classic uses foundation components in the operating system: core services (Quartz, OpenGL, QuickTime, and so on) and the core operating system (Darwin kernel). This enables Classic to use printing, device drivers, and networking as though you were booted in Mac OS 9.

Classic supports applications that run in Mac OS 9.2 and later. In mixed Mac OS 9/Mac OS X installations, this allows you to retain your investment in older Macintosh applications. Classic provides a fully-featured Mac OS 9 environment, with virtually all of the functionality that is available when running Mac OS 9 as the primary operating system on your Macintosh.

The Classic environment requires a Mac OS 9.2 or later System Folder, with fonts, extensions, control panels, and system preferences. However, you use Classic preferences in Mac OS X to manage Classic. That is where you can perform maintenance tasks, such as restarting or stopping Classic, rebuilding the Classic desktop, or starting Classic with extensions off.

For ease of use, and due to the legacy nature of Mac OS 9, Classic components are easier to identify than components for other application environments such as Java and X11. In this appendix, you will learn about Classic components, the architecture of the Classic Environment, and troubleshooting issues.

> **NOTE ▶** Although this appendix covers how Classic provides Mac OS 9 functionality from within Mac OS X, it assumes you are already familiar with the basic concepts and operation of Mac OS 9.

Exploring the Classic Process

Unlike Cocoa or Carbon applications, Classic applications do not operate as standalone processes. Instead, Classic applications open and run within a single, shared process named TruBlueEnvironment. This single memory space contains Mac OS 9, along with any Classic applications and extensions.

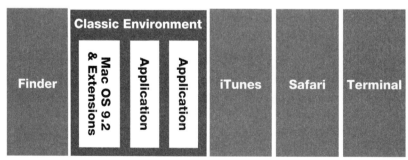

TruBlueEnvironment

Because Classic applications share a common process and memory space, just as they do in Mac OS 9, they are not protected from each other. If a Classic application crashes, it can crash other applications running in the Classic environment or the Classic environment itself. It cannot crash native Mac OS X applications, because they run in separate, memory-protected spaces.

You should remember that quitting or forcibly quitting the Classic environment shuts down Mac OS 9 and all running Classic applications. If you are having problems quitting a specific Classic application, save your work in other applications before you try the Mac OS X Force Quit command (Command-Option-Escape). You can attempt to force quit the offending application without disturbing the rest of the Classic environment. If the operating system cannot quit the Classic application, it will automatically quit the Classic environment instead.

NOTE ▶ Although Classic and all Classic applications run in a single memory space, Force Quit will list Classic applications separate from the Classic environment. This is shown in the screenshot above, where SimpleText is a Classic application.

Starting the Classic Environment

When Classic starts, it must initialize itself, identify hardware components, and present a user interface. Here's an example of a Classic application starting when Classic is not already running:

1   You open a Classic application, such as SimpleText.

2   The application icon appears in the Dock. Classic Startup (an application that starts the Classic environment) starts, and a "9" icon appears in the Dock to represent the Classic Startup process.

As the Classic environment loads, the Classic icon in the Dock "fills in" as a progress monitor, in addition to the progress bar in the Classic window.

3   The TruBlueEnvironment process starts. This is the Classic environment.

4   Mac OS 9.2.x starts, and a window displaying the Mac OS 9 startup screen appears. If an error occurs during startup, the system expands the window to show the error message.

5 The Classic application (in this case, SimpleText) starts up, and the Classic Startup icon disappears from the Dock.

NOTE ▶ Once started, the Classic environment runs until it is stopped or the system restarts. If it is started in this manner, it will run in the background after you quit the Classic application, so reopening a Classic application—or opening a second Classic application—would be much faster than outlined here.

Additions to Mac OS 9 for Classic

When the Classic environment starts for the first time on a specific computer, it presents a dialog requesting permission to copy a set of files to its System Folder. These files include updates to such items as Startup Disk and AppleScript, and new files such as Classic, Classic RAVE, Classic Support, and Classic Support UI. The files are required; if you click Quit in the dialog, Classic will not start.

To view the files that Mac OS X uses to update Mac OS 9.2, do the following:

1 In the Finder, choose Go > Go to Folder (Shift-Command-G).

2 In the "Go to the folder" field, enter the following path:

/System/Library/CoreServices/Classic Startup.app/Contents/Resources/ English.lproj/SystemFiles

3 Click Go.

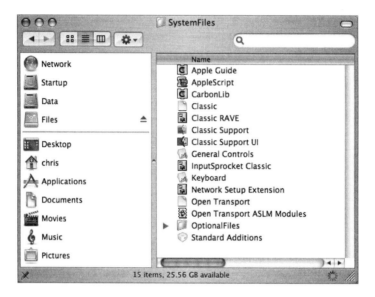

If Classic develops startup problems and you suspect that file corruption may be an issue, you can use this archive to replace the corresponding files in your Classic System Folder.

Limited Control Panel Usage in Classic

Some Mac OS 9 control panels configure system components that are already configured by System Preferences in Mac OS X. When Mac OS X detects a redundant control panel during Classic startup, it does not load the control panel. However, redundant control panels are still visible in Classic when you choose Apple > Control Panels. If you try to use the Mac OS 9 version of a redundant control panel, you will see an alert prompting you to perform the task in Mac OS X System Preferences instead. You should also be aware that third-party control panels and extensions might not work properly in Classic. Contact the third-party vendor to ensure compatibility.

MORE INFO ▶ Refer to Knowledge Base document 107135, "Mac OS X 10.2: About Using Mac OS 9 Control Panels in the Classic Environment."

The following Mac OS 9 control panels are not used in Classic (Classic will use the settings you assign in Mac OS X System Preferences instead):

▶ AppleTalk

▶ Control Strip

▶ Date & Time

▶ Energy Saver

▶ File Exchange

▶ Infrared

▶ Location Manager

▶ Memory

▶ Modem

▶ Mouse

▶ Multiple Users

▶ Password Security

▶ PowerBook SCSI Disk Mode

▶ Remote Access

▶ Startup Disk

▶ TCP/IP

▶ Trackpad

▶ Web Sharing

TIP ▶ Use General Controls in Classic to avoid managing two Documents folders. In the General Controls control panel, select "Documents folder." This sets the default save location for Classic applications to the ~/Documents folder.

Starting/Stopping with Classic Preferences

Use the Start/Stop pane in Classic preferences to select the Mac OS 9.2 folder you want the Classic environment to use. This pane lists all Mac OS Standard and Mac OS Extended volumes, including those on mounted disk images. Volumes with valid Classic system folders are selectable; all others are dimmed.

> **NOTE ▶** Classic on Mac OS X 10.2 or later does not require a system folder to be "blessed."

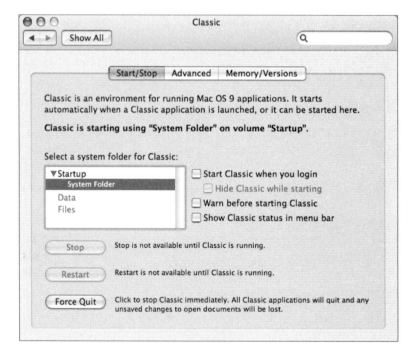

The Classic environment opens automatically the first time you open a Classic application. However, in Classic preferences, you can manually start, restart, force quit, or stop Classic. The Stop button performs the equivalent of the Shut Down command in Mac OS 9. Select the "Start Classic when you login" checkbox to automatically start Classic when you log in to the computer.

Selecting the "Show Classic status in menu bar" checkbox gives you a menu extra in Mac OS X where you can see if Classic is running; start, stop, or restart Classic; and open Classic preferences. You can use the Startup Items folder in the Mac OS 9.2 System Folder to set applications to open when the Classic environment starts.

Using Advanced Classic Preferences

Click Advanced in Classic preferences to set startup options, configure sleep, or rebuild the Classic desktop. You can set the following options for starting Classic. These execute only on the first Classic startup after you set them, and are usually used for troubleshooting:

▶   Turn Off Extensions — Allows starting Mac OS 9.2 in Classic with all extensions disabled. This is useful for troubleshooting because it loads the bare bones Mac OS 9 components, avoiding all potential third-party extension conflicts.

▶   Open Extensions Manager — Brings up the Extensions Manager when Mac OS 9.2 starts in Classic. This is useful for resolving extension conflicts because you can selectively load items for testing.

▶   Use Key Combination — Lets you specify simulating key combinations when Classic starts up. For instance, some extensions can be disabled individually by pressing particular keys during startup. You can configure these keys in Use Key Combination.

By default, all user accounts on your computer use the same Classic System Folder, which can cause problems with unique settings, such as user names in Classic applications. Select the "Use Mac OS 9 preferences from your home folder" checkbox to give each user unique preferences. This option copies the Preferences folder and other user-specific parts of the Mac OS 9 System Folder (/System Folder/Preferences) to the user's home folder (~/Library/Classic). After selecting this option on a multiuser computer, Classic Startup prompts each user to make a copy of the preferences from /System Folder/Preferences.

You can configure the Classic environment to sleep after a set amount of time with no Classic foreground applications running. Changes made to the inactive time will take effect the next time the Classic environment runs. While Classic sleeps, it puts no load on the system. For this reason, if Classic is configured to start upon login, it's a good idea to also configure it to sleep when inactive. The environment will wake from sleep with a little delay when you open a Classic application. No background Classic applications run while the Classic environment sleeps. If you need Classic background applications to remain running (for scanner button monitoring, for example), set the value to Never. Otherwise, the default value of 5 minutes is a good choice.

You can manually rebuild the desktop in Classic by clicking the Rebuild Desktop button. This process rebuilds only the desktop on the Classic startup volume. To rebuild the desktop on all volumes, start Classic from the Advanced pane with the Use Key Combination option set to Command-Option. This preference item is persistent, so unless you want to rebuild the desktop on every startup, click Clear Keys.

> **MORE INFO** ▶ Refer to Knowledge Base document 10182, "Mac OS: Rebuilding Desktop File and Icon Recovery."

Viewing the Memory/Versions Pane in Classic Preferences

The Memory/Versions pane shows details about the state of the Classic environment, including active applications, memory usage, and the version of Mac OS 9. This pane's information is similar to that provided by the "About This Mac" menu item in the Finder for Mac OS 9.

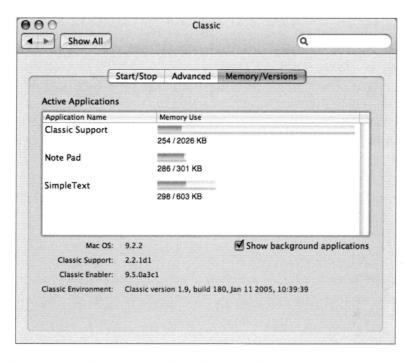

In the Active Applications area, all of the currently running Classic applications are listed with memory usage and allocations. In Mac OS 9, applications are assigned a fixed amount of memory in the Get Info window in the Finder, and that behavior persists in Classic. While native Mac OS X applications are able to use additional memory as needed, Classic applications cannot use more memory than they have been assigned. Symptoms of a Classic application running out of memory are out-of-memory errors, poor performance, erratic behavior, or crashes. If you see these symptoms, check the Memory/Versions pane to see if the application has used all of its memory allocation. If it has, you can quit the application, assign it more memory, and restart it.

Some Classic applications and drivers use background processes to provide their functionality. Selecting the "Show background applications" checkbox will add these processes to the list, helping you determine if you want to set Classic sleep time in the Advanced pane to Never.

Printing in Classic

The Classic environment uses the Mac OS X printing architecture. All the printers you have created in Printer Setup Utility are automatically available in Classic without other configuration. For this reason, you should only set up printers in the Classic Chooser if you need Mac OS 9–specific printing features. Also, any printers you configure in Classic will not be available in Mac OS X, so you should do most of your printer configuration in Mac OS X.

Configured printers in
Mac OS X Printer List

No configured printers
in Classic Chooser

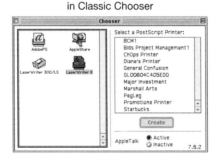

Mac OS X printers automatically
available when printing from Classic

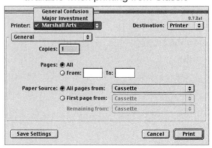

If your printer manufacturer does not make a Mac OS X printer driver, or if their driver requires Mac OS 9 for installation but your computer cannot boot Mac OS 9, you have two options available. You can use a Gimp-Print driver to configure that printer in Mac OS X, or you can try a configuration file for a similar printer. You could also drag the print driver to /System Folder/ Extensions, as you would in Mac OS 9.

You can install a Mac OS 9 PostScript Printer Description file (PPD) in Mac OS X. Most printer manufacturers include an installer to place the PPD in the correct location for Mac OS X. However, in some cases you might have to decompress or install the PPD in Classic, then manually copy the PPD files from /System Folder/Extensions/
Printer Descriptions to /Library/Printers/PPDs/Contents/Resources/en.lproj.

Troubleshooting Classic Applications

Try the following strategies to troubleshoot problems with starting Classic and running Classic applications:

▸ Ensure that a valid Mac OS 9 System Folder is listed and selected in Classic preferences.

▸ If you encounter problems starting Classic, use standard Mac OS 9 troubleshooting techniques to diagnose and resolve the problem. For example, look in /System Folder/Preferences for damaged or corrupted system preferences, try discarding the MacTCP DNR file, or consider fonts or system extensions.

▸ If Classic begins to start up but does not finish, it could be caused by a bad alias in the Servers folder in the Mac OS 9 System Folder. Try dragging the /System Folder/Servers folder to the Trash and restarting Classic.

▸ Choose Turn Off Extensions in the Advanced pane of Classic preferences and click Restart Classic. If Classic is able to fully start up, troubleshoot for an extension conflict just as you would with a regular Mac OS 9 system.

▸ If applications are crashing, check and increase their memory allocations, as needed.

▶ Evaluate any third-party extensions or system enhancers for possible conflicts.

MORE INFO ▶ Refer to Knowledge Base document 106677, "Troubleshooting the Classic environment in Mac OS X."

What You've Learned

This appendix discusses the Classic Environment: how it works, and how it interacts with the Mac OS X operating system. You have also learned some troubleshooting options and approaches.

▶ To use the Classic environment, Mac OS 9 must be installed and properly configured. You select which Mac OS 9 System Folder to use and configure Classic options in Classic preferences.

▶ If an application does not respond to input from the keyboard or mouse, switch to Mac OS X and choose Apple > Force Quit, or press Command-Option-Escape to display the Force Quit Applications window. Select the application to quit, and click Force Quit.

References

The following Knowledge Base documents (located at www.apple.com/support) will provide you with further information regarding Classic:

Classic Troubleshooting

▶ 10182, "Mac OS: Rebuilding Desktop File and Icon Recovery"

▶ 75275, "Mac OS X: About the 'Install Mac OS 9 Drivers' Option in Disk Utility"

▶ 106677, "Troubleshooting the Classic environment in Mac OS X"

▶ 106678, "Mac OS X: Classic doesn't start, Mac OS 9 not installed or recognized"

▶ 106679, "Mac OS X: Classic Will Not Finish Starting Up—Extension Conflict or 'Bus Error'"

▶ 106719, "Mac OS X: How to Use Mac OS 9 Applications"

▶   106874, "Mac OS: Web Browser Quits Unexpectedly or Stops Responding"

▶   107135, "Mac OS X 10.2: About Using Mac OS 9 Control Panels in the Classic Environment."

Classic Printing

▶   106710, "Mac OS X: How to Print From a Classic Application"

▶   107060, "Mac OS X 10.2, 10.3: Sharing a printer with Mac OS 9 computers"

Glossary

64 bit A computing term that refers to using 64-bit addressing (2 to the power of 64) or 18,446,744,073,709,600,000 memory addresses (4 billion times more than 32-bit computing). 64-bit addressing is new in Mac OS X 10.4.

802.1x Standard for access control on both wireless and wired local area networks. It provides a way to authenticate and authorize devices that attach to the network port.

A record A DNS entry on a server that identifies a host. It represents the canonical name of the server, and maps an IP address to its host name.

A

administrator user (Admin user) Type of user account. When logged in as an administrator user, you can add user accounts, change system settings, and install applications and resources to be accessed by any user on the computer.

AFP (Apple Filing Protocol) A protocol that allows a computer on a network to access AppleShare file servers and view the items in them as though they were stored locally.

AirPort Apple's implementation of the wireless Ethernet standard, Ethernet 802.11.

alias A feature of the Mac OS Extended volume format that provides a lightweight reference, or pointer, to files or folders.

API (Application Programming Interface) A set of routines, protocols, and tools that allows application developers to use features of the computer and operating system without writing low-level code.

Apple events A messaging tool used to transfer information, commands, and requests between applications, networks, and Mac OS X.

AppleTalk A set of networking protocols developed by Apple. Largely replaced by zero-configuration networking via Bonjour.

application environment Consists of the frameworks, libraries, and services (with associated APIs) necessary for the runtime execution of programs developed with those APIs. For example, applications developed with Carbon APIs run in the Carbon application environment.

Aqua Human interface for Mac OS X and Mac OS X Server.

archive A collection of files and folders, compressed into a single file for space savings or transfer to non-native file systems.

B

binary file File with contents that include arbitrary data, such as executable code, graphics, and application-specific text formatting.

BinHex (Abbreviated term for binary hexadecimal) Encoding format that converts 8-bit binary files into 7-bit flat files. BinHex format preserves file attributes as well as Macintosh resource forks.

Bluetooth Short-range (less than 30 feet) wireless technology for file transfer and device communication and synchronization. Bluetooth 2.0 + Enhanced Data Rate is the current version of the protocol, which allows data transfer up to 3 MB/s.

Bonjour The Apple implementation of the Zeroconf protocol. Used for automatic discovery of computers, devices, and services on IP networks. Formerly known as Rendezvous.

BOOTP (Bootstrap Protocol) A method for acquiring an IP address in which a particular address is assigned to a particular host machine each time the machine starts up. It is used primarily for computers that start from a network server rather than their own hard disk.

BootROM Hardware that contains the first code to be activated at startup. Its two primary responsibilities are to initialize system hardware and select an operating system to boot.

BSD (Berkeley Software Distributions) A version of the UNIX operating system developed at the University of California at Berkeley. Applications that run at the command line execute in the BSD application environment.

bundle A folder in the file system that stores executable code and the software resources related to that code. Many applications are bundles. A bundle is a special type of package.

burn folder A Finder feature in Mac OS X 10.4. It contains aliases that can be quickly burned to optical media.

Carbon Application environment. Carbon is a set of programming interfaces derived from earlier Mac OS APIs that have been modified to work with Mac OS X, especially its kernel environment.

C

CGI (Common Gateway Interface) A script or program that adds dynamic functions to a website. It sends information back and forth between a website and an application that provides a service for the site. For example, if a user fills out a form on the site, a CGI could send the message to an application that processes the data and sends a response back to the user.

CIFS (Common Internet File System) A protocol that allows applications to make requests for files and services on remote computers. It is used by SMB and the open-source SAMBA, among others.

Classic (Abbreviated term for Classic application environment) Classic makes it possible for Mac OS 9 and Mac OS 9–compatible applications to run on a Mac OS X system.

Cocoa An application environment based on object-oriented frameworks that offer both Java and Objective-C APIs.

ColorSync Color management software used by the Quartz graphics system.

command-line interface Application environment used to execute BSD commands; accessed via Terminal, single-user mode, >console, X11 Terminal application, and Telnet (SSH).

CUPS (Common UNIX Printing System) Cross-platform printing solution for UNIX environments, based on the Internet Printing Protocol (IPP).

D

Darwin Core operating system in Mac OS X. It is an open-source operating system (XNU) built on the Mach 3.0 kernel.

data fork See *file fork*.

DAT files Virus definition files used by virus protection software. They contain information about virus threats and their cures, and must be kept up-to-date.

Desktop folder User-specific location for items on the user's desktop. Found in the file system at ~/Users/*Username*/Desktop.

DHCP (Dynamic Host Configuration Protocol) A method for acquiring an IP address in which a range of unique addresses are assigned to computers.

directory (file system) See *folder*.

directory (service) A database that keeps track of the resources available to the users of that database. Common directories are LDAP, Open Directory, and Active Directory.

discovery The method by which an application finds computers and services on a network. Bonjour is a method of automatic service discovery used by many programs, such as the Finder and iChat. AppleTalk is still used in some environments for printer discovery.

disk image In Mac OS X, a disk image is a file that works like a drive volume. When opened, it mounts in /Volumes and appears on the desktop. Disk images can be compressed, encrypted, and resized.

DNS (Domain Name System) DNS servers are host machines that can translate domain names into IP addresses.

Dock Tool in the Mac OS X Finder that allows users to quickly access and open applications, documents, and other frequently used items.

driver A program that enables a user to access and interact with a hardware device.

DSL (Digital Subscriber Line) A high-speed connection to an Internet service provider using the same wires as a regular telephone line.

E

encryption The process of password-protecting data with the use of a one-time hash called an encryption key. You can establish a network tunnel to pass encrypted data over a network, and you can encrypt a network session using SSH and SSL. In the file system, encrypted data can be stored in encrypted disk images, in FileVault-protected home folders, and with encrypted virtual memory.

Exposé A Mac OS X feature that automatically tiles open windows.

extension Software that extends the functionality of an operating system. See *kernel extension*.

F

FAT (File Allocation Table) A common volume format used by PC operating systems such as Windows.

favorites User-selected aliases to frequently accessed folders, files, network volumes, or websites.

file extension Multicharacter suffix preceded by a period in a filename. File extensions are used to identify the correct application to execute the file.

file fork Method of storing data in a Mac OS file system where each file has two portions: a data fork that contains the data, and a resource fork that contains information about the file itself.

file system A combination of disk formatting and operating system features that defines how files are stored and retrieved.

FileVault A Mac OS X feature that secures a user's home folder with AES-128 encryption.

Finder Carbon application that manages the user's access to any item in the file system.

firewall Hardware or software system designed to prevent unauthorized access to or from private networks.

FireWire Apple's implementation of the IEEE 1394 serial bus standard.

firmware Software contained in read-only memory, such as BootROMs or EPROMs.

folder A named group of related files at a particular location in the file system hierarchy.

framework A type of bundle that packages a dynamic shared library with the resources that the library requires, including header files and reference documentation.

FTP (File Transfer Protocol) A networking protocol used to transfer files over a TCP/IP network, such as the Internet.

G

Get Info Finder command that opens Info window revealing Spotlight terms, permission settings, application settings, previews, and general information about an item; accessed using the Command-I keyboard shortcut.

GID (Group Identification Number) An identification number used in multiuser operating systems to uniquely identify groups of users.

GPU (Graphics Processing Unit) Refers to the video card or chipset that a computer uses to draw objects on the screen. Older computers that don't have a separate GPU use the CPU to draw images on the screen. A separate GPU speeds up computer operation by keeping the CPU free to process data.

host machine A computer that provides a network service (a web server is an HTTP host), or more broadly, any computer with a host name and IP address.

HTML (Hypertext Markup Language) A set of symbols or codes inserted in a file to control display in a web browser. The markup tells the web browser how to display a web page's words and images for the user.

HTTP (Hypertext Transfer Protocol) A networking protocol used to transfer information to web browsers and WebDAV clients.

H

IANA (Internet Assigned Numbers Authority) An organization responsible for allocating IP addresses, assigning protocol parameters, and managing domain names.

ICMP (Internet Control Message Protocol) A message-control and error-reporting protocol used between host servers and gateways. For example, some Internet software applications use it to send a packet on a roundtrip between two hosts to determine roundtrip times and discover problems on the network.

IEEE (Institute of Electrical and Electronics Engineers) An engineering group that defines electrical interconnect standards.

IGMP (Internet Group Management Protocol) An Internet protocol used by hosts and routers to send packets to lists of hosts that want to participate, which is known as multicasting. QuickTime Streaming Server uses multicast addressing, as does Service Location Protocol (SLP).

IMAP (Internet Message Access Protocol) A networking protocol used to access electronic mail stored in a mail server's IMAP database. It is different from POP because the IMAP database is designed to store mail on the server for more flexible user access.

IPv6 (Internet Protocol version 6) The latest version of the protocol, which includes improvements over IPv4, including 128-bit addresses rather than 32-bit addresses, and defines the rules for unicast, anycast, and multicast. These improvements were included to anticipate future growth of the Internet.

I

ISO 9660 Standard CD-ROM file system that allows you to read the same CD-ROM disc whether you are on a PC, Mac, or other major computer platform.

ISP (Internet Service Provider) A company that provides a connection between client computers and the Internet.

J

Java An application environment built around an object-oriented programming language and set of APIs; developed by Sun Microsystems.

journaling A feature of advanced file systems that tracks changes in an effort to prevent the disk catalog from getting into an inconsistent state and to aid in file system recovery if a problem occurs.

K

KDC (Key Distribution Server) A server that maintains a list of user principles for a Kerberos authentication system.

Kerberos Authentication system based on a unique key, or ticket. Allows encrypted information to be transferred between two parties with valid assigned tickets.

kernel Also known as a microkernel. The kernel is the underlying core of an operating system.

kernel extension Also known as KEXT. A kernel extension is a type of loadable bundle that low-level system routines recognize and load into the kernel environment. KEXT bundles have a file extension of .kext.

kernel panic A system error that terminates core system processes, requiring a restart. It occurs when the kernel receives an instruction that is in an unexpected format or that it fails to handle properly.

keychain Tool in Mac OS X that stores passwords and user identifications for applications, servers, and other resources, in an encrypted database.

LAN (Local area network) A network of devices (computers, printers, and so forth) that are in the same general physical location.

launchd The startup manager for Mac OS X 10.4 that starts up services and launches loginwindow. After startup, it manages daemons in the same manner as the watchdog daemon in Mac OS X 10.3 and earlier.

LDAP (Lightweight Directory Access Protocol) A networking protocol used to access directory services that run over TCP.

link-local address An address assigned by an IP host in the absence of outside configuration information. It is part of the Zeroconf standard.

links In UNIX, a method of referencing files. A hard link provides a file with more than one name and allows the name to be stored in different folders. A symbolic link is a lightweight reference to a file or folder using the path in the file system. Finder aliases are an example of symbolic links.

localhost Name given to a host machine if its IP address has no domain name associated with it.

location A set of network configurations consisting of network ports and the protocols that run on those ports. The location is an organization tool used to manage network connectivity.

LPD (Line Printer Daemon) A process that sends print commands from the computer to an LPR printer.

LPR (Line Printer Remote) A network printer that is configured by identifying the IP address of either the printer itself or the printer queue it is connected to.

L

Mac OS Extended, Mac OS Extended (Journaled) The standard volume formats for Macintosh operating systems. Both Mac OS Extended and Mac OS Extended (Journaled) support case-sensitivity. Mac OS Extended (Journaled) is the default format for new volumes in Mac OS X.

M

master password Feature of FileVault that allows the passwords of encrypted user accounts to be reset using a single system-wide password.

m-DNS (Multicast Domain Name Service) A means of translating host names to addresses without a dedicated domain name server. It is part of the Zeroconf standard.

MBONE (Multicast Backbone) A virtual network that supports IP multi-casting. It uses the same physical media as the Internet, but it is designed to repackage multicast data packets so they appear to be unicast data packets.

metadata Data about your data. If a document is your data, metadata is the document's file type, version, creator, filename extension, comments, author, number of pages, size, duration, color space, exposure setting, date created, and date modified or opened.

MIME (Multipurpose Internet Mail Extension) An Internet standard for specifying what happens when a web browser requests a file with certain characteristics. A file's suffix describes the type of file it is, and you determine how you want the server to respond when it receives files with certain suffixes. Each suffix and its associated response is called a MIME type mapping.

MX record (Mail Exchange record) An entry in a DNS table that specifies how mail is handled for a domain. When a mail server on the Internet has mail to deliver to a domain, it requests the MX record for the domain, and the record directs the mail to the computer specified in the MX record.

N

NetBIOS (Network Basic Input/Output System) A program that allows applications on different computers to communicate within a local area network.

NetInfo A hierarchical database system used for directory services.

network port (network interface unit) In Mac OS X, a device that serves as a common interface for various other devices within a local area network, or as an interface to allow networked computers to connect to a network.

NFS (UNIX Network File System) A client/server application that allows a user to access files on a remote computer as though the files were part of the user's own file system.

normal user See *standard user*.

NSL Provides a protocol-independent way for applications to discover network services. See *SLP*.

NTFS (Windows NT File System) The volume format used by Microsoft Windows NT.

O

Open Firmware Cross-platform standard for controlling hardware. Open Firmware is used by all PCI-based computers running the Mac OS.

OpenGL Industry-standard API for 2D and 3D graphics systems.

open source Software that is developed, tested, and improved through public collaboration and distributed with the intent that it be shared with others.

ORBS (Open Relay Behavior-Modification System) A database, accessible via DNS lookups, that tracks known spammers (senders of junk mail). It contains SMTP servers that are known to allow third-party relay; senders of junk mail use these servers to forward their junk mail.

P

package A special kind of folder that can have embedded executable instructions. Often used to install application or operating system components, or files that must be placed in specific locations. An application package is called a *bundle*.

pane Any region of changeable content within a dialog or window.

path Route through a file system to a particular item.

partition Discrete section of a hard disk. Also known as *volume*.

PC Card A standard that contains the physical, electrical, and software specifications for an integrated circuit card usually used in portable systems. Also known as *PCMCIA*.

PCI (Peripheral Component Interconnect) Bus standard that provides a channel or path between the components in a computer.

PDF (Portable Document Format) A standard graphics format used for rendering and printing. It was developed by Adobe.

permission In a multiuser operating system, authorization that provides a measure of security needed to keep one user from modifying or viewing another user's items on the computer. The three permissions are read, write, and execute.

PID (Process identification number) The number used in multiuser operating systems to uniquely identify running processes.

plug-in A software module that extends the functionality of an application or framework.

POP (Post Office Protocol) A networking protocol used to access electronic mail from a mail server. It relies upon user-specific mailboxes that reside on the mail server, and as a result can be much more resource-intensive than IMAP.

POSIX (Portable Operating System Interface for UNIX) A set of standard operating system interfaces based on the UNIX operating system.

PostScript A programming language developed by Adobe that describes the appearance of a printed page.

PPP (Point-to-Point Protocol) A networking protocol used to connect two peer machines using a common solution, such as a modem.

PPPoE (Point-to-Point Protocol over Ethernet) A networking protocol used to connect two peer machines using a broadband solution, such as a DSL modem.

preemptive multitasking Method of running multiple processes simultaneously where the operating system can interrupt, or preempt, a currently running task to run another task.

process A task; a running program or set of threads.

protected memory Memory scheme in which an operating system allocates a unique memory address space in RAM for each application or process running on the computer, and prevents applications from accessing memory outside of their allocated space.

protocol Networking language. A special set of rules that relate to intercommunication between systems.

Quartz 2D Graphics application programming interface based on PDF. **Q**

QuickTime Multimedia development, storage, and playback standard developed by Apple.

RAID (Redundant Array of Independent Disks) Software or hardware **R** system that uses two or more disk drives at the same time to improve fault tolerance and performance.

Rendezvous Former name for Apple's implementation of the Zeroconf protocol. See *Bonjour*.

receipt A bundle that acts as a record of what was installed by the Mac OS X Installer. The receipts are stored in /Library/Receipts.

resource fork See *file fork*.

root (user) Short name for System Administrator. Root has read and write permissions to all areas of the file system.

root (file system) Beginning of a file path. The root of the file system is designated by /.

router Gateway between two networks that determines the next network point to which networking information should be forwarded, on the way toward its destination.

RTP (Real-Time Transport Protocol) A networking protocol used to transmit, or stream, QuickTime data.

RTSP (Real-Time Streaming Protocol) A networking protocol used for two-way communication with a unicast streaming server.

S

SCSI (Small Computer System Interface) A fast communications bus that allows multiple devices to be connected to a computer.

SDP (Session Description Protocol) Protocol used with QuickTime Streaming Server; an SDP file contains information about the format, timing, and authorship of the live streaming broadcast.

search domain Domain that provides the TCP/IP configuration with a domain name or list of domain names to use in the event that one is not specified in an IP search or request.

Section 508 The section of the U.S. Rehabilitation Act that requires any electronic information developed, procured, maintained, or used by the federal government to be accessible to people with disabilities.

Secure Empty Trash A Mac OS X 10.4 feature that repeatedly overwrites deleted files when the Trash is emptied, making the files nearly impossible to recover.

share point A server volume that can be mounted by a network user.

sheet Modal dialog attached to a particular document window.

single-user mode Mode in which Mac OS X is started without the multi-user components or graphical user interface. Single-user mode is enabled by pressing Command-S at startup.

SLP (Services Location Protocol) A networking protocol used to discover and advertise TCP/IP-based services, such as personal file sharing, personal web sharing, or USB printer sharing. Some of these discovered services are viewed in the Finder by choosing Go > Connect to Server (Command-K).

SMB (Server Message Block) A networking protocol that allows a computer on a network to access Windows and Samba file servers and view the items on them as though they were stored locally.

SMTP (Simple Mail Transfer Protocol) A networking protocol used to send electronic mail using a mail server.

Spotlight Desktop search technology introduced in Mac OS X 10.4 for searching file data and metadata.

SSH Program to log in to another computer over a TCP/IP network, and execute commands on the remote computer. SSH provides authentication and secure communications over unsecure channels.

SSL (Secure Sockets Layer) An Internet protocol that allows you to send encrypted, authenticated information across the Internet.

standard user A user account type in which a user can use a basic set of applications and tools. It is limited to making configuration changes that only affect the user's own account; a standard user cannot make changes to system-wide settings or use Directory Setup and NetInfo Manager to change configurations. Also called *normal user*.

subnet mask A filter used to determine what part of an IP address identifies a network and what part identifies an individual host machine.

superuser Another name for root. See *root (user)*.

System Administrator Long name for root. See *root (user)*.

System Preferences Application used to configure system settings and preferences in Mac OS X.

TCP/IP (Transport Control Protocol/Internet Protocol) The primary networking protocol used to communicate over the Internet.

T

Telnet Program used to log in to another computer over a TCP/IP network, execute commands on the remote computer, and move files from one computer to another. It provides authentication, but not encryption of information.

thread Information needed to serve a particular service request or set of instructions.

ticket In a Kerberos authentication system, an embedded unique key that allows private information to be passed between parties.

TTL (Time-to-Live) The specified length of time that DNS information is stored in a cache. When a domain name–IP address pair has been cached longer than the TTL value, the entry is deleted from the name server's cache (but not from the primary DNS server).

U

UDF (Universal Disk Format) Standard CD-ROM and DVD file system designed to ensure consistency in optical media.

UDP (User Datagram Protocol) A communications method that uses the Internet Protocol (IP) to send a data unit (called a datagram) from one computer to another in a network. Network applications that have very small data units to exchange might use UDP rather than TCP.

UFS (UNIX File System) This volume format is used primarily by UNIX and UNIX-based operating systems.

UID (User identification number) The number used in multiuser operating systems to uniquely identify a user.

UNIX Pronounced YEW-nihks. Nonproprietary operating system used on computers.

URL (Uniform Resource Locator) An address of a file or resource accessible on a network server, such as a website on the Internet or a shared volume on a local file server. The URL prefix determines the protocol used: HTTP, AFP, SMB, and so on.

USB (Universal Serial Bus) A serial interface between a computer and add-on devices.

Universal Access Mac OS X accessibility software for improving human interface usability and functionality.

verbose mode Setting that displays all of the startup messages (drivers loading, services starting, and so forth) generated as Mac OS X starts up. It is enabled by pressing Command-V at startup.

V

virtual memory Scheme for managing the protected memory space and allocating the amount of memory needed by applications. Uses a swap file where inactive code segments are stored on disk.

VoiceOver A spoken English interface introduced in Mac OS X 10.4.

VPN (Virtual Private Network) Private data network that uses public telecommunications infrastructure but maintains privacy with tunneling protocols.

WebDAV (World Wide Web Distributed Authoring and Versioning) An extension of HTTP that allows the viewing of a web server file system as though it was a local file system.

W

WEP (Wired Equivalent Privacy) Security protocol for wireless networks designed to offer the same level of security as wired networks.

WINS (Windows Internet Naming Service) A name resolution service used by Windows computers to match client names with IP addresses. A WINS server can be located on the local network or externally on the Internet.

X11 The X Window System, a common windowing environment for UNIX.

X

XML (Extensible Markup Language) A universal format for documents and data accessed on the web.

Zeroconf An Internet standard for Zero Configuration IP Networking. Zeroconf implementations allow computers to self-assign link-local IP addresses for basic IP-based network connectivity. Bonjour is the Mac OS X implementation.

Z

Index